EARLY MODERN ACADEMIC DRAMA

In this essay collection, the contributors contend that academic drama represents an important, but heretofore understudied, site of cultural production in early modern England. Focusing on plays that were written and performed in academic environments such as Oxford University, Cambridge University, grammar schools, and the Inns of Court, the scholars investigate how those plays strive to give dramatic coherence to issues of religion, politics, gender, pedagogy, education, and economics. Of particular significance are the shifting political and religious contentions that so frequently shaped both the cultural questions addressed by the plays, and the sorts of dramatic stories that were most conducive to the exploration of such questions. The volume argues that the writing and performance of academic drama constitute important moments in the history of education and the theater because, in these plays, narrative is consciously put to work as both a representation of, and an exercise in, knowledge formation. The plays discussed speak to numerous segments of early modern culture, including the relationship between the academy and the state, the tensions between humanism and religious reform, the successes and failures of the humanist program, the social profits and economic liabilities of formal education, and the increasing involvement of universities in the commercial market, among other issues.

Jonathan Walker is Assistant Professor of English at Portland State University, USA.

Paul D. Streufert is Associate Professor of Literature and Languages at the University of Texas at Tyler, USA.

General Editor's Preface

Helen Ostovich, McMaster University

Performance assumes a string of creative, analytical, and collaborative acts that, in defiance of theatrical ephemerality, live on through records, manuscripts, and printed books. The monographs and essay collections in this series offer original research which addresses theatre histories and performance histories in the context of the sixteenth and seventeenth century life. Of especial interest are studies in which women's activities are a central feature of discussion as financial or technical supporters (patrons, musicians, dancers, seamstresses, wigmakers, or 'gatherers'), if not authors or performers per se. Welcome too are critiques of early modern drama that not only take into account the production values of the plays, but also speculate on how intellectual advances or popular culture affect the theatre.

The series logo, selected by my colleague Mary V. Silcox, derives from Thomas Combe's duodecimo volume, *The Theater of Fine Devices* (London, 1592), Emblem VI, sig. B. The emblem of four masks has a verse which makes claims for the increasing complexity of early modern experience, a complexity that makes interpretation difficult. Hence the corresponding perhaps uneasy rise in sophistication:

> Masks will be more hereafter in request,
> And grow more deare than they did heretofore.

No longer simply signs of performance 'in play and jest', the mask has become the 'double face' worn 'in earnest' even by 'the best' of people, in order to manipulate or profit from the world around them. The books stamped with this design attempt to understand the complications of performance produced on stage and interpreted by the audience, whose experiences outside the theatre may reflect the emblem's argument:

> Most men do use some colour'd shift
> For to conceal their craftie drift.

Centuries after their first presentations, the possible performance choices and meanings they engender still stir the imaginations of actors, audiences, and readers of early plays. The products of scholarly creativity in this series, I hope, will also stir imaginations to new ways of thinking about performance.

Early Modern Academic Drama

Edited by

Jonathan Walker
Portland State University, USA

and

Paul D. Streufert
University of Texas at Tyler, USA

ASHGATE

Published by
Ashgate Publishing Limited
Wey Court East
Union Road
Farnham
Surrey GU9 7PT
England

Ashgate Publishing Company
Suite 420
101 Cherry Street
Burlington, VT 05401-4405
USA

Ashgate website: http://www.ashgate.com

British Library Cataloguing in Publication Data
Early modern academic drama. – (Studies in performance and early modern drama)
1. English drama – Early modern and Elizabethan, 1500–1600 – History and criticism
2. English drama – 17th century – History and criticism 3. College and school drama, English
I. Walker, Jonathan II. Streufert, Paul D.
822.3'09

Library of Congress Cataloging-in-Publication Data
Early modern academic drama / edited by Jonathan Walker and Paul D. Streufert.
  p. cm. — (Studies in performance and early modern drama)
Includes bibliographical references (p.   ) and index.
ISBN 978-0-7546-6464-2 (alk. paper)
1. English drama—Early modern and Elizabethan, 1500–1600—History and criticism.
2. English drama—17th century—History and criticism. 3. College and school drama, English.
4. Knowledge, Theory of, in literature. 5. Theater and society—England—History. I. Walker, Jonathan. II.
Streufert, Paul D.

PR651.E26 2008
822.3'09—dc22
                                                                        2008011888
ISBN: 978-0-7546-6464-2

Printed and bound in Great Britain by MPG Books Ltd, Bodmin, Cornwall.

Contents

Notes on Contributors

EMILY D. BRYAN is Assistant Professor of English at Dominican College of Blauvelt, and has published on early modern drama and nineteenth-century theater. Her research interests include boy actors, Renaissance children, rhetorical training, theatrical companies, the circulation of children in the Americas, and performance pedagogy. Emily is currently working on a book project titled *In the Company of Boys: The Place of the Boy Actor in Early Modern England.*

HELEN HIGBEE is Assistant Professor of English at Kentucky State University. She has co-edited Robert Weimann's *Author's Pen and Actor's Voice: Playing and Writing in Shakespeare's Theatre* (with William N. West, 2000). Her research interests include Renaissance pedagogical theory and humanism, humanist drama, and the historical figure of Sir Thomas Gresham.

ODAI JOHNSON is the author of *Rehearsing the Revolution* (2000) and *Absence and Memory in Colonial American Theatre* (2006), and co-author of *The Colonial American Stage, 1665–1774: A Documentary Calendar* (with William J. Burling and James Coombs, 2002). He has published articles in *Theatre Survey, Theatre Journal,* the *Virginia Magazine of History and Biography,* and the *New England Theatre Journal.* Odai runs the Ph.D. program at the University of Washington's School of Drama.

SARAH KNIGHT is Lecturer in Shakespeare and Renaissance Literature at the University of Leicester. She has published essays on early seventeenth-century satire and on academic print culture in Elizabethan and Jacobean England, and has translated and co-edited Leon Battista Alberti's *Momus* for the I Tatti Renaissance Library (2003). Sarah is associate general editor of *John Nichols's The Progresses and Public Processions of Queen Elizabeth I: A New Edition of the Early Modern Sources* (forthcoming), for which she has edited and translated the material relating to the University of Oxford. She is co-editor of *The Progresses, Pageants, and Entertainments of Queen Elizabeth I* (with Jayne Elisabeth Archer and Elizabeth Goldring, 2007), and is editing and translating Milton's *Prolusions* for vol. 11 of *The Complete Works of John Milton* (forthcoming).

ERIC LEONIDAS is Assistant Professor of English Literature at Central Connecticut State University, where he teaches early modern poetry and drama as well as Greek and Roman literature. He is currently at work on a book examining the role of Renaissance drama in the social acceptance of empirical knowledge.

Ursula Potter is an Honorary Associate in the English Department at the University of Sydney. She has published on Tudor school drama in *Domestic Arrangements* (2002) and in *Tudor Drama Before Shakespeare, 1485–1590* (2004). Her current research examines the education of daughters in Elizabethan England, the pedagogical theories of Juan Luis Vives (forthcoming in Brepols, Disputatio 15), and the social conditions that gave rise to greensickness, the disease of virgins. Dr. Potter has also published in *Early Theatre* and *English Language Notes*, and has an article on Tudor drama and education forthcoming in *Parergon*.

Linda Shenk is Assistant Professor of English at Iowa State University, where she teaches Shakespeare, drama, and early modern literature. She has published on Elizabeth I as a learned queen, on Shakespeare, and on the seventeenth-century mnemonician John Willis. Linda's book project, *Learned Queen: The Imperial Image of Elizabeth I* (forthcoming, Palgrave Macmillan), explores the relations between Elizabeth I's political image as a learned prince and the literary texts associated with some of her most internationally ambitious courtiers.

Paul D. Streufert is Associate Professor of Literature and Languages at The University of Texas at Tyler, where he teaches Latin and World Literature. His research interests include dramatic literature, particularly Athenian tragedy and its influences. Paul has translated Euripides' *Bacchae*, *Iphigenia at Aulis*, and *The Trojan Women* from the ancient Greek, and five separate productions of his translations have appeared around the United States, two of which he directed. He is currently working on a book project titled *Staging the Supernatural: A History of Ghosts on Stage from Ancient Greece to Modern America*. In addition to an article on Umberto Eco's fiction, Paul has published on a wide range of dramatic subjects, including Aeschylus, Euripides, Shakespeare, and Sam Shepard.

Jonathan Walker is Assistant Professor of English at Portland State University in Portland, Oregon, where he teaches English Renaissance drama and critical theory. His research interests include medieval and Renaissance drama in English, performance theory, feminism and gender studies, and print and manuscript culture in early modern England. Jonathan was managing editor of Clark Hulse's *Elizabeth I: Ruler and Legend*, a catalogue for an exhibition of the same name at the Newberry Library in Chicago. His current book project is titled *Theater of the Obscœne: Offstage Action on the English Renaissance Stage*. Jonathan has published on transvestism in medieval hagiographic literature, on lesbianism in Ovid and Augustan Rome, and on the place of "offstage action" in classical dramatic criticism.

Acknowledgements

Producing a book of this nature requires a great number of people to learn and adapt to new roles, to collaborate in unfamiliar and unforeseen ways, and to be willing to improvise their parts when the working script is, for whatever reason, no longer working. The co-editors would therefore like to express appreciation to the volume's contributors for the professionalism they have shown and for the education they have provided. We are also happy to give thanks to Erika Gaffney at Ashgate for her support of this volume, and to Helen Ostovich for selecting *Early Modern Academic Drama* to be a part of her series Studies in Performance and Early Modern Drama. The anonymous reader for Ashgate offered us valuable suggestions on the manuscript, for which we are very grateful.

For permission to reproduce the cover image, we thank the British Library, particularly Sandra Powlette, and for their assistance in hunting down many essential volumes and references, we are indebted to the Branford P. Millar Library at Portland State University, to the Robert R. Muntz Library at the University of Texas at Tyler, and to Geoff Wexler at the Oregon Historical Society.

Jonathan Walker wishes to express appreciation to David Bevington and Carla Mazzio, who kindly chaired two conference sessions at the Thirty-Seventh International Congress on Medieval Studies, whereat this volume was conceived. Although perhaps unaware of their contributions, Mary Beth Rose and Clark Hulse have both been influential forces in the shaping of this project.

Paul Streufert would like to thank Paul Whitfield White and Victor I. Scherb for their encouragement and help in researching the early modern dramatic texts of Cambridge and Oxford. He would also like to thank Sara Steinbrueck for her editorial assistance. Both Dean Donna Dickerson and Dean Alisa White of the University of Texas at Tyler generously contributed research support for this volume.

Introduction

Learning to Play

Jonathan Walker

In the midst of a discussion about "the trew vse of perfite Imitation," the pedagogue
Roger Ascham recalls his days as a Cambridge University student in the 1530s:

> Whan *M. Watson* in S. Johns College at Cambrige wrote his excellent Tragedie of
> *Absalon, M. Cheke*, he and I, for that part of trew Imitation, had many pleasant talkes
> together, in comparing the preceptes of Aristotle and *Horace de Arte Poetica*, with the
> examples of *Euripides, Sophocles*, and *Seneca*. Few men, in writyng of Tragedies in our
> dayes, haue shot at this marke. Some in *England*, moe in *France, Germanie*, and *Italie*,
> also haue written Tragedies in our tyme: of the which, not one I am sure is able to abyde
> the trew touch of *Aristotles* preceptes, and *Euripides* examples, saue onely two, that
> euer I saw, *M. Watsons Absalon*, and *Georgius Buckananus Iephthe.*[1]

Although reminiscing about "trew Imitation," Ascham stops short of either
setting the scene or reproducing the dialogue from his "many pleasant talkes"
with Thomas Watson and Sir John Cheke. Nor does THE SCHOLEMASTER spell out
either the specific content of their conversations or their assessment of where
classical dramatic practice meets classical dramatic theory. But even in its brevity
the anecdote is evocative. For, like the unlocalized settings and uncluttered
stages that so many early modern plays make a virtue of, Ascham economically
dramatizes a perfect humanist moment with but a few words and little action. His
story presents, in other words, the epitome of an academic play, one in which the
actors converse informally within a formal educational environment, enhancing
their understanding "togither" by refining the necessary skills that facilitate the
production of knowledge. Inviting the reader to participate imaginatively in
the scholarly exchange, Ascham's scene portrays the humanist reclamation of
classical learning, whose "preceptes" and "examples" furnish its pupils with
modern standards for critical judgment, while at the same time supplying them
with models for contemporary education and praxis.

Besides adding a measure of narrative delight to THE SCHOLEMASTER's lesson on
imitatio, Ascham's story illustrates for the reader the humanist program's ideals
in action. The form in which he casts the scene, moreover, pays homage to one
of humanism's predominant methodologies: the extraction of universal principles
from particular examples, which proceeds from the assumption that such principles
are contested and, therefore, that the historical or fictional examples from which
one draws them are in need of careful interpretation. As Joel Altman has argued,

These [methodological] emphases lay the foundation for a mimetic fiction of explorative character, one that teaches and delights by examining through exempla which engage the emotions the diverse existential claims that govern human life. The concern to link the universal principle with the particular example—which lies at the heart of Renaissance poetic theory—and the interest in developing the ability to see both sides of the question remain constants throughout the program.[2]

In addition to offering young scholars rich instructional opportunities through the dramatic mode—for invention, the imitation of classical exemplars; for rhetoric, the *disputatio* of the dramatic *agon*; for oratory, the practical delivery of well-formed speeches—academic plays seek to articulate humanistic ideals within the unpredictable circumstances of concrete social relations, which students can inhabit and observe through the simulacrum of dramatic performance. Such an approximative enterprise, however, has the inexorable consequence of producing a gap between the ideals that humanism encoded as universal principles and the practices that it read as embodiments of those ideals. This gap is one that academic plays both enact and examine.

Our investigations into early modern academic drama aim to account for this differential between practices and ideals by tracing two trajectories at once: first, the forces of influence and resistance that the academy exercised over England's political, religious, and economic relations and, second, the ways that English culture influenced and resisted the power of academic institutions, the appeal of education, and the value of humanistic knowledge. If academic drama is a platform for humanistic scholars to imagine how they might inaugurate change for the interests of a more ideal social sphere, then it is equally a means of confronting and negotiating the social realities of early modern England that impede such change on national and cultural scales.

* * *

Each of the essays in this volume explores academic plays as sites of cultural contestation. Such plays often take the form of academic exercises devised to give participants and spectators alike practical experience with Latin and Greek, with declamation and debate, and with ancient myths and histories, which yield valuable lessons despite their remoteness in time and place. The expressly pedagogical nature of much academic drama has tended to limit its critical reception as an elite and secluded undertaking in schools. Yet the collective thesis that this volume of essays argues is that—however elite and secluded they might be in their composition, performance, audience, and objectives—academic plays actively engage with urgent social, religious, and political questions of the period. The field of academic drama certainly consists of plays that originate from within educational environments or that offer representations of scholars and the academy. But the field also concerns the cultural place, social perceptions, and political uses of the academy. It includes humanist theater that is designed (according to

Horace's dictum[3]) both to instruct and to entertain, whether within the aristocratic household, in grammar schools, or in universities. It involves the connections and competitions between the academy and popular theatrical venues as institutions of formal and informal education. It comprises the technologies of theater, such as the practices of live performance, the oratorical training of the voice and mind, and the disciplining of the actor's body. Finally, academic drama extends to the educative function of role-playing and both the dramatization of learning and the teaching of theatricality.

Scholars on the Continent seem to have embraced drama as a method of formal instruction earlier and more frequently than those in England, although by the mid-sixteenth century the statutes of several Cambridge and Oxford colleges stipulate yearly funds to be expended on "comoedias et tragoedias."[4] On the one hand, it is important to recognize a continuity between humanist academic drama and a large proportion of medieval theater, whose objectives usually included the spiritual edification of its audiences. But, on the other hand, the formalization of drama as a component of educational programs marked a shift toward theatrical practices with less exclusively religious motivations, which was significantly enhanced by the performance, translation, and imitation of classical dramatic texts. From the available evidence, academic plays were most often written or adapted by schoolmasters, fellows, and lecturers to be performed by their students. The contributions to this volume, however, interpret "academic drama" more widely to include plays written by sometime students—as is apparently the case with the trilogy of *Parnassus* plays that appeared around the turn of the seventeenth century—as well as plays that depict academic environs and scholars. With the exception of its concluding essay, which examines American academic drama from the late seventeenth through the eighteenth centuries, the book concentrates on Greek, Latin, and vernacular drama in England that emerged from grammar schools, universities, and the Inns of Court during the early modern period.

With such a vast field in which to conduct their investigations, the volume's contributors can inevitably survey only a narrow stretch of ground so as to attain a significant depth in their particular discussions. The essays thus achieve their depth and coverage, both individually and for the book's common goals, by drawing on and advancing a body of scholarship that traverses literary studies, theater history, pedagogical theory, intellectual history, the history of religious reform, gender studies, cultural criticism, economics, and political history. Especially important is the work of cultural materialist, new historicist, and feminist critics, whose interdisciplinary modes of enquiry have helped to shape our own. Furthermore, the essays in this volume join scholarly conversations about academic drama that are themselves methodologically and ideologically diverse. Frederick S. Boas's *University Drama in the Tudor Age* (1914), G.C. Moore Smith's *College Plays Performed in the University of Cambridge* (1923), and T.H. Vail Motter's *The School Drama in England* (1929) are familiar but indispensable studies which chronicle a chapter of dramatic history whose documentary record is often terribly fragmented and elusive.[5] Supplementing and systematizing the research that Boas,

Smith, and Motter have bequeathed us are the equally indispensable Cambridge and Oxford volumes from the Records of Early English Drama project as well as the research to which Alan H. Nelson and John R. Elliott, Jr., have devoted much of their careers.[6]

While these scholars and the REED project provide a documentary foundation, the work of others has contributed cultural and historical dimensions to our examination of early modern academic drama. In *Ancient Scripts and Modern Experience on the English Stage 1500–1700* (1988), Bruce R. Smith formulates an influential argument for understanding academic plays as part of a broader cultural exchange, one which partook of the medieval *translatio studii et translatio imperii* topos, but which also profited from the traffic of humanism, whose intellectual networks and printed editions of classical texts permitted new transactions of knowledge and culture across many European borders. More recently, Rebecca Bushnell has argued in *A Culture of Teaching: Early Modern Humanism in Theory and Practice* (1996) that the early modern humanist regime frequently registered its own paradoxes and contradictions, stressing the ways in which schools and scholars negotiated and understood their cultural capital. And, by challenging the long-established orthodoxy that the commercial drama of Shakespeare and his contemporaries issued chiefly from the popular morality play tradition, Kent Cartwright makes a persuasive case for humanist school drama's extensive contributions to London's commercial dramatic repertory in his *Theatre and Humanism: English Drama in the Sixteenth Century* (1999).[7]

Arranged in this way, these critics who comprise part of the book's scholarly genealogy exhibit an increasing concern for the kinds of cultural agency that schools and universities brought to bear on early modern English society, particularly in the form of drama. *Early Modern Academic Drama* emphasizes this cultural agency by arguing that the plays articulate points of contact between the academy and the wider English culture, and that the discourse they articulate is political, religious, and economic just as it is intellectual and humanistic. On one hand, this volume attempts to revitalize, rather than displace, an earlier base of knowledge about academic drama—principally established by Boas, Smith, and Motter—by asking of it new kinds of questions that have only become articulable over the last thirty years or so. But, on the other hand, the volume seeks to examine a variety of dramatic texts and theatrical spaces in the academy that have received limited exposure to questions about gender, politics, and the material conditions under which these texts and spaces were produced. We want thereby not to circumscribe the field of academic drama but, rather, to reposition it in relation to dominant questions that have occupied researchers in recent years about the cultural significance of early modern theater. The challenge that this task has posed to our contributors is one that the book extends to other scholars as well, just as the collection itself is impelled by developing research in the field.

Hence the discussions in this volume are carried out with two key questions in mind. The first explores how academic plays negotiate political, religious, and economic issues. Like other early modern institutions, the academy resided within the purview of the state and the church, whose ideological and economic interests it served by regularly producing suitably educated young men to fill governmental, diplomatic, and clerical posts, among other esteemed occupations. At the same time, however, academies like Oxford and Cambridge administered their day-to-day activities in large measure as independent institutions, often insulated from issues of *Realpolitik*. Thus universities, Inns of Court, and even grammar schools not only prepared many students to participate in actual affairs of state, religion, law, and so forth; they also provided a space wherein students were encouraged to test, question, and debate such affairs. Academic plays frequently dramatize a variety of religious, political, and economic problems, sometimes deliberately and directly, sometimes implicitly. The strategies that the plays use as they strive conceptually to resolve these problems make acutely visible both the pedagogical role of the drama and, more broadly, the institutional role of the academy within the larger culture. Many of these plays, in other words, represent an unofficial discourse addressing tensions in the period brought about by contradictions and upheavals in political, religious, and economic relations.

The volume's second guiding question asks how the composition, staging, and reception of the plays helped to produce distinct academic and theatrical cultures. As an essentially pedagogical undertaking, academic drama occupies a fascinating place within the educational structure. Such drama is often instructive and thus purposive, but it also provides entertainment and recreation for players and playgoers alike. In such an atmosphere of profit and delight, the educational system brings a vibrant theatrical culture to life, while in the same breath the academic theater creates an interactive culture of learning. This mutual constitution is no accident. The activity of "performance," of course, comprises a core pedagogical element in the acquisition and demonstration of knowledge, and, steeped in the teachings of humanism, early modern schools and universities frequently exploited the didactic value of theater as a tool for illustrating, modeling, and manipulating forms of knowledge. That academic drama actively engages with and explores cultural issues which are ostensibly non-academic suggests its value for understanding the relation between cultural and intellectual formations in the period. Academic plays therefore record important cultural moments in which the realm of ideas becomes actualized through dramatic performance as it is embodied by students, who both teach and are taught by their experiences onstage.

But herein lay a profound cultural anxiety. While the actor manipulated his role through performance, he was also understood to be manipulated by it, shaped by the identity that he was called upon to perform. Remarkably, however, academic drama is virtually immune to the charges of those critics, such as antitheatrical writers, who most feared the transformative quality of performance and who repeatedly condemned the popular stage for its immoral instruction. Although at variance, such disparate attitudes toward the pedagogical and the professional stages point to the basic early modern belief that dramatic performance was itself a mode of learning, one that possessed an unsettling power to fashion individuals in its own image. In recent years, for example, new historicist and cultural materialist critics have demonstrated how the period's deeply religious and political rituals were both practiced and understood in terms of dramatic display. "[W]e princes," said Queen Elizabeth I in 1586, "are set on stages in the sight and view of all the world duly observed. The eyes of many behold our actions," a sentiment that King James I would echo years later.[8] Furthermore, controversies between Catholics and Protestants often centered on the troubling resemblance of religious rite to dramatic acting. The fact that academic drama tended to elude antitheatrical censure suggests that it occupied an especially meaningful place in the cultural imagination.

If school and university plays inhabited this cultural imagination, however, then they were also distinct manifestations of that imaginary. Academic plays are at once a way of imagining the possibilities of humanist aspirations—of altering the course of social history by narrativizing it otherwise in the present—as well as a way of putting tangible humanist achievements on view. Above all, this drama is about representing and modeling speech and behavior, about modifying student subjects in ways that will allow them to exercise their knowledge within social settings beyond institutional walls. In other words, the proposition that students will effectively undergo verbal, intellectual, and behavioral modifications through their involvement in dramatic events is in fact an investment in the power of narrative to refashion existing social relations, a power which is greatly enhanced by the experience of playing and playgoing itself. Because early modern humanism is a multifaceted discourse—affecting for instance educational reform, political counsel, book production and trade, notions of human meaning and cultural value—academic plays might be viewed as individual dialogues within this larger discourse. We might think of academic plays as cultural dramas allied to humanistic ideals while at the same time constrained by the practicalities of trying to realize those ideals within imperfect social, political, religious, and economic systems.

Academic plays literally represent narratives of early modern learning. Some of these narratives take the form of fictional conflicts that activate a process of humanistic assumptions, explanations, and solutions. Other narratives account for actual events and controversies that often surrounded academic performances themselves. Still others consist simply of the dramatic action that scholars and students have scripted and staged for the edification of their minds and for the pleasure of their senses. Yet, from a compositional standpoint, academic plays *narrativize* knowledge as much as they are narratives *about* knowledge and its uses. These scriptings and stagings attest, then, to the peculiar double-nature of knowledge, which students must experience as an a priori phenomenon—as something to be encountered anew, practiced, and mastered—but which is also an epistemological construction that forever depends on its own rehearsal and recapitulation, a process that necessarily, if subtly, alters the constitution of that knowledge through the re-creation of theater. Conceiving of the field in these terms, we propose to examine how early modern academic drama mediates such transactions of knowledge, how it organizes its own ways of knowing, and how it participates in the work of cultural reproduction and social change.

* * *

The sequence of the essays in this volume reflects a process of historical change within broad cultural trends such as humanism, the English Reformation, Tudor and Stuart absolutism, and proto-capitalism. While it resists a developmental narrative about how these broad trends constitute early modern history, the book nonetheless proceeds along an arc that considers, first, how residual cultural values confront changing political and religious circumstances during the sixteenth and seventeenth centuries; second, how the dominant educational force of humanism exhibits both vitality in its pedagogical variety and limitations in its ideological disunity; and, third, how academic drama meets with an emergent proto-capitalist market, an escalating centralization of state power, and finally a revitalized religious orthodoxy in and beyond the seventeenth century. On one hand, the taxonomy of "residual," "dominant," and "emergent" provides a way of locating academic drama within the broad cultural and historical trends mentioned above.[9] But, on the other hand, the language promotes the scrutiny of terms like humanism and the Reformation, which enables us to foreground the plays less as clear-cut examples of broad trends and more as complex material events that bring those cultural and historical trends into existence in the first place. In its emphasis on the collective cultural work of individual academic plays, the volume uses a method of enquiry that first appropriates the humanist objective of extolling universal principles by extracting them from particular examples, and then inverts and reverses that objective.

The thematic organization of the essays follows the volume's cultural and historical arc by grouping the discussions into four interconnected clusters. The first is comprised of essays that address political and religious issues, both within academic plays and surrounding their composition and production. Opening this group is Linda Shenk's examination of the changing relationship between royal patrons of Cambridge and Oxford and the advisory role of the two universities in matters of state. The change in this relationship, she argues, reached a crisis point in 1592 when Queen Elizabeth I requested both universities to produce distinctly non-academic plays for her Christmas festivities at court. Shenk demonstrates how university officials—who were possessed with a keen institutional memory of offering their princes academic demonstrations that imparted good counsel— experienced Elizabeth's request as an active erosion of their political significance. The university administrations entreated William Cecil, Chancellor of Cambridge and the queen's chief advisor, to intervene on their behalves, but whether the festivities proceeded according to her desire, we have no evidence. Yet the confrontation that we witness between the crown and the gown in 1592 is an event that records a crucial moment in the history of the two universities, concerning not only the influence they exercised with the queen but also the power that they commanded in a rapidly changing culture. Because Shenk's analysis also situates the academy and its drama within sixteenth-century English politics generally, it provides a valuable contextualization for the wider field and for the volume's subsequent essays.

The concern in Shenk's essay with the shifting political circumstances that university officials negotiated under Elizabeth takes on a pronounced religious dimension in Paul D. Streufert's essay on John Christopherson's *Jephthah*, a Cambridge play in Greek from about 1544. "Ιεφθάε," Frederick Boas explains, "is of peculiar interest as the only English academic play in Greek known to have survived."[10] Streufert argues that Christopherson, a vocal Catholic proponent, manages to synthesize divergent and far-flung cultural elements into a vehicle for Greek-language acquisition, for proper ethical training, and for teaching conciliatory solutions to the religious controversies afflicting England under King Henry VIII. By deploying three separate dialects of Greek (including Homeric, Classical, and New Testament Greek) into an ancient Hebraic story from the Book of Judges, *Jephthah* effectively appropriates non-native cultural values to suggest how divisions between English Catholics and Protestants might be remedied through common national interests. Simultaneously, the play emphasizes how Christopherson's appropriation of other cultures is itself a means of creating early modern Englishness through the education and acculturation of its students.

Taken together, the two opening essays reveal the extent to which academic plays were used to effect political and religious change, whether by redefining established institutional traditions or by fashioning the language and ethical behaviors of individual scholars. While *Jephthah* aims to transform esoteric knowledge into the everyday practices of Catholic faith within an unpredictable Protestant milieu, Elizabeth takes up drama as an instrument to reduce the advisory responsibilities of university dons, who anxiously witness the devaluation of their knowledge as it is put to increasingly exoteric ends. The consideration that Streufert gives to *Jephthah*'s reworking of earlier cultural traditions serves as a link to a second group of essays concerned with challenges to the humanist tradition. As the dominant educational mode of early modern Europe, humanism exerted a sweeping authority over its ranks, whose subjects ranged from the most powerful heads of state to the most junior of grammar school boys. Yet such a characterization of humanism—even if in the first instance a relatively accurate one—has a tendency to totalize its ideological program and to paper over the many skirmishes that would come to define its theoretical terrain. Through its methodological interest in questioning assumptions and in exploring many sides of an issue, this dominant mode of learning produced the intellectual conditions that would encourage internal critique, both at the macrocultural level of humanist ideology and at the microcultural level of individual humanists.

As Ursula Potter shows in her essay, Thomas Ingelend is one individual who formulates his own vision of humanism in *The Disobedient Child*, a mid-sixteenth-century grammar-school play that is preoccupied with recuperating the poor image and diminished authority of schoolmasters. Potter examines how *The*

Disobedient Child advocates formal education among the gentry and aristocracy by suggesting that, contrary to popular belief, a school education will develop in boys the necessary skills and masculinity that they will need to maintain authority in their own households. We see here the residual aristocratic values that disfavor literacy confronting the dominance of humanism, but the play also resists that dominance by representing the elementary schooling of girls as a threat to male authority. The play thus challenges a variety of leading contemporary scholars like Juan Luis Vives and Desiderius Erasmus, who promote as an ideal of the humanist project the education of young girls, at least among the socially privileged classes. In order to shore up his own authority as an educator, Ingelend makes an appeal through his play to more powerful social classes than those historically represented in grammar schools, and Potter argues that he makes his appeal persuasive by portraying formal schooling as the solution to a social crisis in authority, which has been brought about by an educational crisis in gender. Potter's essay demonstrates how Ingelend's play sets up its own humanist paradigm, which competes with more familiar and esteemed pronouncements from scholars like Vives and Erasmus, revealing one process by which humanism understands and critiques itself.

In another essay that explores challenges to the humanist tradition, Emily D. Bryan takes up the question of authority introduced by Potter and addresses a specific production of *Ignoramus*, a play by George Ruggle that was performed before King James I at Cambridge in March of 1615. Unlike *The Disobedient Child*, which contests the authority of prominent European scholars in order to garner its own authority from wealthier classes, *Ignoramus* engages in a biting satire of English lawyers, which brought the play and apparently many of its student-players into the favor of the king. Bryan reveals that the dispute instigated by the production of Ruggle's play was in fact acted out behind the scenes in the more intimate relationship between tutors and students, who disagreed about how far the university could exercise its power over the individual principles of its students. One student, she explains, categorically refused to perform despite the influence of university authorities, while another student disobeyed his tutor's instructions and proceeded to perform in the play before the king. Recalling Potter's concern with ideological conflicts between individual humanists, and also Shenk's concern with the declining political significance of the Elizabethan universities, Bryan investigates how the confrontations occasioned by *Ignoramus* point to a discrepancy in what were once believed to be common interests between tutors and students, on the one hand, and, on the other, to a kind of self-determination that capitalizes on the opportunities that an increasingly competitive culture offers to those individuals.

One joint observation that both Potter's and Bryan's essays furnish is that the educational reforms experienced by early modern Europe were contested as much within the boundaries of humanism as along them. The disputes that humanist methodologies fostered amongst its practitioners were therefore not marginal affairs, but were instead constitutive of the educational program itself. Influential and prolific as they were, writers like Vives and Erasmus face the undue burden of speaking rather monologically on behalf of early modern humanism when the voices of other individuals go unheard, like those of the schoolmaster Ingelend or the tutors and students involved in the 1615 production of *Ignoramus*. In other words, humanism qualifies as what Michel Foucault would call a "transdiscursive" field, one which generates "an endless possibility of discourse" by producing the conditions for "a certain number of divergences—with respect to [... its] own texts, concepts, and hypotheses—that all arise from the [...] discourse itself."[11] Hence the expansion of humanism entails the transformation of its discursive practices from within, and the apparently isolated struggles for authority that we see depicted vividly in especially Potter's and Bryan's essays necessarily belong to the historically more visible dialogues in which eminent European humanists are engaged. Moreover, the renovations that humanism sought to carry out within early modern European culture were often simultaneously renovations to its own discursive practices, which were heterogeneous enough to accommodate major pedagogical texts like those of Vives and Erasmus as well as academic plays by little-known schoolmasters like Ingelend writing from unknown grammar schools.

If the essays by Potter and Bryan emphasize divisions within and challenges to early modern humanist ideology, then the next group of essays explores how academic solidarity and common scholarly hardships emerge from the rigorous application of humanist principles of study. This group of essays also considers how students leverage academic drama in order to understand and grapple with their institutional environments. Following Bryan's discussion of satirized lawyers in *Ignoramus* at Cambridge, Eric Leonidas moves us to the Inns of Court in London, where English students received formal training and experience in the practice of law. Leonidas focuses on the *Gesta Grayorum*, a series of Christmas revels staged at Gray's Inn during 1594–95 where the dramatic activities were framed as an evolving social experiment. The Gray's revels, he argues, allowed students to construct an artificial environment within which the audience was invited to test and adapt their knowledge through the shifting experiences of performance. Ultimately culminating in a performance before Queen Elizabeth I at Whitehall, the *Gesta Grayorum* is marked by a series of "occasions" or moments when revelers pause and reflect so they may determine proceedings as they go, incorporating what they learn into the order of their fictional kingdom. Leonidas demonstrates that the revels put into conversation two modes of knowledge production, one which was based in community and the shared experiences of students, and one which was based in individual observation and the independent substantiation of knowledge.

This juxtaposition of collective and individual epistemologies, which helps the students of Gray's Inn to navigate a variable field of experience, also serves to structure the second essay in this group by Sarah Knight. While the *Gesta Grayorum* tends to foreground a productive and socially unifying application of students' knowledge and intellectual skills, other dramatic ventures in the academy emphasize the destructive and socially isolating effects that individual study and scholarship too often educe. Knight situates such dramatic ventures within the early modern discourse on humors psychology, arguing that "fantasy" or the faculty of imagination was understood both to aid and to vex scholars in an erratic and progressively debilitating manner. Since "fantasy" has the ability to promote creativity while also inspiring melancholia in the intellectual life of every student, the mind's imaginative faculty itself becomes an object of study in a number of dramatic satires hailing from universities, including Thomas Tomkis's *Lingua* (1607), Barten Holyday's *Technogamia* (1617), and the *Parnassus* trilogy (circa 1598–1601), presumably written by out-of-work Cambridge alumni. Treatises on psychopathology and educational theory provide Knight with a backdrop that shows how the debates staged by university dramatists over the pedagogical utility of imagination are in fact symptomatic of broader transformations in the culture of humanism. Knight argues that while these debates reduce the epistemological value that scholars might derive from "fantasy," scholars are themselves experiencing a very real sense of decreased social value as the universities overproduce learned men for a market that has fewer and fewer positions to offer them.

The academic plays examined by Leonidas and Knight represent the most self-reflexive drama in the volume. Together, their essays underscore the relationship between public and private spheres: while the *Gesta Grayorum* depicts an optimum—if perhaps idealized—interaction between communal and individual experiences, wherein the production of knowledge becomes process-oriented and facilitated by regular adaptation and improvisation, then the satirical academic plays that are the focus of Knight's essay illustrate how scholars tend to face the communal problem of a shrinking job market by withdrawing more frequently into unhealthy private study, which gives rise to ruminating melancholia. That the texts both essays discuss appear around the same period of time suggests that the individual scholar's relationship with his community is an especially topical issue at the turn of the seventeenth century. These two representations of academic communities and individual scholars indicate two different perspectives on the same cultural problem, one in which the dominant ideals and optimism of humanistic learning are, on one hand, staving off and, on the other, succumbing to emergent forces in politics and the market economy, to which the academy too slowly adapts. In other words, if nearly a century earlier humanist scholars were busy theorizing and institutionalizing a programmatic endeavor to alter politics and social relations for the better through systematic educational reforms, then by the end of the sixteenth century political, social, and economic relations have begun to outstrip humanism's influence. The result of such a shift is the subjection of the academy in general and of scholars in particular to powers that humanists had once dreamt of appropriating and maintaining according to their own rational principles.

The question of the individual scholar's relationship with his academic community and, even more, the academic community's relationship with its surrounding culture provides a bridge to the volume's last group of essays. Helen Higbee opens this group with a consideration of John Ricketts's *Byrsa Basilica* (circa 1633), a play that overtly speaks to topical debates occurring within the London market. Set in the Royal Exchange, Ricketts's play takes as its subject a variety of business relationships between London merchants, which it then structures using the conventions of Plautine comedy. In her essay, Higbee argues that the play's preoccupation with the growing business of marine insurance and with the decline of the competing practice of judicial astrology marks a radical departure from the typical concerns that academic plays had historically addressed. Whereas in Knight's essay we see a deterioration of humanism's influence over the social sphere at the dawn of the seventeenth century, Higbee's essay shows how, by the 1630s, at least one drama has begun to imagine ways to meet the demands of an emergent market-based economy, one which international trade and imperialism have helped to engender. That *Byrsa Basilica* essentially stages a debate around the mercantile issues of marine insurance and judicial astrology indicates just how far humanistic ideals have been transmuted into residual values within Caroline England.

Whether we understand these changing cultural formations as academic drama expanding into the marketplace or as the market infiltrating the academy, *Byrsa Basilica* clearly argues that the educational and economic systems might cultivate a mutually profitable relationship in the 1630s, one which plays like the *Parnassus* trilogy at the turn of the seventeenth century seem more at pains to imagine. The commercial and maritime themes that Higbee's discussion highlights both provide links to the second essay in this group, which closes the volume. Odai Johnson's essay departs from the others in both disciplinary and geographic terms as it crosses the Atlantic from early modern England to colonial America, where commercial theater faced manifold cultural difficulties that the academic theater found much easier to navigate. By surveying a number of recorded performances as well as a series of *curricula vitae* for students involved in dramatic activities, Johnson shows how theatrical cultures existed virtually only within the academy in seventeenth- and eighteenth-century New England. Yet he also argues that the distinction between commercial and academic drama in early America is much more troubled than it at first seems, especially because students often profited from their performances—which were usually advertised simply as rhetorical demonstrations—and also because ventures in commercial theater tended to draw on the language of the academy in an effort to validate their existence. Thus Johnson finds that popular theater could at times circumvent Puritan resistance in America by associating itself with academic drama, but as a result public fears about theatricality more readily attached themselves to student-players.

As Johnson's essay looks forward and outward toward the eighteenth century and the development of American dramatic cultures, it also returns to the volume's earliest concerns (in Shenk's and Streufert's discussions) with the political and religious issues that helped to shape the early modern theater in England. In this concluding group of essays, Higbee's analysis of *Byrsa Basilica* reveals a drive toward expansionism and colonialism, both from the academy into the marketplace, and from the domestic market into international trade relations.

Johnson's discussion, in contrast, transports us to the American colonies where the residual values of English culture confront new and uncertain ways of knowing, which are dependent as much upon familiar narratives of self and nationhood as they are upon imagining novel forms of identity. As this volume argues, such narratives and forms always manifest themselves not simply in sweeping trends like humanism or colonialism but also in more intricate structures that have specific material dimensions and chartable socio-historical coordinates. Because especially Johnson's essay in this group reprises some of the issues that other contributors examine in earlier English contexts, the cultural and historical arc that the volume sets out to trace acquires a reverse trajectory. This reversal furnishes a dynamic perspective whereby our self-consciously back-constructed narrative about early modern culture overlays a chronological model of development in the period, which throws into relief the residual, dominant, and emergent forces that inspired and produced early modern academic drama.

These forces can be glimpsed in the manuscript leaf that adorns the cover of this book. The annotated drawings represent a design for the adaptation of the great hall at Christ Church, Oxford, into a theater for a visit by James I in 1605: the Court's visit in late August corresponded with "the week of ceremonies at Oxford called the Act, an annual celebration when public debates were held by day in St Mary's, the University Church, and in the evenings the colleges fell to feasting and sometimes by custom to dramatic entertainments."[12] The drawings, moreover, can be viewed as "academic" in a variety of ways, for they include classical, contemporary, and prospective intellectual currents. Whereas the classical influence was mainly generic, the contemporary came in the form of original dramatic compositions in Latin. "The plays," John Orrell explains,

> were of an academic sort, at once learned and facetious. The three evening productions, in Latin, represented the whole range of the drama, for in accord with the ancient division found in Vitruvius and his Renaissance commentators the authorities had chosen a tragedy, a comedy, and a satyr play. The satyr play, *Alba*, was performed first, on the Tuesday night; it was followed successively by the tragedy, *Ajax Flagellifer*, and the moral comedy, Matthew Gwinne's *Vertumnus*. All were staged at Christ Church, as was an English pastoral, Samuel Daniel's *Arcadia Reformed*, given on the morning after the main series had concluded.[13]

The influences that I am calling prospective were in a sense the future not of the academic stage but of English court productions, which took advantage of the latest Continental and the most esoteric theatrical innovations, both for perspective staging and for seating arrangements designed to optimize the perspectival effects. These innovations were "academic" insofar as they had scarcely been seen in England except in books and in the Whitehall production of *The Masque of Blackness* earlier that same year.

Not yet affiliated with the Royal Works during the Oxford visit, Inigo Jones was nonetheless responsible for the stage set and machinery, as indeed he had been for *The Masque of Blackness* in January. For the Christ Church productions, Jones probably used modified versions of classical *periaktoi*, and he certainly employed a raked stage, the first recorded example in England. On the other side, the responsibility for designing the auditorium fell to the Comptroller, Simon Basil, who modeled much of the spectatorial space on woodcuts and descriptions in Sebastiano Serlio's *Tutte l'opere dell'architettura* (1566 edition).[14] Yet, despite the confluence of classical authority, modern learnedness, and cutting-edge technical innovations in staging and seating, the plan for the auditorium had to be changed because several of James's courtiers objected to the placement of "the Isl for the kinge, a foote eleuated aboue the grounde."[15] Disrupting the intended perspective effects, James's Council required the workmen to move the king's halpace further back in the auditorium to a more conventional location, where he could be more easily viewed by all those present. The ironic result was that James ended up being "too farr from the stage (vizt) xxviij. feete, soe that there were manye longe speeches delivered, which neyther the kinge nor anye neere him could well heere or vnderstand."[16]

The annotated drawings for the theater at Christ Church, then, might represent the most erudite and astonishing neoclassical developments in theater technology in 1605. But they also form only a single stage in a larger narrative, one in which complex negotiations between the culture of learning and the culture of the Court play themselves out with compromised and disproportionate results. Such negotiations with external forces, we argue, are what the academy both encounters and puts on display when producing its own dramatic events.

* * *

Together, the essays collected in this volume aim to present a series of challenges to the reader. The first of these challenges regards the place of early modern academic drama within the critical consciousness of the various disciplines with which the essays engage, especially that of literary studies and theater history. From the sixteenth century alone, Boas accounts for some seventy-one extant university plays in English, Latin, and Greek, more than half of which are original compositions written on a wide range of classical, biblical, and contemporary subjects during the Tudor period.[17] As with the hundreds and hundreds of plays surviving from the commercial theaters that have historically failed to meet canonical standards, plays issuing from academic environments tend to remain peripheral or specialized concerns. Moreover, academic plays are often less accessible to scholars because of a dearth of available or affordable editions, and to some degree either because of language barriers in the case of Greek and Latin texts or because training in archival research and paleography is now less common in many graduate curricula. Yet our contemporary retrieval of academic drama might be seen to parallel the humanist recovery of "the examples of *Euripides*, *Sophocles*, and *Seneca*," which had once lain neglected or undiscovered for well over a millennium. Just as the advent of feminism, cultural materialism, new historicism, and post-colonialism has encouraged a reevaluation of the texts and materials we study—in terms of canonicity, of distinctions between "high" and "low" culture, and even of the notion of a field called the "Renaissance"—this volume, too, promotes the continued reassessment of these issues within the halls and upon the stages of the early modern academy.

This first challenge of centralizing academic plays within the general study of early modern English drama is greatly dependent upon the work of recent scholars and the REED project, who have begun to give more visibility to the dramatic output of educational institutions in the period as well as to the microcultures that helped to produce such plays.[18] Like the conversations that Roger Ascham recalls having with Sir John Cheke and Thomas Watson, the work of these scholars opens up a discourse about academic drama while at once modeling a critical practice for its study. Therefore the intellectual affiliations that I have emphasized between this volume and recent research in the field I also want to extend to scholarship in the early modern period itself. Since the intellectual work that humanists performed was also a kind of cultural architecture, one which both influenced and was influenced by the period's political, religious, and economic relations, there are not a few continuities between the place that scholars and their educational system occupied in early modern England and the ones that we occupy in North America, England, and Australia, which are the regions represented by our contributors. If the first challenge offered by the volume chiefly involves critical awareness and disciplinarity, then the second is epistemological, insofar as academic drama presents us not only with narratives of early modern learning to be studied, but also with ways to understand and narrativize our own relationships with scholarly subject-matter and with the intellectual and cultural communities to which we belong.

Such a restructuring of our ways of knowing amounts to far more than a rhetorical conceit about the stories we tell, or an idealized vision of the scholarly life. Quite to the contrary, the poststructuralist precept that narrative organizes social relations and constitutes a form of belief continues to be a potent incitement to take stock of how intellectual work affects our cultural surroundings, and even actively to cultivate change within them, much as early modern humanists did. Hence the volume's last challenge is one that we have set for ourselves as well as for our audiences: as I have said, the essays seek to examine academic drama in order to understand the relationship between cultural and intellectual formations. But this examination also entails a reconsideration of a body of scholarship devoted to academic drama, which enables us to hear, instead of neglect, the stories that critics such as Boas, Motter, and Smith have told about it, while also offering new arguments about the work that such plays achieved—and failed to achieve— within early modern culture. While the essays in this volume are examples of new critical narratives about the field of academic drama, we also await the work of others who will extend and enhance our conclusions.

Indeed my argument in this introduction is that—from "the preceptes of Aristotle and *Horace de Arte Poetica*" discussed by Ascham, Cheke, and Watson, to the subsequent research that we hope this book will stimulate—this particular dramatic criticism participates in a scholarly dialogue that is itself a kind of academic drama, one which features many perspectives on and disagreements over the aesthetic merits and the cultural significance of plays written and performed by scholars and students. And though, for us, the intersection between theater and learning may not always take the form of "many pleasant talkes togither" with colleagues and friends, the academic drama of early modern England invites us to imagine both new and old ways of experiencing the production of knowledge.

Notes

1   Roger Ascham, THE SCHOLEMASTER *Or plaine and perfite way of teachyng children [...]* (London: by Iohn Daye, 1570), 57.

2   Joel Altman, *The Tudor Play of Mind: Rhetorical Inquiry and the Development of Renaissance Drama* (Berkeley: University of California Press, 1978), 44.

3   Horace, *Ars Poetica*, in *Satires, Epistles and Ars Poetica*, trans. H. Rushton Fairclough (Cambridge: Harvard University Press, 1999), ll. 333–4: "Aut prodesse volunt aut delectare poetae / aut simul et iucunda et idonea dicere vitae" ("Poets aim either to benefit, or to amuse, or to utter words at once both pleasing and helpful to life").

4   J.E.B. Mayor, *Early Statutes of the College of St. John the Evangelist in the University of Cambridge* (Cambridge: Cambridge University Press, 1859), 139.

5   Frederick S. Boas, *University Drama in the Tudor Age* (Oxford: Oxford University Press, 1914); G.C. Moore Smith, *College Plays Performed in the University of Cambridge* (Cambridge: Cambridge University Press, 1923); and T.H. Vail Motter, *The School Drama in England* (London: Longmans, Green and Co., 1929).

6   Cf. Alan H. Nelson, ed., *Records of Early English Drama: Cambridge*, 2 vols. (Toronto: University of Toronto Press, 1989); John R. Elliott, Jr., and Alan H. Nelson (University), Alexandra F. Johnston and Diana Wyatt (City), eds., *Records of Early English Drama: Oxford*, 2 vols. (Toronto: University of Toronto Press, 2004); Alan H. Nelson, *Early Cambridge Theatres: University, College, and Town Stages, 1464–1720* (Cambridge: Cambridge University Press, 1994); and John R. Elliott, Jr., "Plays, Players and Playwrights in Renaissance Oxford," in *From Page to Performance: Essays in Early English Drama*, ed. John A. Alford (East Lansing: Michigan State University Press, 1995), 179–94.

7   Bruce R. Smith, *Ancient Scripts and Modern Experience on the English Stage 1500–1700* (Princeton: Princeton University Press, 1988); Rebecca Bushnell, *A Culture of Teaching: Early Modern Humanism in Theory and Practice* (Ithaca: Cornell University Press, 1996); Kent Cartwright, *Theatre and Humanism:*

English Drama in the Sixteenth Century (Cambridge: Cambridge University Press, 1999).

8 "Queen Elizabeth's first reply to the Parliamentary petitions urging the execution of Mary, Queen of Scots, November 12, 1586" (version 2), in *Elizabeth I: Collected Works*, ed. Leah S. Marcus, Janel Mueller, and Mary Beth Rose (Chicago: University of Chicago Press, 2000), 194. For James I's remark addressed to his son Prince Henry, see his *Basilicon Doron*, in *King James VI and I: The Political Writings*, ed. Johann P. Sommerville (Cambridge: Cambridge University Press, 1994), 4: "Kings being public persons, by reason of their office and authority, are as it were set (as it was said of old) upon a public stage, in the sight of all people; where all the beholders' eyes are attentively bent to look and pry into the least circumstance of their secretest drifts."

9 See Raymond Williams, *Marxism and Literature* (Oxford: Oxford University Press, 1977), 121–7.

10 Boas, *University Drama*, 43.

11 Michel Foucault, "What Is an Author?," in *Textual Strategies: Perspectives in Post-Structuralist Criticism*, ed. and trans. Josué V. Harari (Ithaca: Cornell University Press, 1979), 153, 154, 155. Foucault, it should be said, would likely disagree that humanism is a transdiscursive field because he believes Marxism and psychoanalysis "to be both the first and the most important cases" (154).

12 John Orrell, *The Theatres of Inigo Jones and John Webb* (Cambridge: Cambridge University Press, 1985), 24.

13 John Orrell, *The Human Stage: English Theatre Design, 1567–1640* (Cambridge: Cambridge University Press, 1988), 120. Incidentally, King James did not attend the performance of *Arcadia Reformed*, which seems to have been "played in English as a treat for the queen and Prince Henry" (Orrell, *The Theatres of Inigo Jones and John Webb*, 30).

14 For detailed discussions of Jones's and Basil's influences, see especially Orrell, *The Theatres of Inigo Jones and John Webb*, 24–38; and Orrell, *The Human Stage*, 119–29. In "The Theatre at Christ Church, Oxford, in 1605," *Shakespeare Survey* 35 (1982): 129–40, John Orrell is less confident about attributing the drawings to Basil (132–3), but he appears to have accepted the attribution by the time he writes *The Human Stage*.

15 The quotation is from annotation "K." for the upper drawing on the manuscript, "Theater at Christ Church, Oxford, August 1605," British Library, Additional MS. 15505, fol. 21a. Cf. the classic study by Stephen Orgel, *The Illusion of Power: Political Theater in the English Renaissance* (Berkeley: University of California Press, 1975).

16 Cambridge University Library, Additional MS. 34, fol. 30a; quoted in Orrell, *The Human Stage*, 127. For a sensitive discussion of just how unfamiliar the Christ Church theater design was in 1605 England, see Stephen Orgel, "The

Poetics of Spectacle," *New Literary History* 2 (1971): 367–89, especially 376–9 and 385–6.

17 See Boas, *University Drama*, "Appendix IV," 385–90.

18 For exciting recent work on academic drama see, for instance, Lynn Enterline on grammar schools: "Rhetoric, Discipline, and the Theatricality of Everyday Life in Elizabethan Grammar Schools," in *From Performance to Print in Shakespeare's England*, ed. Stephen Orgel and Peter Holland (New York: Palgrave Macmillan, 2006), 173–90; Carla Mazzio on universities: "The Three Dimensional Self: Geometry, Melancholy, Drama," in *The Arts of Calculation: Quantifying Thought in Early Modern Europe*, ed. David Glimp and Michelle R. Warren (New York: Palgrave Macmillan, 2004), 39–65; and Matthew Steggle on the Inns of Court: "Varieties of fantasy in 'What You Will,'" in *The Drama of John Marston: Critical Re-Visions*, ed. T.F. Wharton (Cambridge: Cambridge University Press, 2000), 45–59.

CHAPTER 1

Gown Before Crown: Scholarly Abjection and Academic Entertainment Under Queen Elizabeth I

Linda Shenk

In 1592, Queen Elizabeth I and the Privy Council made a rather audacious request of their intellectuals at the Universities of Oxford and Cambridge. The Christmas season was fast approaching, and a recent outbreak of the plague prohibited the queen's professional acting company from performing the season's customary entertainment. To avoid having a Christmas without revels, the crown sent messengers to both institutions, asking for university men to come to court and perform a comedy in English. Cambridge's Vice Chancellor, John Still, wished to decline this royal invitation, and for advice on how to do so he wrote to his superior, William Cecil, Lord Burghley, who was not only the Chancellor of Cambridge but also Elizabeth's chief advisor. In this letter, Vice Chancellor Still implies the impropriety of having academics participate in such a performance:

> how fitt wee shalbe for this that is moued, havinge no practize in this Englishe vaine, and beinge (as wee thincke) nothinge beseeminge our Student*es*, specially oute of the Vniu*er*sity: wee much doubt; And do finde our principale Actors (whome wee haue of purpose called before vs) very vnwillinge to playe in Englishe; Wherefore wee thoughte it not only our duties, to giue intelligence hereof vnto yo*ur* Lo*rdshi*p as being our cheife hedd and governor; but also very expedient for vs, to craue your Lordships wisdome, either to disswade the matter withoute any displeasure vnto vs, yf wee shall not seeme meete in yo*ur* Lo*rdshi*ps iudgment for that purpose; or to advise vs by your Honorable direcc*i*on, what ma*n*ner of argument wee should ch[o]use, and what course is best to followe. Englishe Comedies, for that wee neuer vsed any, wee presentlie haue none.[1]

Finding that the request is "nothing beseeminge our Student*es*, specially oute of the Vniu*er*sity" and emphasizing that they "neuer vsed any" English comedies, Still insinuates that the crown has crossed a line by asking university men to perform in the vernacular—especially the lighter fare of a comedy. They are academics, after all, not professional stage-players.

By asking intellectuals to come *to court*, to perform *a comedy*, and a comedy *in English*, the crown is treating its university subjects as entertainers who can be called upon to provide diversion solely for amusement. The issue here is not simply that the crown wants scholars to perform a play, for the universities had already prepared many productions for the crown—some even in English.[2] The issue, rather, is that the crown requested a rather *un*academic combination: a stand-alone comedy, in English, at court. In the past, university productions for the queen and nobility had always been produced on university soil, always performed at the end of a day of learned activities, and always scheduled between evenings that contained plays treating weightier material. When the crown asks for performances that occur without these learned contexts and the medium of Latin and Greek, it is asking for performances that ignore university men's identities as intellectuals. As such, the state treats them as court players rather than future political advisors, clerics, and ambassadors.

The crown's request to the universities crystallizes a trend that had become a uniquely Elizabethan phenomenon in English history: university men repeatedly performing for the crown. Before Elizabeth's reign, university plays were private, university-only affairs, but after her first progress to Cambridge in 1564, the queen and court frequently attended university productions. The importance of these performances has not been lost on theater and university historians. Scholars such as Frederick S. Boas, John Elliott, Jr., and Alan H. Nelson have mined the accounts and university records, and their descriptive work has contributed substantially to our understanding of university culture and early modern staging practices. What scholars have not yet fully examined are the *implications* of these performances—the implications, essentially, of the gown entertaining the crown. How does having the monarch in the audience affect university drama? How might these performances, on a more profound level, affect the relationship between the monarch and intellectuals? Lastly, how might this relationship imply that the Elizabethan regime had created its own version of the humanist idea that the scholar should serve the state as a wise counselor?[3]

Answering these questions, in part, involves looking at the choices the universities made when preparing plays for the court. These performances begin with Elizabeth's 1564 and 1566 progresses to the Universities of Cambridge and Oxford (respectively) and then include a series of later interactions when the universities hosted and performed either for the court or on the court's behalf, such as for the Polish Palatine Alberto Laski's visit to Oxford in 1583. These historical examples reveal that the universities (especially Oxford) increasingly linked drama with the crown by tailoring their productions to satisfy the court's preferences for lavish spectacle and royal flattery. As Nelson has demonstrated, some private university productions did contain elaborate, costly spectacle.[4] The university productions for the court, however, not only made much of highly scenic effects but specifically involved court-affiliated alumni to assist in making these productions pleasing to the courtly audience.

This interest in making university productions more court-like, though, had changed direction by 1592—a year full of events that shared a common concern: the need to distinguish university "actors" from professional stage-players. Early in the year, the famous controversy over academic drama flared between John Rainolds and William Gager,[5] and Gager had defended university men, emphasizing that "ludii nos nec sumus, / nec esse cupimus" ("We are not professional players nor do we care to be").[6] Similarly, during the queen's final visit to Oxford that September, Gager and the university overall continued to emphasize that their productions were bookish and inexpertly executed instead of spectacle-filled and skillfully performed. The meteoric rise of the professional theater, now put alongside an increasingly theatrical connection between crown and gown, was taking its toll. Before the rise of the public theater, performances for royalty were often conducted in aristocratic homes and at the Inns of Court, but the high visibility of the professional actor on the popular public stage began to loosen dramatic entertainment's previously exclusive connections. University men faced the conjoining of two separate trends: the popularity of the professional actor (who, unlike the intellectual, possessed no established right to a political voice) and the rise of the universities' dramatic connections with the crown. Pressed to keep these two trends from becoming conflated, many university men had a change of heart sometime around 1592 when the controversy over academic drama raged and Vice Chancellor Still wrote his letter to Lord Burghley. University men seemed to realize that their performances for royalty had cast them in the role of royal entertainers—a role that, particularly through its similarity with professional players, diminished the political authority their learning was supposed to give them.

These trends in drama offer a perspective on the political relationship between crown and gown, which is central to the idea of humanism and the scholar's authority in early modern England. When the crown turned to university men for diversion more than disputation, it undercut the humanist mythology of the scholar serving the state as a learned advisor. I have argued elsewhere that the Latin orations Elizabeth delivered at the ends of her university visits reveal that the queen sought to contain the scholars' authority through a language of learned absolutism and, later, of divinity.[7] Turning to university men for entertainment similarly worked to contain the scholars' influence by redirecting intellectual energy into a form that focused on pleasing Elizabeth. I contend that even university-educated playwrights for the professional stage recognized this trend and sought to capitalize on it. In the small window of years surrounding 1592, university "wits" Robert Greene, Christopher Marlowe, and Thomas Nashe wrote works that portray university men performing spectacle *to please royalty*. In *Friar Bacon and Friar Bungay* (circa 1589–92), Greene's Friars Vandermast and Bungay compete to out-magic each other, while the Emperor and visiting royal dignitaries cheer them on; the protagonist in Marlowe's *Doctor Faustus* (circa 1588–1592) sells his soul for empowering knowledge, yet ends up creating merriment for Emperor Carolus and Duke Vanholt; and in *The Vnfortvnate Traveller* (1594), Nashe's intellectuals at Wittenberg try to impress their visiting Duke with ridiculous orations and a poorly acted comedy, but end up making fools of themselves.[8] In his article on the magician-scholars in *Friar Bacon and Friar Bungay*, *Faustus*, and *The Tempest*, Andreas Höfele explains that these characters, in their acts of performance, provide "a portrait of the artist, especially of the artist in society."[9] The theatrical spectacle-making that these figures depict, I propose, also provides a portrait of the university scholar in relation to his monarch. Modern historians have not examined in detail how these literary representations speak to the historical relationship between crown and gown. University drama implies that these institutions and their scholars were becoming satellites of the state. This trend matches university historian Penry Williams's observation that the crown's influence over the universities increased during Elizabeth's reign so that, by the end of the sixteenth century, "the university's independence had been heavily mortgaged."[10] By 1592, university men were beginning to acknowledge that their role as entertainers for the court tied them more closely (and abjectly) to the crown's authority.

Despite this power dynamic, the decisions regarding drama did not arise as top-down, crown-imposed scenarios but, rather, evolved through a slow compilation of choices and requests made by both crown and gown. Though I began with the universities' wary unease of 1592, I will now return to the early stirrings of this trend in the 1560s and then trace the subsequent events that comprise the gradual progression. Moving through the early university productions for the court and crown, through the literary representations, and finally to the events of 1592, I will demonstrate how the image of the scholar as a royal entertainer not only came into being but also revealed the universities' increasing focus on the court's preferences and authority. In fact, Oxford tended to follow this trajectory more so than Cambridge. The early modern period celebrated the scholar's role in political life, but the dramatic activity between the crown and the universities in Elizabeth's reign added entertainment to this idea of service. This idea, in turn, helps explain the rise of the entertaining intellectual throughout the 1590s—from the numerous scholars who did go on to perform for the court while still studying at the universities to the scholars hired to write entertaining prose against Martin Marprelate.

Elizabeth's Early Progresses: Cambridge in 1564 and Oxford in 1566

On 12 July 1564, William Cecil, then Chancellor of Cambridge, notified his university that the rumors were indeed true: the queen intended to spend nearly a week visiting the university, and the university was to prepare orations, disputations, sermons, and plays for her visit. Elizabeth's progress was unprecedented in English history. Never before had an English monarch conducted such a lengthy visit to one of the universities, and never before had an English monarch slept on university soil as a guest.[11] Over the course of her reign, Elizabeth would eventually conduct three such lengthy progresses to her universities (1564 to Cambridge; 1566 and 1592 to Oxford), and through these visits Elizabeth fostered a relationship between crown and gown that was markedly different from that created by the previous

Tudor monarchs—a difference that underscores the image of the intellectual as an entertainer.

Throughout the sixteenth century, Elizabeth's Tudor predecessors had occasionally called upon the universities to offer learned opinion regarding important matters of political policy. Henry VIII asked both institutions to provide public responses concerning the "great matter" of his divorce; Edward's administration staged a disputation against the Mass at Cambridge; and Mary countered this disputation by organizing one in support of the Mass at Oxford. Even though the universities always produced the desired "answer" and affirmed the current monarch's agenda, these demonstrations acknowledged the humanist notion that the enlightened prince should consult the wisdom of educated subjects. Elizabeth, however, never asked the universities to participate in political policy. Instead, her administration asked them to act as the queen's hosts in a fashion similar to her progresses to private, aristocratic homes. They were to lodge her and prepare suitable entertainment. Cecil's initial letter to Cambridge before the first progress makes these two priorities clear, asking the university to "*co*nsider what lodgynge shalbe metest for her ma*ies*tie & nexte what man*er* of [plaies]/ plesures/ in lernyng may be p*r*esented to her ma*ies*tie."[12] As editor Alan H. Nelson's brackets above denote, Cecil initially wrote "plaies" before striking through this choice and replacing it with "pleasures." Cecil's initial impulse was to specify dramatic entertainment before deciding to broaden the possibilities. His emphasis on pleasure (and his conflation of this idea with plays) is in harmony with the repeated use of "entertain" and "entertainment" in the accounts of the progresses. In essence, the universities were called upon to entertain their queen—a role that did not necessarily have a condescending air in the 1560s because many royal entertainments were staged in aristocratic homes and through connections with the Inns of Court. These two venues help explain why the universities would not have taken offense at royal requests for plays. The universities, after all, had a long-standing dramatic tradition in England and, as Siobhan Keenan notes, these plays offered a venue for university men to counsel their monarch.[13] In these performances of the 1560s, both Oxford and Cambridge sought to balance court-pleasing theatrical elements with material that retained a connection to learning's association with political comment. Even within this balance, however, the foundations for the image of sheer (non-academic) entertainment were being built and would soon be strengthened with the rise of professional theater.

For Elizabeth's visit, Cambridge planned a series of plays that demonstrated not only breadth of learning and an interest in showcasing the university's Protestant affinity with the court but also intellectual opinion on current political issues. In fact, the topics of three of the four plays the Cambridge men prepared hinted at the two most politically sensitive issues for Elizabeth in 1564: marriage and religion. On the first evening of the queen's visit, the university presented Plautus' *Aulularia* in Latin, which culminates with the main character, Euclio, giving the pot of gold alluded to in the title to his virtuous daughter as a wedding present. The next night, Elizabeth watched another play that included a tale of love (but now with a tragic ending) when she attended *Dido*, written in Latin by Cambridge's own Edward Haliwell. For the third performance, the university switched the subject-matter to religion and presented *Ezechias* in English, a revival of Nicholas Udall's comedy about the Old Testament King Hezekiah.[14] Because Hezekiah had ordered the destruction of idolatrous images and the brazen serpent (an image theologians associated with the cross), this king often served as the biblical model for Protestant rulers. In other venues and even earlier in that day's academic exercises, others had already likened Elizabeth to King Hezekiah, and what is more, Udall himself had similarly alluded to Hezekiah when he lauded Henry VIII's Protestant reforms. As Margaret Aston notes, however, the production of *Ezechias* for Elizabeth may have also housed criticism with compliment. Elizabeth still kept a cross in her private chapel (hence, the significance of a reference to the brazen serpent), and certainly many Protestants felt that her private devotions as well as her public policies were not sufficiently reformed.[15] These potential aspects of criticism may explain the cryptic phrase in Nicholas Robinson's account that "after the performance had been *viewed long enough*, it was time for rest."[16] Did the queen leave partway through the performance?[17] If so, the production may have smacked too much of counsel. If she did retire before the play concluded, this act may suggest a subtext to her claims of fatigue the next night as the reason for canceling that evening's performance, which was to be a Latin version of Sophocles' play *Ajax Flagellifer*.

The queen may have had enough of such politically driven entertainment, but a few of her Cambridge men were not finished using drama to make their points about religion. In a letter written to the Duchess of Parma, the Spanish ambassador Guzmán de Silva relates that several intellectuals from the university followed Elizabeth to her next stop at Hinchinbrook where they put on a baldly anti-Catholic performance:

> The actors came in dressed as some of the imprisoned Bishops. First came the bishop of London carrying a lamb in his hands as if he were eating it as he walked along, and then others with devices, one being in the figure of a dog with the Host in his mouth. They write that the Queen was so angry that she at once entered her chamber using strong language.[18]

According to the Spanish ambassador, Elizabeth was none too pleased to have her subjects offer such a strident depiction of Catholic practice. Considering that this description occurs in a letter written by a Spanish (hence Catholic) figure to the wife of another prominent Spanish leader, Elizabeth's reaction may have been exaggerated; however, it would be no surprise if Elizabeth did react negatively. Not only were diplomatic affairs with Catholic Spain rather delicate at the moment but also such blunt and radical representations were hardly in tune with Elizabeth's much more religiously conservative *via media*. As with this representation and the production of *Ezechias*, Cambridge men may have taken too much political license with their entertaining fare. On the one hand, their choice to use Udall's play shows, in part, an interest in calling upon a playwright who had successfully entertained previous Tudor monarchs, but on the other, these men may have strayed too far from their entertaining role. Oxford, especially with its dangerously Catholic recent history, would not make the same choice.[19]

Two years after the visit to Cambridge, Oxford stayed more clearly in the realm of entertainment by selecting and commissioning pieces that more overtly incorporated royal compliment and awe-inspiring spectacle. Oxford also added another factor to ensure success—not just a playwright who had pleased a previous monarch but one who was doing so currently—Richard Edwardes. Elizabeth had appointed Edwardes, an Oxford alumnus, as her Master of the Children of the Chapel Royal in 1561. Oxford had him come to campus two months early both to complete an English comedy for the visit (*Palamon and Arcyte*) and to share his expertise in courtly performance for the other productions.[20] As a university graduate, Master of the Children of the Chapel Royal, and member of Lincoln's Inn, Edwardes had a career that integrated the three premiere institutions that fostered drama: the court, the universities, and the Inns of Court.[21] The productions associated with the 1566 progress represent the height of this fusion—learned sources grounded in English tradition, political themes, and impressive spectacle reminiscent of court masques. Perhaps through Edwardes's expertise, Oxford's productions surpassed those at Cambridge in that they better resembled the strategies playwrights were using at court to honor their queen's power. Though these plays still possessed political posturing, they also mark an increased focus on university productions as entertainment.

Oxford tapped into Edwardes's court experience throughout the progress, beginning with the opening production, *Marcus Geminus*. In this performance, Edwardes had helped with the staging, and the set for this production reveals how the performance used staging and topicality both to honor Elizabeth's supreme authority and to forge good relations with her. As Heather Kerr notes, *Marcus Geminus* was based on chapters thirty-eight and thirty-nine of Sir Thomas Elyot's *The Image of Governaunce* (1540).[22] Choosing this story and this author was particularly shrewd. The tale's legal scenarios would have given the appropriately learned air to the dramatic action, and Elyot had been one of Elizabeth's father's supporters (at least for awhile) as well as a champion of the learned prince. Kerr notes that even the arrangement of the stage, when considered with the action in the story, emphasized Elizabeth's enlightened status as a wise ruler-judge. "Elizabeth was to sit in 'a state' placed on the stage raised at the western end of the Hall. Alexander Severus, sitting 'in astate' [*sic*] in 'The Theatre of Pompey,' and giving his 'last judgement in his own person,' is a potential mirror-image for the Queen as wise judge," for it was "a flattering allusion to Elizabeth as an ideal ruler."[23] Unfortunately, all this careful deference was almost completely for naught. Elizabeth made her feelings about Oxford's historically strong ties to Catholicism quite known and avoided all activities on the Sunday of the scheduled performance. Even so, this play shows how Oxford shaped its entertainment to honor Elizabeth, using the stage configuration (much like a court masque) to showcase her power over all, even over their scholarship.

Just as Edwardes applied his court experience to the staging, he also incorporated his particular forte: court-pleasing spectacle. On the next two evenings, his flair for the visually and dramatically pleasing was evident when the university men put on his two-part play *Palamon and Arcyte* (an adaptation of Chaucer's *The Knight's Tale*). All were thoroughly entertained. It was "acted with very great applause in Christ Church Hall. [...] Afterwards the Actors performed their parts so well, that the Queen laughed heartily thereat, and gave the Author of the Play great thanks for his pains." Merriment and enthusiasm typified the audience's reaction to this play, which was full of energetic spectacle. In the scene when Theseus goes hunting with his hounds, some students stood in the quadrant outside to create the effects of the "howndes w*ith* a trayle at a ffox." Apparently, they were so successful that "ye ladyes in ye wyndowe crydd nowe nowe & hallowed oh excellent said ye Quen*es* ma*iest*ie those boyes ar readye to leape oute of ye windowe to follow ye hownd*es*."[24] In choosing Edwardes, Oxford elicited the desired response: Elizabeth was delighted. Edwardes (and even Udall, to a lesser extent) demonstrates the beginnings of a fusion between performances for crown and gown. Their plays, while not diminishing the learned aura of academic productions, show how diversion at the universities begins to possess many of the trappings of diversion at court.

The Court's Intellectuals: Performance and Honoring the Crown

In entertaining the queen, the universities, particularly Oxford, were so successful that these "performances" begat more productions. The court began to call upon the universities to host court figures and even foreign dignitaries on its behalf. This string of entreaties in the 1570s and '80s opens the door for the crown's explicit request in 1592 to intellectuals to perform at court. Through these events, the court treats the universities as an extension of itself, and, similarly, the universities use drama to express increased association with queen and court. Plays become one facet of a growing intimacy between crown and gown, and this intimacy heightens the academy's focus and emphasis on the crown, which erodes the semblance of it as an autonomous institution. The image of the performing academic, rather unwittingly, becomes a symbol of the crown's power to have its intellectuals at its bidding. Having drama as a central form of service additionally separates the intellectual from his serious, political stature that was the source of his authority. Events of the 1570s and '80s do not represent such a clear portrayal of these power dynamics, but they set into motion the ingredients that will later facilitate them.

The first of the crown's requests for entertainment came in 1569 when Robert Dudley, Earl of Leicester, planned to bring to Oxford Odet de Coligny, Cardinal de Châtillon (an ambassador representing the Huguenot leader Condé). The university began preparations, which included a play, *The Destruction of Thebes*.

Although this visit was eventually cancelled, a sufficient number of the university population would have known about the plans, because they were announced during Convocation. In 1578, Cambridge scholars were given the opportunity to perform—this time for Elizabeth—when she visited nearby Audley End. This event was like a mini-university progress, and for it they prepared a shortened itinerary of a comedy, orations, and disputations. This connection between the queen and performing comedy (even though Still will downplay this connection in 1592) was already forming, and this visit was an instance when intellectuals traveled to perform for the queen (though they did not travel far). Unlike the comedy that would be requested in 1592, the comedy the Cambridge men prepared was still performed alongside learned demonstrations. In keeping with this idea of staging comedy for the queen, St. John's started an annual tradition, sometime before 1588, of performing a comedy on Elizabeth's Accession Day.[25] These performances may have begun far earlier; in fact, records at King's College begin listing expenses paid to musicians for work contributing to festivities on the Queen's Day in 1577.[26] Although Elizabeth would not have attended these performances, it is interesting that, at least by 1588, the university started to honor this day with drama—and a comedy, no less. By choosing this more festive genre, St. John's helped solidify the relationship between entertainment and royalty.

Such focus on the court as a force that prompts and inspires drama, in turn, would have encouraged university men to believe that the crown was now a potential audience for university productions. Nelson speculates that university playwright Thomas Legge wrote his ambitious trilogy *Richard Tertius* with Elizabeth in mind, and certainly this trilogy's grand spectacle and theme of Tudor propaganda would have made it a crown-pleaser.[27] Several of Legge's actors were Robert Greene's classmates, and this connection may help explain why Greene chose to depict scholars performing for royalty in *Friar Bacon and Friar Bungay*. Greene and his Cambridge peers Marlowe and Nashe may have received further inspiration from the repeated university hostings that became quite frequent at Oxford throughout the 1580s. In 1580/81, John Harington and Robert Devereux, Earl of Essex, attended a university production of *Pedantius*, the infamous production that playfully satirized Gabriel Harvey. On a much larger and well-publicized scale, Oxford was called upon in 1583 and 1585 to entertain court and foreign dignitaries with an itinerary similar to that prepared for Elizabeth years earlier. In 1585, Oxford hosted Leicester, and to make this event sufficiently sumptuous for their Chancellor, officials contacted John Lyly at court to assist them with costumes. This visit, however, paled in comparison to the elaborate visit that had taken place at Oxford in 1583. For this earlier visit, Oxford received a request directly from the crown to host the Polish Palatine Laski, and entertainment remained clearly on the agenda.[28] On the first night of his visit, because the palatine "sought rather rest in his lodging than recreation in anie academicall pastimes, strange fire works were shewed."[29] The next day, these "academicall *pastimes*" (my emphasis) of orations, disputations, and plays began, and once again the plays provided an opportunity for the university men to present a learned product that contained strong courtly influences. The university prepared two plays—the comedy *Rivales* and the tragedy *Dido*—both in Latin and both by in-house playwright William Gager. The two plays offered much opportunity for spectacle, especially *Dido*, whose special effects prompted the following admiration in Holinshed's *Third Volume of Chronicles* (1587), beginning with Dido's banquet scene:

> wherein the queenes banket (with Eneas narration of the destruction of Troie) was liuelie described in a marchpaine patterne, there was also a goodlie sight of hunters with full crie of a kennell of hounds, Mercurie and Iris descending and ascending from and to an high place, the tempest wherein it hailed small confects, rained rosewater, and snew an artificiall kind of snow, all strange, maruellous, and abundant.[30]

With a tempest, artificial snow, and even a hunting scene (perhaps reminiscent of Edwardes's theatrical coup years earlier), this play included all the spectacle of a courtly presentation. Christ Church spent a total of £86 on the productions—almost one fourth of the entire cost (£350) for Laski's visit.[31]

The similarity to courtly presentation stemmed, at least in part, from the university again seeking assistance from its alumni who had landed employment entertaining the court. For this visit, the university called upon George Peele to help with the theatrical arrangements.[32] Peele, just like Edwardes before him, had proven himself a successful court dramatist, as his recent play *The Arraignment of Paris* attested. He, like Edwardes, provided tested success with courtly audiences. As Thomas John Manning notes, the two plays performed during Laski's visit also called for staging techniques that Peele particularly liked. For example, the same kind of machinery that Peele's play used to make the tree of gold rise and Pluto ascend from the underworld could have been used for Sichaeus' entrance from below in *Dido*, and both plays include a storm. Peele may even have suggested the rosewater and confectionary hailstones used in the production, for as Manning also observes, they "seem more appropriate to the sumptuous world of Peele's mythological pastoral than to the austerity of Gager's neo-Senecan tragedy."[33] With such spectacular productions in conjunction with the care put into the rest of Laski's visit, it was no wonder that "yᵉ Prince Laskey [...] made such report here of yᵉ great entertainement you gaue him." Leicester, then Chancellor of Oxford, wrote these words in a letter dated 28 June 1583. In this letter—read during Convocation—the Chancellor expresses thanks not only on his behalf but also on behalf of Elizabeth.[34] It is one thing for Leicester as Chancellor to express his thanks, but when he indicates that Elizabeth expresses hers as well, he implies that the university entertained on the crown's behalf, thus making this entertainment an extension of the court's hospitality. In effect, the crown was treating the university as a royal ancillary.

The Entertaining Academic: Character in Vogue on the Public Stage

One year before assisting Oxford University with preparations to entertain Leicester, Lyly took his play *Campaspe* to court. In the play, he represents such famous philosophers as Plato and Aristotle entertaining their ruler, Alexander the Great. This dramatic scene, which David Bevington and Eric Rasmussen call "the royal quiz-show,"[35] is a precursor to the trend that will materialize historically in the next few years. In *Campaspe*, Alexander not only charges the intellectuals "to instruct the young with rules, confirm the old with reasons,"[36] but, more importantly, goes on to question them for his own amusement. Throughout this scene, the philosophers are all deference, eagerly expressing such sentiments as "We are all here ready to be commanded, and glad we are that we are commanded" (1.3.75–6). The scholars' willingness to provide entertainment, Lyly implies, goes hand-in-hand with submission. Lyly, however, lightly criticizes their subservient stance by juxtaposing it with the cynic Diogenes and his resistance to comply with Alexander's summons to court. According to Melippus' report of Diogenes' response, the Cynic had said, "If Alexander would fain see me, let him come to me; if learn of me, let him come to me" (1.3.17–18). Refusing to budge, Diogenes stands firm on his position as an advisor, more fit to instruct than to entertain. As of *Campaspe*'s court-performance in 1584, England's academic men had not yet been requested to entertain the crown at court, but Lyly is already associating scholars with entertainment and at-court entertainment with a subservient position— connections that, eight years later, come into literary vogue and royal request.

In the late 1580s and early '90s, the figure of the academic enjoyed brief popularity on the professional stage and in the bookstalls.[37] Although scholars have long noted the popularity of the foolish scholar character in this period (and the frequent representations of this figure as a magician), they have not stressed that these examples all involve performing for royalty. These literary representations written by university alums suggest that some university men did notice that the traffic between crown and gown had become increasingly focused on courtly entertainment. While these university wits surely over-represent the foolishness of the entertaining scholar to boost sales and box office revenues, their works make evident why Vice Chancellor Still expressed such nervousness at having his university men called upon as professional stage-players, and why, earlier that same year, William Gager emphasized that his university men were not like Roscius, the famous professional actor from Roman antiquity. These literary representations express the concerns that the university men themselves could not voice so overtly: that when scholars perform for royalty, the nature of the learned activities is skewed towards entertainment, and without this emphasis on their learned authority, they become disempowered.

Greene in *Friar Bacon and Friar Bungay* and Nashe in *The Vnfortvnate Traveller* each took particular care to depict university scenes that pointedly matched Elizabeth's progresses.[38] In *The Vnfortvnate Traveller*, narrator Jack Wilton and the Earl of Surrey witness a royal visit when, from "the verie pointe of our enterance into Wittenberg, we were spectators of a verie solemne scholasticall entertainment of the Duke of Saxonie thether."[39] Jack proceeds to describe a visit almost identical to Elizabeth's progresses. The Duke is greeted with orations by both university figures and a town dignitary, is honored with shouts of well-wishes from the university men lined up according to degree, and then proceeds to attend disputations and plays. Likewise, Greene bases *Friar Bacon and Friar Bungay* somewhat on the visit to Oxford in 1583 when Polish Palatine Laski was lavishly entertained with sumptuous banquets and entertainments full of spectacle. Friar Bacon honors the royal entourage with an exotic buffet, and Greene emphasizes that such a gluttonous feast[40] is sharply out of place at a university by having Bacon first bring out the scholar's meal of broth and pottage (scene 9). Greene also alludes to Laski's visit when he has Friar Bacon, as England's pride,[41] soundly defeat Germany's scholar, Friar Vandermast—an event that exacts revenge on one of the visitors present at the 1583 visit: hermetic philosopher Giordano Bruno. Bruno, who visited Oxford in Laski's train, had mocked Oxford men in his *La Cena de le Ceneri* (1584). Greene turns the tables on Bruno's expressions of triumph by depicting his Vandermast as clearly inferior to Bacon.[42]

Greene similarly demeans Vandermast by including this character as part of the sequence that links scholars with royal entertainment. This theme begins before the royal entourage arrives at Oxford, when the university officials are deliberating about what events to prepare for the royal guests. Significantly, they suggest only plays until they realize they should plan a disputation because Vandermast is coming: "We must lay plots of stately tragedies, / Strange comic shows, such as proud Roscius / Vaunted before the Roman emperors."[43] Their ideas for plays cover the standard range typically prepared for important royal guests: both tragedies and comedies; however, they liken the kind of plays to those that Roscius—a *professional* actor from antiquity—put on for his political leaders. They take a professional actor's choices as their model. Interestingly enough, though, we never see any of these plays, and the closest we get to entertainment for the royalty is the disputation between Vandermast and England's own Bungay. The disputation begins quasi-seriously with a discussion of "whether the spirits of pyromancy or geomancy be most predominant in magic" (9.24–5); yet, this hermetic question soon devolves into a conjuring match. And the royal company actually prefers the change in tone. After watching in silence as Vandermast and Bungay dispute, they suddenly perk up with interest when the learned men try to out-magic each other. Enthusiastically, the Emperor of Germany cheers, "Now, English Harry, here begins the game, / We shall see sport between these learned men." After Bungay responds with his (rather inferior) magic, King Henry chimes into this "sport" with pride in his own team, saying, "What say you, royal lordings, to my friar? / Hath he not done a point of cunning skill?" (9.76–7, 9.84–5). These royals prefer spectacle to entertain them. Intellectual contest cannot compare.

Although this disputation in Greene's play begins as learned demonstration, Nashe implies that entertainment is already built into academic demonstration when scholars perform for royalty. Throughout the scene at Wittenberg, Nashe repeatedly emphasizes this theme of mirth. Jack describes the Duke's visit as "scholasticall entertainment"; the events the scholars plan for the Duke are "the chiefe ceremonies of their intertainment" (2.246); the University Orator's speech is described as "pageant" (2.247); and Jack bores easily when Luther and Carolostadius dispute about the Mass: the "particulars of their disputations I remēber not [...]. [T]hey vttered nothing to make a man laugh, therefore I will leaue them. Mary, their outwarde iestures would now and then afford a man a morsel of mirth: of those two I meane not so much as of all the other traine of opponents & respondents" (2.250). Jack cares not at all for the substance of the arguments—he gauges the success of the whole progress solely on the basis of amusement. Although this interest is clearly in line with Jack's own pleasure-seeking nature, Nashe uses his narrator to make a point. Nashe plants this emphasis on entertainment through Jack's voice but then extends it to the ridiculous nature of the events themselves—acts that clearly are trivial pleasures. Several of the disputants sink particularly low. One intellectual, "seeing the Duke haue a dog he loued well, which sate by him on the tarras, conuerted al his oration to him, and not a haire of his tayle but he kembd out with comparisons" (2.251). Another scholar "commented and descanted on the Dukes staffe, new tipping it with many queint epithites" (2.251–2). Although speeches on such frivolous themes occur frequently in the tradition of oratory, they still reduce the scholar to a foolish comedian, wishing more to please than to enlighten. Once the monarch becomes an audience sheerly for entertainment, the semblance of wise counsel is gone.

Marlowe, too, gets in a jab at intellectuals who seek to amuse royalty—an amusement that repeatedly resembles theater. In fact, scholar Thomas Healy comments on theater-making as perhaps the dominant force in *Faustus*, observing that this "play's preoccupations with creating theatre, with organizing performances, may come to seem its ultimate rationale."[44] When Faustus returns from his world-tour with Mephistopheles, his colleagues at Wittenberg respond appropriately to Faustus's role as a scholar. The Chorus relates that,

> Touching his journey through the world and air,
> They put forth questions of astrology,
> Which Faustus answered with such learnèd skill
> As they admired and wondered at his wit.[45]

When Faustus arrives at the Emperor's court, however, his learned skill is called upon for entertainment. He presents the Emperor with life-like representations of Alexander and his paramour and then satisfies this ruler's ridiculous curiosity about whether Alexander's paramour had a mole or wart on her neck. In the B-text, this moment is presented essentially as theater, specifically as a dumb show: Alexander slays Darius and then crowns his paramour. Although the extent of Marlowe's hand in the B-text is controversial, it is interesting that the 1616 text emphasizes the theatricality of this moment. Even after this scene, Marlowe continues the vein of foolish performance for rulers when Faustus next visits the

Duke and Duchess of Vanholt. As Faustus enters with the Duke, the Duke thanks him for "merriment." Faustus continues to amuse him by putting horns on the knight's head and then getting grapes for the pregnant Duchess.

In such instances of entertainment, one could argue, as Alan Shepard does, that the ruler looks as foolish as the academic because the ruler is so easily pleased with ridiculous pranks and trivial knowledge.[46] Like Sir Philip Sidney's discussion in *A Defence of Poetry*, pleasing literature is ideally suited to sugarcoat virtue and wisdom for children.[47] These moments in the plays thus depict royalty as having the academic maturity of a child. Yet the scholar-figures do not seem to notice the discrepancy; in fact, they follow along, completely willing to pander to and sustain the monarchy they amuse. Friar Bacon begins Greene's play hoping to serve England by surrounding it with a protective wall of brass (an appropriate interest for Greene to include, considering the recent defeat and continuing threat of the Armada). In the end, however, Bacon abjures all magic except for one last prophecy in which he foretells the arrival of a queen (Elizabeth) who will reign in peace. Interestingly, his emphasis on Elizabeth's ability to create peace negates any need for the service of protection he originally hoped to create.[48] Elizabeth is a queen who does not need such service. Bacon's position of flattering this future "Diana's rose" also represents the complete reversal of authority. As Peter Mortenson notes, Bacon's powers are repeatedly "related to aspects of the moon goddess: celestial Luna; earthly Diana, chaste goddess of love and beauty; and underworld Hecate, witch goddess of death, destruction, and necromancy."[49] Early in the play, Bacon likens himself to Luna-Hecate, when he vows to "circle England round with brass" (2.171), but at the end, he gives over his connection with Luna-Hecate to honor instead another Luna-figure: Elizabeth as Diana. His power, connected to his "scholarly" service, is subsumed into royal flattery.

In *Faustus*, Marlowe follows a similar trajectory that leads to abject adulation. Faustus initially turns to magic because it promises "a world of profit and delight, / Of power, of honour, of omnipotence" (1.1.55–6), but he ends up performing superficial spectacle and voicing obedience to rulers. He pulls a prank on the sarcastic knight by putting cuckold's horns on the nobleman's head and claiming that he did it not so much to revenge the knight's nasty comments as to delight the Emperor: "My gracious lord, not so much for the injury he offered me here in your presence as to delight you with some mirth" (4.1.90–92).[50] In his interest to amuse, appropriately enough, Faustus is all humility and deference: "My gracious sovereign, though I must confess myself far inferior to the report men have published, and nothing answerable to the honour of your Imperial Majesty, yet, for that love and duty finds me thereunto, I am content to do whatsoever your Majesty shall command me" (4.1.13–18). He uses similar language again right before he exits: "Now, my good lord, having done my duty, I humbly take my leave" (4.1.96–7). No longer the Faustus who stood ready to pursue forbidden knowledge to gain absolute political power, he ends up voicing duty and obedience. This change is particularly striking in his obeisance to the Duke of Vanholt who has minimal authority as the ruler of a small kingdom. Faustus's last line to him echoes his earlier humility to the Emperor: "I humbly thank your Grace" (4.2.37). The Faustus who began the play hoping to have the world bow to him has been reduced to performing trivial spectacle and acts for royalty—and thanking them for the favor they promise as reward for his acts of amusement.

Although such instances of entertainment demean the scholar, Greene and Nashe save the greatest degradation for scholars performing plays (which makes Nashe's prose work particularly appropriate). By 1594 when Nashe wrote *The Vnfortvnate Traveller*, Elizabeth had already made her requests for a comedy in English to both Oxford and Cambridge. Nashe may have included the Duke's progress to the University of Wittenberg in *The Vnfortvnate Traveller* to comment on this situation or, more generally, on the crown's repeated requests for plays during the various progresses. Pointblank, Nashe has Jack explain that having scholars perform a comedy is as ridiculous as having a drunk "townie" attempt a learned oration. Jack explains that "The Duke laught not a little" at the townsman's "ridiculous oration, but that verie night as great an ironicall occasion was ministred, for he was bidden to one of the chiefe schooles to a Comedie handled by the scollers" (2.249). True to the scholars' ineptitude for theater, they prove to be terrible actors—able only, appropriately enough, to portray hunger convincingly. In *Friar Bacon and Friar Bungay*, Greene takes this emphasis on theater one step further. He overtly blurs the boundaries between professional and academic drama—an idea that he has already hinted at through humor earlier in the play. Rafe, who is Prince Edward's fool (and is posing as the prince), declares, "Doctors, whose doting nightcaps are not capable of my ingenious dignity, know that I am Edward Plantagenet, whom if you displease, will make a ship that shall hold all your colleges, and so carry away the Niniversity with a fair wind to the Bankside in Southwark" (7.69–73). Playing on the idea of the ship of fools, Rafe not only teasingly likens academics to his own vocation as a fool but also describes moving the university to the Bankside—the current location of the professional Rose theater and the district that would later house both the Swan (1595) and the Globe (1599) theaters as well.[51] Indeed, the accounts place both recorded Elizabethan productions of the play at the Rose (1592 by Lord Strange's Men and 1594 by a joint effort between the Queen's Men and Sussex's Men). Through this allusion, Greene begins to merge the university and the public stages, the scholar and the professional actor, and, interestingly enough, he puts these words into the mouth of a character who is impersonating royalty.

1592: University Man vs. Professional Player

Rafe's playful, "royal" threat to bring the university to a professional theater may have seemed pure humor in 1589–92 (or it may be the professional theater's attempt to solidify its status as artistically superior to the socially elite university men). This parallel between professional and academic theater is not so farfetched, however, when the crown expected university men to present comedies in English for its entertainment in 1592. What makes the queen's expectations so striking is not that the academic and the courtly stages were worlds foreign to each other, for they had crossed over repeatedly and increasingly during the reign. What is striking is that the crown makes this request in the *same year* that the university stage has made particularly pointed efforts to distinguish itself from the professional theater. Throughout the 1580s, university officials had sought such distinction by repeatedly prompting the crown to issue injunctions that banned professional players from performing within a five-mile radius of each university. Yet the events of 1592 suggest a new urgency in separating the university actor from the professional player. This pivotal year began with controversy over academic drama when John Rainolds openly condemned it as immoral and frivolous. This attack prompted William Gager to defend academic drama as precisely that—academic. Gager stressed the educational and pedagogical functions of university productions, emphasizing that they allowed scholars to practice Latin and Greek as well as essential skills in oratory. Within days of Gager's response, his position received (perhaps quite by accident) the highest official support: the crown announced its plans to revisit Oxford. The crossover between Gager's defense of university drama and the choices the university made for (what would be) Elizabeth's final university progress reveal that, by 1592, university men, like their fellows writing popular plays professionally, were becoming aware of the implications of their and the crown's frequent interactions involving entertainment—and they realized that the crown needed reminding of the distinction just as much as anyone else. In response, they sought to preserve and to emphasize their identity as university men.

At the heart of Gager's defense of university drama is the separation between academic and professional playing. Gager begins this distinction in the final two epilogues to his play *Hippolytus*—the two epilogues that will eventually spark Rainolds's ire. For the first epilogue, Gager created the figure of Momus, a figure Rainolds believed referred to him. Then, the speaker in the second epilogue answered all of Momus's objections by emphasizing that, in part, university men are not professional actors who are skilled in this art, for "non histrionam didicimus, Roscii / nescimus artem. ludii nos nec sumus" (ll. 369–70) ("We have not studied acting, we are ignorant of Roscius' art. We are not professional actors" [2.215]). When Gager responds to Rainolds's attack five months later, he continues this argument. He claims that he thought Rainolds's original criticisms were "spoken agaynst *Histriones*, and not agaynst Schollares" (4.258), and then emphasizes later in the letter how different (and essentially lacking) university playing is from its professional counterpart:

> Next I denye that we are to be termed *Scenici, or Histriones*, for cumminge on the Stage once in a yeere, or twoe yeere, sevne, ten, or somtyme twentye yeeres. [...] First therfor I saye, we differ from them alltogether in the manner bothe of setting owte Playes, and of actinge them. thay did it with excessyve charge; we thriftely, warely, and allmost beggerly; thay acted theire Playes in an other sorte than we doe, or can, or well knowe

howe; but so exquisytly, and carefully, that we may seeme, compared with them, eyther for skill, or diligence, rather *Recitare,* which you doe not dislike, than *Agere.* [4.263]

Gager claims that university productions pale in comparison to the professional stage in "beggerly" production and careful but not skillful acting, and yet history—specifically the productions of Gager's own plays—contradicts his claims. Gager is selective in his memory of what university productions have entailed, particularly at Oxford. In the previous nine years alone, the university had mounted lavish entertainment and productions of Gager's plays for Laski's and Leicester's visits. Even if Gager considered these productions as anomalies, many typical productions at the universities included spectacle throughout the sixteenth century.[52] Significantly, Gager disregards the high-profile instances that contradict his claims—instances that would not have escaped Rainolds who had acted at Oxford for Elizabeth in 1566. Rainolds had played Hippolyta in *Palamon and Arcyte* and had received a financial reward from the queen herself, no less, for his *skillful* performance.

Such productions for the queen would seem to offer perfect support for university drama, and yet Gager does not draw attention to the fact that Elizabeth had attended numerous university productions. Because Gager glosses over these events, it is no wonder that he similarly emphasizes university productions as private, university-only affairs: "We contrarywise doe it to recreate owre selves, owre House, and the better parte of the *Vniversitye* [...] to practyse owre owne style eyther in prose or verse; to be well acquantyed with *Seneca* or *Plautus*; honestly to embowlden owre yuthe; to trye their voyces, and confirme their memoryes; to frame their speeche" (4.263).[53] Considering that Gager emphasizes private performances and drama's educational function, it is most ironic that, ten days after he writes his letter, the crown notifies Oxford that Elizabeth will visit. Although his works are back in the court's limelight, Gager and the university officials do not take steps to create productions that so clearly resemble court performances. Gager's emphasis on academic drama in his letter to Rainolds can explain the choices made for Elizabeth's final visit. The university does *not* demonstrate the same enthusiasm for performing for the queen, as both it and Cambridge had done in the 1560s. Modern scholars have often attributed some of this waning exuberance to Elizabeth's age. In fact, the visit prompted only one rather lackluster account, which was not written until James I's reign. When the university's choices are placed in the context of the controversy and topical literary representations of the scholar, these decisions resonate with anxiety over the issue of the intellectual as courtly entertainer. The plays Oxford chooses to perform for the queen, the amount of money spent on the productions, and even the fact that the surviving account is written by Philip Stringer, who was a Fellow and Senior Bursar of St. John's College, Cambridge, as well as one of the University's Esquire-bedels,[54] all point to the university's interest in debunking any connections the crown may make between its university subjects and those studied actors who perform at court.

Although the queen stayed at Oxford for seven days (22–28 September), the university prepared only two plays (in Latin), spent only £31 on those productions, and selected plays already written rather than commissioning new works. They performed *Rivales* by Gager and *Bellum Grammaticale*, thought to be by Leonard Hutton. In the epilogue that Gager wrote for the latter play, we find him making claims similar to those he articulates to Rainolds when he emphasizes the lack of finesse and spectacle that comes with university productions:

> nullus ubi dulcis puer,
> nec vestis exquisite, nec symphonia.
> non histrionis Roscii hic vel discitur,
> vel ars docetur. Nostra superavit modum
> inscitia. [ll. 8–12]

> [There is no sweet boy here, no elegant costumes nor instrumental music. Here Roscius' art is neither learned nor taught. Our lack of skill surpasses all bounds. (2.249)]

Drawing attention to the lack of both spectacle and skill in acting, Gager reminds his queen that she is watching learned men, not individuals who have studied acting. To emphasize this contrast, Gager mentions that "nullus ubi dulcis puer" ("There is no sweet boy here"), and his use of "puer" may allude to pupils from such grammar schools as his alma mater (Westminster with Udall as its headmaster for years). Because this phrase comes after the idea of teaching and learning acting, however, this reference most likely alludes to the professional troupes of boy-actors who often performed at court as well as the masters who taught them, such as Edwardes, Lyly, and Peele. Significantly, many of those masters of the children's companies were the same men who had come to Oxford to help the university men prepare for the court's visits. No Udall, Edwardes, Lyly, or Peele had been summoned from court to assist with these later productions.[55] Without such court-focused assistance, these productions are indeed only university drama, which Gager makes quite clear in the prologue he wrote for *Bellum Grammaticale*, noting the play's purely academic subject-matter: "rex nominalis rexque verbalis solent, / academica mera iurgia ac rixae irritae" (ll. 14–15) ("That is to say, the sort that the Noun King and the Verb King are accustomed to hurl, really [are] just academic wrangling and ineffectual squabbles" [2.249]).[56]

Clearly, though, Gager's and the university's efforts to depict a gulf between their productions and the professional stage were not successful, for less than three months later, the crown made its request to both universities for a comedy at Christmas. Vice Chancellor Still's letter is dated 10 December, and the timing of this letter begins to shed light on why Stringer, in his meager account of the plays for the Oxford progress, may have purposely written his descriptions so sparingly. In December of 1592, Stringer had also participated in Cambridge's attempts to distinguish between professional and academic productions. According to Still's papers, a Mr. Stringer was also sent to court on what looks like 10 December—the same day that Still wrote his letter to Lord Burghley. The entry reads: "Alowed vnto Mr Stringer for his charges in A iourney to the Courte the [x] w*hic*h laye then at Hampton Courte beinge then sent vp with *lett*res for thaduertisinge of the Lo*rd* Treasurer of thelecc*io*n of the Vicechauncellor and the others of the councell for the Renewal of a sute made for the restrainte of <......> the plaiers beinge then abroad seuen daies."[57] If Stringer was at court to encourage the continued ban on professional players and was there at the time when other representatives from Cambridge came bearing Still's letter, it would explain why his descriptions of the plays are so uninspired. Stringer clearly was not in favor of the professional stage and probably knew about the crown's request. He certainly would have known about it by the time he wrote the account years later when Oxford was preparing to host James I and wanted descriptions of the visits that had been prepared for Elizabeth. Whether in that December or later, he would have been aware that Elizabeth had treated her university subjects as performing academics. He might not have wished to proliferate this image and thus encouraged Cambridge not to continue on this trajectory.[58]

Just as Gager's efforts did not affect the crown's request, so in turn Stringer's no-nonsense description did not deter the universities from perpetuating and even intensifying the image of university productions as courtly diversion. For James's visit in 1605, Oxford had the court's arch spectacle-maker, Inigo Jones, assist them in the preparations. By Charles I's visit in 1636, university and courtly productions were essentially one and the same: "Although the texts of the royal plays of 1636 were written by Oxford men, the performances themselves were, in every other respect, the product of the king's usual purveyors of court entertainment."[59] By looking back at Elizabeth's reign, we can see this blurring of the boundaries already beginning early on; in fact, the notion of university men as entertainers for the court continued through at least the 1590s, if not the rest of Elizabeth's reign. In 1595, some university scholars temporarily did become professional actors performing for the crown when Francis Bacon and the Earl of Essex hired scholars from both Oxford and Cambridge to perform in their Accession Day piece, *Of Love and Self-Love*. Perhaps encouraged by the success of this performance, the crown once again asked the universities to perform at court only a month later, during the Christmas season of 1595. Through such instances, some scholars were indeed becoming entertaining academics for the court.

As Elizabeth and her court increasingly turned to the universities for theatrical entertainment, they diminished the public image of the scholar as a serious figure, and this treatment, I believe, sparked literary production beyond the fawning, entertaining academics that Marlowe, Greene, and Nashe created in their plays for the professional stage. It is in harmony with the crown's decision to hire scholars such as Lyly and Nashe to write humorous rebuttals to Martin Marprelate's mocking tracts—requests that call upon intellectuals to adopt an entertaining persona and support the crown's authority in doing so. In turn, the connection between entertainment and subservience may also explain the popularity of the underemployed satirist in the 1590s. Literary critics often depict these men as humanist failures of sorts, and yet these writers, by claiming failure to obtain court and government service, articulated a position outside the bondage of entertainment that yoked their university fellows to the crown. University productions for the queen and court were far more than entertaining performances. They altered the intellectual landscape in Elizabethan England and prompted university men to reconsider the type of humanist service they offered to their monarch.

Notes

1   Alan H. Nelson, ed., *Records of Early English Drama: Cambridge*, 2 vols. (Toronto: University of Toronto Press, 1989), 1.347.

2   In fact, intellectuals at Cambridge had performed a few comedies in English—and one of those (Nicholas Udall's play *Ezechias*) for Elizabeth herself in 1564. By 1592, Cambridge had performed the following comedies in English: *Gammer Gurton's Needle*, *Ezechias*, and *Comedy Satirizing the Mayor of Cambridge*. (The latter play is no longer extant but was most likely in English.) For a list of all productions at both universities, see "Appendix IV" in Frederick S. Boas, *University Drama in the Tudor Age* (Oxford: Oxford University Press, 1914), 385–90. In addition, university plays had long been included in the academic curriculum, particularly with the rise of humanism, and many colleges in Cambridge, for example, had gone so far as to institutionalize the performance of plays in their college statutes: St. John's 1545, Queen's 1559, and Trinity 1560. See Alan H. Nelson, "Contexts for Early English Drama: The Universities," in *Contexts for Early English Drama*, ed. Marianne G. Briscoe and John C. Coldewey (Bloomington: Indiana University Press, 1989), 141. For a discussion of humanism's influence on Tudor theater, see Kent Cartwright, *Theatre and Humanism: English Drama in the Sixteenth Century* (Cambridge: Cambridge University Press, 1999).

3   For a discussion of the effect of the monarch's presence on early modern plays, see Stephen Orgel, *The Illusion of Power: Political Theater in the English Renaissance* (Berkeley: University of California Press, 1975).

4.   Alan H. Nelson, "Cambridge University Drama in the 1580s," in *The Elizabethan Theatre 11*, ed. A.L. Magnusson and C.E. McGee (Port Credit: P.D. Meany, 1990), 20.

5.   Critics had long attacked public stage-plays, but 1592 marks the year when university drama also came under attack, beginning with John Rainolds's letter to William Gager. For an overview of antidramatic texts, see chapter seven of J.W.H. Atkins, *English Literary Criticism: The Renascence* (New York: Barnes and Noble, 1947); and also Paul D. Streufert's essay in this volume.

6.   William Gager, *The Complete Works*, 4 vols., ed. Dana F. Sutton (New York: Garland Press, 1994), ll. 370–71; 2.215. For all citations from Gager's Latin works, I follow the quotation in Latin with Sutton's translations, and each

reference includes first the line numbers for the Latin and then the volume and page numbers for the translation. Subsequent citations will appear parenthetically in the text.

7　Linda Shenk, "Transforming Learned Authority into Royal Supremacy: Elizabeth I's Learned Persona in Her University Orations," in *Elizabeth I: Always Her Own Free Woman*, ed. Carole Levin, Jo Eldridge Carney, and Debra Barrett-Graves (Burlington: Ashgate, 2003), 78–96.

8　Even the upstart crow William Shakespeare was intrigued by the entertaining academic. Not only does he liken the artisans to scholars who greet Theseus in *A Midsummer Night's Dream* but also in *Love's Labors Lost*, his comic, learned characters Holofernes, Don Armado, and Sir Nathaniel perform a pageant of the Nine Worthies for the king, the princess, and their followers.

9　Andreas Höfele, "'So Potent Art': Magic Power in Marlowe, Greene and Shakespeare," in *The Iconography of Power: Ideas and Images of Rulership on the English Renaissance Stage*, ed. György E. Szónyi and Rowland Wymer (Szeged: JATE, 2000), 54.

10　Penry Williams, "Elizabethan Oxford: State, Church and University," in *The Collegiate University*, ed. James McConica (Oxford: Clarendon, 1986), 440, vol. 3 of *The History of the University of Oxford*, 8 vols., 1984–97.

11　In the thirteenth century, Henry III had used Oxford as one of his royal residences, but Elizabeth's status as a visitor staying at an English university was unprecedented.

12　Nelson, *Cambridge*, 1.227.

13　Siobhan Keenan, "Spectator and Spectacle: Royal Entertainments at the Universities in the 1560s," in *The Progresses, Pageants, and Entertainments of Queen Elizabeth I*, ed. Jayne Elisabeth Archer, Elizabeth Goldring, and Sarah Knight (Oxford: Oxford University Press, 2007), 86–103. Also in this collection, Jayne Elisabeth Archer and Sarah Knight include commentary on Elizabeth's first two university progresses in their essay "Elizabetha Triumphans" (especially 13–19). These two essays, in addition to Louise Durning's edition of *Queen Elizabeth's Book of Oxford* (trans. Sarah Knight and Helen Spurling [Oxford: Bodleian Library, 2006]) are important recent studies that demonstrate the political centrality of Elizabeth's progresses to the universities.

14　Scholars suggest the last few years of Henry's reign as the possible date of composition for *Ezechias* because, in 1545, Udall made an explicit reference to Hezekiah in the preface to *The Paraphrase of Erasmus*, which he addressed to Henry VIII. See William L. Edgerton, *Nicholas Udall* (New York: Twayne, 1965), 82.

15　Margaret Aston, *The King's Bedpost: Reformation and Iconography in a Tudor Group Portrait* (New York: Cambridge University Press, 1993), 123.

16　Quoted in Edgerton, *Nicholas Udall*, 83, my emphasis.

17　Elizabeth may indeed have stood up and left this performance. She was never bashful about expressing her disagreement in this fashion, as when she walked out of a Christmas service in 1559. The Bishop of Carlisle refused to heed her instructions not to elevate the host. Elizabeth made known her (Protestant) disapproval by getting up loudly, turning her back on the priest, and leaving right after the reading of the Gospel. See Wallace MacCaffrey, *Elizabeth I* (London: Edward Arnold, 1993), 51.

18 Quoted in Boas, *University Drama*, 383. This section from Guzmán de Silva's letter reads as follows: "entraron los representantes, en habitos de Algunos de los obispos que estan presos, fue el primero, el de Londres, lleuando en las manos vn cordero, como que le yua comiendo, y otros con otras deuisas, y vno en figura de perro, con vna hostia en la boca La Reyna se enojo tanto segun escriuen que se entro, a priesa en su camara, diziendo malas palabras" (Nelson, *Cambridge*, 1.242–3).

19 Unlike Oxford, Cambridge felt sufficiently comfortable in its affiliation with Elizabeth's religious policies to produce plays that touched on religion. As Edward VI's disputation against the Mass at Cambridge suggests, this university had a strong Protestant tradition. Oxford, in contrast, had been not only the site of the disputation *for* the Mass but also the site where Elizabeth's godfather Thomas Cranmer was burned at the stake for his Protestant practices. In response to religious tensions with Oxford, Elizabeth did not attend any activities on the Sunday of her progress to that university—no sermons, no disputations—not even the play.

20 For Nicholas Robinson's account of Richard Edwardes's participation in the visit, see Charles Plummer, ed., *Elizabethan Oxford: Reprints of Rare Tracts* (Oxford: Clarendon, 1887), 178–9. See also Ros King, *The Works of Richard Edwards: Politics, Poetry and Performance in Sixteenth-Century England* (Manchester: Manchester University Press, 2001), 63–87.

21 Thomas John Manning, "The Staging of Plays at Christ Church, Oxford, 1582–1592" (Ph.D. Thesis, University of Michigan, 1972), 60.

22 Heather Kerr, "Sir Thomas Elyot, 'Marcus Geminus' and a Comedy for Elizabeth I at Oxford, 1566," *AUMLA: Journal of the Australasian Universities Language and Literature Association* 73 (1990): 142.

23 Kerr, "Sir Thomas Elyot," 145–6.

24 John R. Elliott, Jr., and Alan H. Nelson (University), Alexandra F. Johnston and Diana Wyatt (City), eds., *Records of Early English Drama: Oxford*, 2 vols. (Toronto: University of Toronto Press, 2004), 1.129. In "Queen Elizabeth at Oxford: New Light on the Royal Plays of 1566," *English Literary Renaissance* 18 (1988): 220–21, John R. Elliott, Jr., provides both extant versions, and I think the other text more clearly encapsulates this moment of mirth: When the cries of the hounds were mimicked outside, "the young Scholars, who stood in the windows, were so much taken (supposing it was real) that they cried out 'Now now!—there there—he's caught, he's caught.' All which the Queen merrily beholding said, 'O, excellent! those boys in very troth, are ready to leap out of the windows, to follow the hounds.'" These two accounts are also found

in John Nichols, *The Progresses and Public Processions of Queen Elizabeth*, 3 vols. (London: Printed by and for J. Nichols and son, 1823), 2.210–12.

25 Nelson, "Contexts," 142.

26 Nelson, *Cambridge*, 1.278.

27 Nelson, "Cambridge University Drama in the 1580s," 21.

28 "The Queen's Matie hath willed me to signifie unto you y^t ye Palatin Lasky ye nobleman that is nowe out of Polonia mindeth shortly to come downe and see ye universitie of Oxford, & that her highnes pleasure therefore is y^t he be receaved of you wth all ye curtesy & solemnitie y^t you maye" (Quoted in Manning, "The Staging of Plays," 113, from Bodleian, Twyne MSS. xvii, fol. 170).

29 Raphael Holinshed, THE *Third volume of Chronicles* (London, 1587), 1355.

30 Holinshed, *Chronicles*, 1355.

31 "Such an entertainment it was, that the like before or since was never made for one of his degree; costing the University with the Colleges (who contributed towards the entertainment) about £350" (Nichols, *Progresses*, 2.409).

32 In Christ Church's disbursement book for 1582/83, Peele has given his signature to confirm receipt of £20 "in respect of the playes & intertaynment of the Palatine laskie etc. Receiued by me George Peele the xxvj^th day of May anno 1583" (quoted in Manning, "The Staging of Plays," 133). In addition, two other items suggest Peele's assistance: one that University Archivist Philip Bliss told to Peele's first editor Alexander Dyce "It(e)m the chardges of a Comedye and a Tragedye and a shewe of fi[r]e works," and another document listing a Mr. Pille (quoted in David H. Horne, *The Life and Minor Works of George Peele* [New Haven: Yale University Press, 1952], 62).

33 Manning, "The Staging of Plays," 135. Peele teaming up with Gager was a win-win combination, because even Gager would most likely have brought with him some experience performing for the court. Gager had received his grammar education at Westminster School, whose students, under Udall's direction, had often performed before Elizabeth at court.

34 Quoted in Boas, *University Drama*, 191, from Bodleian, Twyne MSS. xvii, fols. 172–3.

35 David Bevington and Eric Rasmussen, "Introduction," in Christopher Marlowe, *Doctor Faustus, A- and B-Texts* (Manchester: Manchester University Press, 1993), 15.

36 John Lyly, *Campaspe*, in *The Complete Works of John Lyly*, 3 vols., ed. R. Warwick Bond (Oxford: Clarendon, 1902), vol. 2, 1.3.91–2. Subsequent citations will appear parenthetically in the text.

37 In fact, these representations form an early cluster, but their effects continue beyond this period, as Shakespeare has his Sir Nathaniel and Holofernes put on the laughable pageant of the Nine Worthies for the king in *Love's Labor's Lost*; the scholar-figures Studioso and Philomusus consider becoming professional

actors in the *Parnassus* plays; and Bacon in *John of Bordeaux* conjures up the rape of Lucrece for Emperor Ferdinand.

38 University historian Roderick Robertson actually begins his article on drama at Oxford with a quote from *Friar Bacon and Friar Bungay*, making clear the parallels between this play and Elizabeth's progresses; see his "Oxford Theatre in Tudor Times," *Educational Theatre Journal* 21 (1969): 41.

39 Thomas Nashe, *The Vnfortvnate Traveller*, in *The Works of Thomas Nashe*, 5 vols., ed. Ronald B. McKerrow (New York: Barnes & Noble, 1966), 2.246. Subsequent citations will appear parenthetically in the text.

40 For a discussion of this feast as a demonstration of gluttony, see Albert Wertheim, "The Presentation of Sin in 'Friar Bacon and Friar Bungay,'" *Criticism: A Quarterly for Literature and the Arts* 16 (1974): 273–86.

41 Frank Ardolino discusses the role of national pride in this play, and he mentions a particularly interesting idea about the close relationship between Oxford and Henry III in the thirteenth century. At this time, Oxford served as a royal residence and the site of many key councils. See his "'Thus Glories England Over All the West': Setting as National Encomium in Robert Greene's *Friar Bacon and Friar Bungay*," *Journal of Evolutionary Psychology* 9.3–4 (1988): 227. This close relationship reveals the reverse of what I see happening in Elizabeth's reign where the universities were encouraged to be more like the court (and at court) rather than bringing the court to the academy.

42 For more discussion of Bruno's visit to Oxford, see Robert McNulty, "Bruno at Oxford," *Renaissance News* 13 (1960): 300–305. Also, see Frances A. Yates, *Giordano Bruno and the Hermetic Tradition* (Chicago: University of Chicago Press, 1964). For connections between Marlowe's *Faustus* and Bruno, see Hilary Gatti, *The Renaissance Drama of Knowledge* (New York: Routledge, 1989).

43 Robert Greene, *Friar Bacon and Friar Bungay*, ed. Daniel Seltzer (Lincoln: University of Nebraska Press, 1963), 7.8–11. Subsequent citations will appear parenthetically in the text by scene and line number.

44 Thomas Healy, "Doctor Faustus," in *The Cambridge Companion to Christopher Marlowe*, ed. Patrick Cheney (Cambridge: Cambridge University Press, 2004), 189.

45 Christopher Marlowe, *Doctor Faustus, A- and B-Texts*, ed. David Bevington and Eric Rasmussen (Manchester: Manchester University Press, 1993), 4.Chorus.8–11. Subsequent citations, which are taken from the 1604 A-text, will appear parenthetically in the text.

46 Alan Shepard, *Marlowe's Soldiers: Rhetorics of Masculinity in the Age of the Armada* (Burlington: Ashgate, 2002), 188–95.

47 Sir Philip Sidney, *A Defence of Poetry*, ed. J.A. Van Dorsten (New York: Oxford University Press, 1966), 39–40.

48 Depicting Elizabeth as a queen who can replace a learned character's contribution to national defense makes sense in light of my recent work on Elizabeth's learned persona. I demonstrate that Elizabeth's educated status

was often conjured to augment England's image of strength when the nation faced international threat. See my "'To Love and Be Wise': The Earl of Essex, Humanist Court Culture, and England's Learned Queen," *Early Modern Literary Studies* 13.2, Special Issue 16 (2007): 3.1–27; and "Queen Solomon: An International Elizabeth I in 1569," in *Queens and Power in Medieval and Early Modern England*, ed. Robert Bucholz and Carole Levin (Lincoln: University of Nebraska Press, forthcoming).

49 Peter Mortenson, "*Friar Bacon and Friar Bungay*: Festive Comedy and 'Three-Form'd Luna,'" *English Literary Renaissance* 2 (1972): 202–3.

50 In the B-text, this moment may contain a reference to the oft-praised scene with the hounds during the performance of *Palamon and Arcyte* before Elizabeth in 1566. Faustus elaborates on the knight's appearance as Actaeon, threatening that "I'll raise a kennel of hounds shall hunt him so / As all his footmanship shall scarce prevail / To keep his carcass from their bloody fangs" (4.1.146–8).

51 I am indebted to Jonathan Walker for noting that Rafe's allusion refers specifically to the Rose.

52 Nelson, "Cambridge University Drama," 20.

53 In contrast, Alberico Gentili, who will enter the fray with Rainolds in 1593 and 1594, defends university playing by emphasizing that Elizabeth and the court have attended productions. See Alberico Gentili and John Rainolds, *Latin Correspondence by Alberico Gentili and John Rainolds on Academic Drama*, trans. Leon Markowicz (Salzburg: Institut für Englische Sprache und Literatur Universität Salzburg, 1977), 45.

54 Boas, *University Drama*, 253.

55 This connection between boy-actors and university men performing for the queen merits further study.

56 Not only is *Bellum Grammaticale* a wise choice because its subject-matter is exclusively academic but also this choice proves that a moral man can write plays. Hutton had his B.D., and his education in divinity perhaps was useful in disproving Rainolds's criticism that university drama corrupts intellectuals. Rainolds was present at this progress; in fact, on the Tuesday of the visit (26 September), he gave a divinity lecture at 9 A.M., and Gager's play *Rivales* ended that day's activities. The juxtaposition was obvious, and Elizabeth evidently supported her university playwright, for after she delivered her Latin oration at the end of the visit, she "schooled Dr. John Rainolds for his obstinate preciseness, willing him to follow her lawes, and not run before them" (Nichols, 3.146). Such reprimand may have included both Rainolds's Puritan views, which often conflicted with Elizabeth's more conservative Protestantism, as well as his opinions regarding academic drama.

57 Nelson, *Cambridge*, 1.346.

58 Stringer also wrote an account of James's visit to Oxford in 1605—an account that theater historian John Orrell describes as "rather sniffy"; see his "The Theatre

at Christ Church, Oxford, in 1605," *Shakespeare Survey* 35 (1982), 130. Clearly, Stringer did not approve of plays, either for the court or for anyone else.

59 John R. Elliott, Jr., "Plays, Players, and Playwrights in Renaissance Oxford," in *From Page to Performance: Essays in Early English Drama*, ed. John A. Alford (East Lansing: Michigan State University Press, 1995), 191.

CHAPTER 2

Christopherson at Cambridge: Greco-Catholic Ethics in the Protestant University

Paul D. Streufert

This story [of Jephthah and his daughter] is frightening.
It is so frightening that I wish it could be erased from scripture.

—Elie Wiesel, *Sages and Dreamers*

In an often quoted sixteenth-century letter to John Rainolds, the Christ Church playwright and fellow William Gager writes of the value of playing and play-making for students and scholars at the collegiate level. He argues:

> [Plays serve] to practice our own style either in prose or in verse; to be well acquainted with Seneca or Plautus; honestly to embolden our path; to try their voices and confirm their memories; to frame their speech; to conform them to convenient action; to try what mettle is in everyone, and of what disposition they are of; whereby never any one amongst us, that I know, was made the worse, many have been much the better [...].[1]

Though some like Rainolds, a fellow at Corpus Christi College, Oxford, objected to the curricular use of the drama, perhaps fearing its secular appeal and power, numerous scholars at both Cambridge and Oxford used a variety of play-texts, both original compositions and classical, to entertain and instruct. As John R. Elliott argues, "[such plays] reflected the humanist conception of the practical value that drama was thought to have in the training of young men for public life, either in the church or the state."[2] This training usually included instruction in Christian ethics, either Protestant or Catholic.[3] At several Cambridge colleges, most notably St. John's and Trinity, fellows considered the experience so valuable that they actually required yearly performances.[4]

In addition to the behavioral, social, and religious instruction so prominent in sixteenth-century collegiate drama, the need for linguistic instruction encouraged the proliferation of such plays. Though innovators like Thomas Legge of Gonville and Caius, Cambridge, and Nicholas Udall of Corpus Christi, Oxford, wrote and produced academic plays in English, many of the plays performed in this period were either classical plays in Greek or Latin or original plays composed in those classical languages.[5] The composing, reading, and acting of such plays in Greek or Latin obviously would have helped both students and fellows in their mastery of syntax, morphology, vocabulary, and pronunciation. Even today, students of classical languages are at a disadvantage compared to their colleagues in the modern languages, in that their objects of study are not widely spoken or conversational per se. Like their sixteenth-century counterparts, teachers still use the performance of scenes to bolster the learning of these difficult languages. While it is true that the early modern period witnessed a rebirth of curiosity in all aspects of the classical world, interest in the language and poetics of Rome dwarfed interest in those of Athens. The lists of plays performed at Cambridge in the sixteenth century bear out this point. For instance, according to accounts kept at St. John's, Cambridge, for expenditures on academic drama in 1538 alone, payment was made for "vij comedes and one Greek dialogue."[6] Though the ratio narrowed in the following decade,[7] Latin plays were still twice as likely to be performed at the college than plays in Greek.

Indeed, the learning of Greek became accepted as part of the humanist curriculum in sixteenth-century England only through the concerted effort of continentally trained Cambridge fellows like Erasmus,[8] who famously wrote in 1500, "The moment I get some money I will buy, first Greek books, and then clothes."[9] Early on, the teaching of Greek as part of university curricula met with serious opposition for a variety of reasons both practical and theoretical. When tutors sufficiently educated in the language could be found—and such men were rare in the first third of the sixteenth century—they were sometimes denounced. Arthur Tilley describes the situation as darkly comic:

> The younger partisans of the old learning banded themselves under the name of Trojans and mobbed the Grecians in the streets. The seniors preached against Greek from the pulpit. Indeed, one preacher went so far as to denounce not only Greek, but all liberal learning. Logic and scholastic theology were, he said, the only deserving studies.[10]

Ironically, the learning of Greek, as the language of the New Testament, should have fit comfortably into early modern theological studies. Those who objected to its study at the universities may have feared its connection to Eastern Orthodoxy, preferring Latin, the language of the European Church. Only through the intervention of Henry VIII, prompted by Sir Thomas More, was this conflict resolved and the learning of this classical language officially approved and protected by regal decree.[11]

Despite this initial resistance, the learning of Greek eventually took hold at English universities and, like its more popular counterpart Latin, was even used—albeit sparingly—in the composition of academic drama.[12] According to records for Cambridge, students encountered the Greeks through a range of texts. They performed plays in the original, as evidenced by a production of Aristophanes' *Plutus* in 1536. English translations and adaptations of Greek tragedies, which allowed fellows, students, and audiences greater accessibility to ancient texts, include Thomas Watson's *Antigone* (circa 1581) as well as Roger Ascham's 1543 *Philoctetes*, which he describes as "based on Sophocles' [play] in imitation of Seneca."[13] Rather than simple, dry readings of classical Greek, these productions included blocking and costumes, and evidently were funded well enough to provide a special-effects budget. John Dee, a Greek scholar at St. John's, even used an elaborate device for a *deus ex machina* in a production of Aristophanes' *Peace*, "to the delight and astonishment of the spectators."[14]

This intellectual and theatrical milieu produced a most extraordinary text, one that did not follow the usual pattern for Greek plays at Cambridge. John Christopherson, a fellow at St. John's and later a founding member of Trinity, composed the only extant play of its kind, an original written in Greek: *Jephthah*. Ostensibly the play functions as a linguistic tool, as it combines three distinct dialects of the ancient language into an intriguing literary pastiche. Included are Homeric Greek, with the Chorus at one point referring to the "wine-dark sea"; Attic Greek, the fifth-century dialect of the language spoken in Athens, here modeled closely on the playwright Euripides; and Koine Greek, the dialect of the New Testament writers. This jumble of vocabulary and syntax, though at times inelegant and anachronistic, would have served Christopherson's students well, acquainting them with the principal forms and authors of the language. Additionally, like most academic drama of the early modern period, *Jephthah* addresses moral issues and the behavior of children, lessons aimed squarely at the student actors and the text's potential audience of spectators or readers.

Christopherson belonged to that elite group which originally advocated the value of studying Greek at the university. A student of John Redman's at St. John's, he composed *Jephthah* around 1544, a date not absolutely secure but well supported by the evidence in the dedicatory epistles.[15] The play, along with a preface addressed directly to King Henry VIII, was almost certainly sent to court, providing evidence of its author's erudition and, as Christopher Upton argues, likely secured Christopherson's appointment to a University Greek Chair made available that year.[16] Two manuscripts have survived, one at Trinity, dedicated to William Parr, Earl of Essex, and one at St. John's, dedicated to Cuthbert Tunstall, Bishop of Durham.[17] Christopherson later composed a Latin version of the play, which he dedicated to Henry VIII. Though long thought lost, a manuscript of the Latin text survives at the Bodleian Library.[18]

Yet for Christopherson this biblically based play was perhaps an achievement of secondary importance in his scholastic and theological career. In the years following the composition of *Jephthah*, he was best known for two things: his fervent dedication to Roman Catholicism and his tract *An exhortation to all menne to take hede and beware of rebellion* (1554), in which he attacked Lutheranism and the Wyatt Rebellion of 1554. After a self-imposed exile on the continent during Edward VI's reign, Christopherson returned to serve as confessor to Queen Mary I. She, in turn, appointed him Bishop of Chichester in 1557. With the powers of that office, Christopherson persecuted numerous Protestants, culminating in the public exhumation and burning of the corpse of the militant Protestant Martin Bucer—

himself an advocate of the educational value of playing at the collegiate level.[19] Bucer had likely angered Christopherson in 1550, calling the Catholic Fellows of Cambridge University "either most bitter papists, or profligate epicureans, who, as far as they are able, draw over young men to their way of thinking and imbue them with an abhorrence of sound christian [*sic*] doctrine and discipline."[20] Unfortunately for Christopherson, his patron queen died the following year on 17 November, and a mere ten days later he preached a sermon that offended the newly crowned Elizabeth I, for which he was jailed. He took ill, died, and was buried within a month of his arrest.[21] Though his play may not have secured his reputation as solidly as his *An exhortation*, the composition and possible performance of *Jephthah* would have been a natural outlet for his theological and moral views, as evidenced by similar plays in Latin and even in English that were produced by his colleagues at Cambridge. Indeed Alan H. Nelson calls the period in which Christopherson wrote his play the "heyday of college drama at Cambridge."[22]

Given *Jephthah*'s bastardization of Greek dialects and vocabulary, the play has aroused little interest from classicists, the notable exception being Francis Fobes's 1928 edition and translation of the play. Yet looking at the play in the context of ancient Greek literature reveals a surprising and significant theme left untouched by other critiques. Approaching the text as a classicist, I shall offer here a philologically informed reading of the play's central theme. Christopherson, an avid reader of scripture as well as an enthusiastic proponent of Greek, blended a biblical narrative with terminology and images from Greek poetry, and in so doing offered his students moral and ethical instruction. The theme of kinship loyalty emerges in the text through Christopherson's use of two dichotomous Greek terms, φίλος (transliterated here "philos") and ἐχθρός (here "ekhthros"). Simply defined, a *philos* is a friend, one with whom a person shares some sort of binding love. One shares community with one's *philoi*, the plural form. *Philos* always evokes its antonym, *ekhthros*, an "enemy" or "outsider." Greek poets used these terms to distinguish familial, clannish, and political persons from others. Gregory Nagy notes a particularly significant occurrence of these concepts in *Iliad* IX, where he detects tension between Achilles and Odysseus based on their use of these terms.[23] The dichotomy proved useful to later Greeks as well, as *philos* and *ekhthros* appear frequently in the literature of fifth-century Athens, as Mary Whitlock Blundell observes in her study of friends and enemies in Sophoclean tragedy. Blundell notes that for the Golden-Age Athenian it was natural and indeed an ethical obligation not only to help one's *philoi* at all times, but also to harm one's *ekhthroi* with equal vehemence.[24]

This Greek concept informs the whole of *Jephthah*: the playwright uses the two terms and their verbal and adjectival cognates at least twenty-six times in the script. Moreover, Christopherson cites this Greek ethical code in his more famous work *An exhortation*, claiming, "For men for the most part are naturally enclined to be glad of their enemies harmes."[25] The reading of *Jephthah* offered here will investigate the play's use of this theme in light of Christopherson's theological understanding of the Reformation and its implications for the moral education of his students at Cambridge in 1544. Christopherson's appropriation of the friend/ enemy dichotomy offers a complex and nuanced understanding of English Catholic and Protestant identities at this time. Rather than simply drawing Catholics as *philoi* and Protestants as *ekhthroi*, he carefully circumscribes the groups along national and even ecumenical lines, paying honor to his Protestant king, while encouraging him and England to return their loyalties to Rome.

Though the play primarily functions as an exemplum of Christopherson's classical erudition, it also demonstrates an understanding of and reliance upon biblical literature, particularly the Old Testament. Christopherson states in the dedicatory letter to *Jephthah* addressed to William Parr, "Scriptura plena Exemplorum est" ("Scripture is full of examples").[26] Likewise his later work *An exhortation* would make didactic use of numerous Old Testament figures including Absalom, Solomon, David, and Laban. Jephthah originally appears in the Book of Judges, an Old Testament text that features a variety of colorful and unusual characters.[27] All of the Judges—in reality a series of warlords from Israel's twelve tribes—featured in the text are marked by certain characteristics rarely found in other Israelite leaders. The trickster Ehud is left-handed, Deborah is a woman, and Samson, the text's most famous character, cavorts with his nation's enemies, the Philistines. Unusual patrimony marks the Jephthah character: born to a prostitute by a noble father, his half-brothers send him into exile. Being a courageous and potent military leader, his kinsmen recall him to Israel when the Ammonites, a hostile neighbor, invade their territory. In a fit of religious passion, he makes a contract with God: if God gives victory over the Ammonites to Jephthah and his army, he promises that, upon his return, he will sacrifice the first thing he sees leaving his house. Jephthah and Israel are victorious, but when he arrives his only daughter runs from the house to greet him. Realizing the difficulty of the situation, he mourns, yet keeps his promise and sacrifices her.

With its focus on ethnic, religious, and social identities, as well as its conservative interpretation of humankind's obligation to keep vows made to a superior, it comes as no surprise that the Jephthah narrative enjoyed popularity in the theatrical texts of early modern Europe. Christopherson's fellow academic dramatist George Buchanan wrote a Latin version of the Jephthah story, and at least two others—by Hans Sachs and Joost Van Vondel—followed in the next century.[28] References to Jephthah even make their way into the popular theater; Shakespeare uses the image of the sacrificing father in *Hamlet*, as the title character taunts Polonius.[29] Christopher Upton ties the popularity of this story in mid-sixteenth century Reformation England to "a renewed interest [...] in monastic vows,"[30] and, given Christopherson's interest in the Catholic/Protestant debate, this story serves as an appropriate vehicle for his exploration of the Greek concept of the *philos* and the *ekhthros*.

The play's prologue, a thirty-line speech by Jephthah, reveals several of Christopherson's major themes while it provides exposition. He explains the challenges he faces as the illegitimate son of Gilead, the head of the clan. Rather than dwelling on his circumstances, Jephthah wisely states, "ἀλλ' ἐγὼ / γένει δ' ἀμύμων· ὦφλον αἰτίαν γονεῖς / τίκτοντες ὡς ἀνέγγυον μὲ δ' εἰς τὸ φῶς" (ll. 10–12 ["But I / was born blameless; my parents incur the blame, / who, unwed, brought me into the light"]). These lines, as they evaluate the moral responsibility of parents to their children, foreshadow Jephthah's own complex relationship with his daughter and his failure as a parent. Christopherson will return to this theme later in the play, as Jephthah's daughter willingly accepts execution, thereby paying for her father's mistake in much the same way that Jephthah suffers for the illicit union between his noble father and prostitute mother. Unlike her father, who criticizes his parents' behavior in the lines above, Jephthah's daughter nobly pays her father's debt.

Just a few lines later, Jephthah raises an issue that will prove to be one of the central themes of the play, the construction of the friend/enemy dichotomy. His status as the bastard son of a prostitute has complicated his relationship with his family, particularly his half-brothers, who are trying to force him into exile without his share of Gilead's estate.[31] Jephthah debates with himself, "τλήσω μὲν οὖν κοὐκ ἀντερείσω; φέρτερον. / οὐ γὰρ καλὸν κείνοις μάχεσθ' αὐτὰρ βαρύ· / βροτόλοιγος ὁ πόλεμος, μάλιστα σῶν μέτα·" (ll. 21–3 ["Must I suffer and not resist? Yes, that is the better thing. / It is not good to fight a hopeless cause, however painful; / war is a plague, especially with one's own"]). Though he does not use the specific terminology of *philos* and *ekhthros*, his words here concerning war assert that family should naturally be *philoi*. In Jephthah's next lines, Christopherson overlays the ancient Greek ethical code with a Christian one. To resolve the potentially damaging split between himself and his brothers, Jephthah claims:

μὴ πρὸς Θεοῦ στάσις κυρῇ σὺν αἵματι.
ἄλγος γὰρ εἴη τοῖς γονεῦσι, καὶ Θεοῦ
μέλλοιμ' ἂν ὀτρύνειν χόλον θυμάλγεα·
κἂν ἀνδάνει θυμῷ, Θεῷ δ' οὐκ ἀνδάνει,
καὶ τῷ μὲν εἴκειν κρεῖττον ἢ δ' ἡμῶν χόλῳ. [ll. 26–30]

[A quarrel should not be decided by blood in front of God.
It would be painful for my parents, and I would be inviting
The soul-wrenching wrath of God.
And even if it satisfies my desire, it does not please God,
And it is better to submit to Him than to my own fury.]

In much the same way as the Athenians witnessed Socrates issue a challenge to the helping friends/harming enemies dichotomy,[32] so too Christopherson reminds his academic audience of Christ's instructions to turn the other cheek.[33] His character Jephthah advocates a gospel-based Christian ethic, one not found in the Old Testament character on which he is based.

Jephthah's prologue is followed immediately by the episode that makes the greatest use of the *philos/ekhthros* dichotomy, a conversation between Jephthah and his brothers. In this exchange, Jephthah argues with his two half-brothers, an older one who considers him an *ekhthros* since Jephthah's mother was a prostitute, and a kinder, younger one who sees Jephthah as a *philos* through their kinship:

ΑΔΕΛΦΟΣ ΝΕΩΤΕΡΟΣ
τί ῥέζομεν, τί σπεύδομεν πρὸς τὸν κάσιν;
βαρὺς κότος προσπῖτνέει, καὶ δυσμενὴς
ἐστὶν φόνος τοῦ συγγόνου· χεῖρας δ' ἔχε.
ΑΔΕΛΦΟΣ ΠΡΕΣΒΥΤΕΡΟΣ
ὑθλεῖς, ἀδελφέ. τόνδ' ἐᾶς κληροῦ τυχεῖν;
οὐκ ἂν γένοιτο. μὴ συνὼν τύχῃ δόμοις
ἡμῶν μέτ'. οὐδαμῶς ὁμαίμων λέξεται·
νόθος γάρ ἐστι φαῦλος, ἤδ' ἀτάσθαλος.
κτείνειν χρέων· στείχωμεν ἀρτίως, κάσι.
ΑΔΕΛΦΟΣ ΝΕΩΤΕΡΟΣ
τί, φίλτατ'; οὐ πτώσσεις Θεὸν πανάλκεα
τὸν ἔκδικον; κάτεσχε θυμὸν ἄπλετον.
φρόνει. φλέγεις ἄγαν, κασίγνητον κάρα.
νίκα δὲ τλημοσύνῃ· πέλει γὰρ βέλτιον.
νικᾶν σεαυτὸν ἐστὶ νίκη παγκαλής.
ΙΕΦΘΑΕ
ὦ σύγγονοι μοῦ φίλτατοι, χαίρειν λέγω·
ἦλθον γὰρ ὑμῖν τὴν χάριν διδοὺς πρόφρων.
ΑΔΕΛΦΟΣ ΠΡΕΣΒΥΤΕΡΟΣ
σὺ τὴν χάριν; μᾶλλον μὲν ἐχθρὰν προσφέρεις·
ἔχθιστος εἶ πάντων. τί δ' ὡς ἡμᾶς μολεῖς;
ΙΕΦΘΑΕ
εὔφημα βάζε· μηδὲν ὄμμασι βλέπων
ὕβρισα σὲ μήδε τοῖς λόγοις, ἀδελφὲ μοῦ.
ΑΔΕΛΦΟΣ ΠΡΕΣΒΥΤΕΡΟΣ
ἀδελφὸς οὐκ εἶς, ἀλλὰ δ' αἴσχιστος νόθος·
πόρνη δὲ τίκτεσκε ῥυπαρα, γυνὴ ξένη.
ΙΕΦΘΑΕ
ἀληθὲς αὐδᾶς· εὐκόλως μὲ δεῖ φέρειν,
ἀναίτιος γὰρ ἐγώ. χόλον δεινὸν πνέεις.
ΑΔΕΛΦΟΣ ΝΕΩΤΕΡΟΣ
νῦν παῦε τὰς θυμοῦ πνόας· σχάσον μέτρον.
φίλους ἀεὶ φίλει· σοφὸν γὰρ ἐν βροτοῖς.
ΑΔΕΛΦΟΣ ΠΡΕΣΒΥΤΕΡΟΣ
οὗτος δὲ φίλος ἡμῶν; φρονεῖς οὐκ εὖ, κάσι.
μήτηρ ἀπεχθὴς τὸν τεκοῦσα· σὺ τοῦδ' ἐρᾶς;
ΑΔΕΛΦΟΣ ΝΕΩΤΕΡΟΣ
ἐρῶ μέν, ὡς δέ σοι πρέπει, τέκνου πατρός.
λέγειν μὲν εὖ χρέων· κενὸν κακορροθεῖν. [ll. 31–59]

[YOUNGER BROTHER
What are we doing? Why are you so eager to exile our brother?
A vile grudge has conquered your mind; this is a hostile crime

To commit against a brother. Restrain your hands!
> OLDER BROTHER

Quit your blubbering, brother! Are you thinking clearly?
He's not part of our family. You can't include him in our house.
He must never be called a brother of ours.
He is a worthless, arrogant bastard.
Let him die. Come on now, brother, let's go.
> YOUNGER BROTHER

What are you saying, friend? Aren't you afraid of our omnipotent God,
The avenger? Hold back your passionate anger.
Be wise. You're like a fire burning out of control, brother!
Find victory in misery; it is the better way.
A victory over oneself is the noblest kind.
> JEPHTHAH

My dearest brothers, I'm glad to see you.
I've come to you to make peace. Accept my grace.
> OLDER BROTHER

Grace from you? It is hate that you bring here.
I hate you more than anyone or anything. Why have you come to us?
> JEPHTHAH

Speak kindly to me; I have insulted you
Neither with words nor a reproachful look, brother.
> OLDER BROTHER

You are not my brother; you are an ugly, shameful bastard!
Your mother was dirty, a whore, and a foreigner.
> JEPHTHAH

You're right. I have to listen to your words calmly,
Though I am innocent of my parents' actions. You breathe a terrible
wrath.
> YOUNGER BROTHER (TO OLDER BROTHER)

Won't you stop? Give up the anger in your heart.
Always love your friends; that would be the wisest choice for mortal men.
> OLDER BROTHER

Is this man a friend of ours? You're not thinking straight, brother.
The mother who bore him was repulsive; do you love him?
> YOUNGER BROTHER

Indeed I love the son of my father, just as you should.
You should speak well of him; to abuse him is useless.]

This passage, pure invention by Christopherson—in the Book of Judges the
situation is described in less than two verses—shows a deft blending of the
Ancient Greek ethical code with the alternate Christian notion of forgiveness. The
scene also demonstrates two competing models of behavior as it establishes a clear
moral paradigm aimed directly at both the play's audience and any student actors
performing the parts. The Older Brother, an underdeveloped character whose
motivation for hating Jephthah is scarcely explained, clearly models bad behavior
as he rigidly adheres to the ancient ethic of helping friends and harming enemies.
His words are direct and brutal, labeling Jephthah "φαῦλος" ("worthless") and

"ἀτάσθαλος" ("arrogant") (l. 37). In refusing to entertain the notion that Jephthah might be a friend to him and the Younger Brother, he understands the categories of *philos* and *ekhthros* much like a Homeric hero or a fifth-century Athenian would have understood them. His telling remark about Jephthah's mother—that she is "ξένη" ("a foreigner") (l. 51)—reveals the ancient conceit that all foreigners were considered hostile enemies. He goes even further in rejecting the Younger Brother's claim that a common father makes Jephthah their *philos*.

In obvious contrast stand both the Younger Brother and Jephthah himself. From his first lines, when he calls his brother's actions "βαρὺς" ("vile") and "δυσμενής" ("hostile") (l. 32), the Younger Brother is marked by Christopherson as a reasonable moderate. He approaches the *philos/ekhthros* code in a selfless way, stating, "νικᾶν σεαυτὸν ἐστὶ νίκη παγκαλής" (l. 43 ["A victory over one's self is the noblest kind"]). Intriguingly, he does not go so far as to suggest the Christian ethic of loving one's enemy (Luke 6.27) to the Older Brother. Rather, when he says "φίλους ἀεὶ φίλει" (l. 55 ["Always love your friends"]), the Younger Brother keeps the ancient code intact while hoping to broaden the range of *philoi* to include Jephthah, if not all humanity. In an even more radical move, Jephthah's words in the scene juxtapose the Greek treatment of friends and enemies with Christian behavior. He first tries to establish community with his brothers by calling them "φίλτατοι" (l. 44 ["dearest"]), the superlative form of *philos*. The Older Brother rejects his attempt at reconciliation, calling him "ἔχθιστος" (l. 47 ["most hated"]), the superlative antonym to *philos*. According to the ancient code of harming enemies, Jephthah has every right to attack this man who adamantly defines himself as Jephthah's enemy. Yet like Christ, who condemned retaliation, Jephthah takes his Older Brother's abuse and refuses to allow a family member to become an enemy.[34]

Though Christopherson's moral instruction to his students here superficially reminds them to act kindly and respectfully towards their families when they return home—the boys did, after all, spend most of the year at school[35]—it also suggests the importance of the identification and cultivation of friends in other arenas, for example in political or theological circles, where group identity and cooperation can reunify a state divided by religion. Christopherson uses this biblical family conflict and the Greek ethical code to instruct other English Catholics in Reformation England who, though once disenfranchised by their king's break with Rome, may recently have renewed their hope in England's return to Roman Catholicism. English Catholics like Christopherson were likely heartened not only by the Act of Six Articles in 1539 and the fall of the militant Protestant Thomas Cromwell in 1540 but also by the Act for the Advancement of True Religion of 1543, which condemned Protestant literature and outlawed the private reading of scripture for all but the nobles.[36] Henry complicated the theological issue several months after passing the latter Act by marrying Catherine Parr, a vocal Protestant, on 12 July 1543.[37] While Catholics like Christopherson likely saw the union as a setback, the pro-Catholic climate of 1544 likely inspired him to write the brother scene in *Jephthah*. He argues that *ekhthroi*, through God's mediation and an individual's Christian behavior, may become *philoi* once again. Christopherson himself advocates such a course in his dedicatory epistle to William Parr, the brother of the new queen, stating, "Si cum hostibus pugnare aggrediamur, non tantum viribus, quantum Deo (Sic nanque fecit Iephte) aliquando debemus confidere" (ll. 73–5 ["If we should attempt to fight with enemies, we ought to trust more in God (just as Jephthah did) than in force"]).

As with much humanist academic drama, moral instruction is but one aspect of the educational agenda. Christopherson was also promoting the study of Greek at Cambridge, and this scene would have offered students both practice with syntax and morphology as well as an example of a device common to Greek tragedy. Christopherson's Greek in the passage quoted above is basic. The characters state their ideas in simple, declarative sentences. While Christopherson uses Euripides' *Iphigenia at Aulis* as his classical model—a play that also features a father who must sacrifice his daughter—one finds nowhere in Christopherson's dialogue the linguistic complexity of late fifth-century Attic tragedy. He avoids syntactic obscurity, choosing instead to use verbs in the indicative mood. Gone too are the compound epithets often found in Aeschylus and Sophocles. To help his students gain mastery over Greek vocabulary and verbal forms, he relies heavily on simple words like "to be" (εἰμί) and "to love" (φιλέω).

After the Brothers wrangle over the definition of *philos* and *ekhthros*, Christopherson continues the debate with lengthy, combative speeches from Jephthah and the Older Brother. This rhetorical exercise, common to Greek tragedy, would have introduced students to the formal device of the *agon*, an argument between two characters with opposing viewpoints, given in speeches of roughly equal length. Michael Lloyd notes the presence of "angry dialogue after the speeches, or a judgment speech by a third party" as complementary elements of this device.[38] The *agon* in *Jephthah* begins with a speech by the Older Brother, who considers Jephthah *ekhthros*. In his vitriolic twenty-four line speech (63–87), the character reiterates his evaluation of Jephthah as a worthless bastard and enemy.

The Older Brother's speech closely resembles two speeches from Greek tragedy, that of Oedipus in his *agon* with Creon in *Oedipus Rex* and Pentheus' rant against Dionysus in Euripides' *Bacchae*. Both of these classical examples feature angry tyrants raging at innocent men, who, like Jephthah, calmly accept the abuse of their accusers. Jephthah's response to the speech, just slightly longer than his antagonist's, begins by refuting the Older Brother's logic. He says, "ὅταν δὲ θυμ ωθεὶς τίς ἐστ' ὑπερφυῶς, / λόγος κένος, νοῦς σφάλλεται, καὶ γλῶσσα ῥεῖ" (ll. 88–9 ["Whenever someone is exceptionally angry, as you are now, / his argument is empty. Reason is overthrown and the tongue wags uselessly"]). Compare his words to those of Teiresias in *Bacchae* "ἐν τοῖς λόγοισι δ' οὐκ ἔνεισί σοι φρ ένες. / θράσει δὲ δυνατὸς καὶ λέγειν οἷός τ' ἀνὴρ / κακὸς πολίτης γίγνεται νοῦν οὐκ ἔχων" ("There is no reason in your speech. / A man who uses only self-confidence to speak proves to be / a bad citizen since he has no brain!").[39]

Christopherson embellishes the *agon* with the other elements outlined by Lloyd, particularly the "judgment speech by a third party." After Jephthah delivers his speech, the Younger Brother says, "νῦν εὖ λέλεκται. παῦε τὸν χόλον, κάσι" (l. 121 ["Now he has spoken well. Stop your anger, brother"]). Likewise in *Oedipus Rex* a chorus member praises Creon to Oedipus, "καλῶς ἔλεξεν, εὐλαβουμένωι πεσεῖν, ἄναξ" ("He spoke beautifully, king, though I fear I have made you angry").[40] A similar sentiment is voiced by the Chorus in *Bacchae*: "ὦ πρέσβυ, Φοῖβόν τ' οὐ καταισχύνεις λόγοις, / τιμῶν τε Βρόμιον σωφρονεῖς, μέγαν θεόν" ("Old man, you have not dishonored Apollo with your speech / and you also give honor to Bromios, a great god").[41] Like the lines in Sophocles and Euripides, the Younger Brother's encouragement hopes to bring an end to the verbal warfare of the *agon*. Christopherson's painstaking reproduction of the Greek model here serves two purposes. The *agon* heightens the intensity of the scene, allowing the actors and audience—presumably the Cambridge students learning Greek—to enjoy the play in performance. At the same time, the use of an *agon* reinforces the scholastic value of debate in a university setting. It functions as a rhetorical tool rather than a moral or ethical one. Though Christopherson's goals in composing *Jephthah* were principally behavioral instruction, the presence of the *agon* reveals an educational exemplum of the formal and technical elements of Greek tragedy.[42] The intensity of the *agon* scene in all probability delighted his student actors, allowing them a chance to play at spirited argument while learning the rhetorical techniques of classical antiquity.

Christopherson reiterates both his moral point concerning helping friends and harming enemies and also his instruction on the form of Greek tragedy in the subsequent episode. This second scene reads much like the first, but now the exiled Jephthah is absent, and the playwright has substituted two Gileadite elders for Jephthah's combative brothers. A Messenger arrives to announce the incursion of the Ammonites, an enemy clan, into Israelite territory. The two characters in the scene, whose *agon* resembles the one between the brothers, are designated ΓΕΡΩΝ ("Old Man") and ΓΕΡΩΝ ΕΤΕΡΟΣ ("Other Old Man"). Their conversation reveals several significant points about the Christian refiguring of the ancient Greek ethical code. The Old Man wants to recall Jephthah because he is the best Gileadite general and therefore the clan's greatest hope of victory against the Ammonites. The Other Old Man has his doubts, stating, "ἐκεῖνος εὖ ποιεῖν θέλει, παθὼν κακῶς; / οὐ δῆτα· χεὶρ τὴν χεῖρα νίζει δ' ὡς λόγος" (ll. 256–7 ["Would he ever want to help us, having been so horribly dishonored? / Certainly not. As the saying goes: one hand washes the other"]). His remark classifies Jephthah as *ekhthros* and conservatively assumes that an enemy would only treat his enemies in kind. The Old Man, like the Younger Brother in the prior scene, asserts a revisionist understanding of Jephthah's position:

ὁ μὲν γὰρ ἀδικηθεὶς ἀδικίαν οὐ πάλιν
δράσει. Θεῷ δίκην ἐπιτρέψει σοφός.
κακοῦ γὰρ ἄντι χρηστὸς οὐκ ἔρδει κακόν,

ἀλλ' ἐσθλὸν ἐχθροῖς πολλάκις πόρειν θέλει·
χρυσοθρόνῳ γὰρ οὐ Θεῷ τι φίλτερον
ἢ δ' εὐμαρὲς ἀδίκημα πάσχειν ἐν βίῳ. [ll. 264–9]

[A man like him, treated unjustly, will not repay wrong for wrong,
For the wise man seeks justice from God.
He does not offer evil in return for an offense,
But often wishes to act kindly towards his enemies.
There is nothing dearer to God on his golden throne
Than seeing someone suffer injury in life with a calm spirit.]

In positing God as the deconstructor of the ethical code, Christopherson honors the ideas and philosophy of Ancient Greece while asserting a superior Christian reconfiguration of that code. The Other Old Man still clings to his assertion that Jephthah now sees Gilead as *ekhthros*, claiming, "χαίρειν θέλει μᾶλλον κακοὺς πράττειν κακῶς· / ἐχθροὺς γὰρ ἀθλίους βλέπειν ἧδος φέρει" (ll. 289–90 ["He will rejoice to know that the evil suffer evil. / It is always a pleasure to see one's worst enemies in trouble"]). Citing Jephthah's moral goodness, the Old Man again responds, "ου τοῖσι μόνον εὐεργετεῖν μέλλει φίλος. / πάτρη δὲ τὴν δώσει χάριν καὶ τῷ" (ll. 295–6 ["A good man will help anyone, even them. / He will do it for his country and for God"]). Eventually, the Old Man's rhetoric wins and the two elders agree to recall Jephthah, who now is an *ekhthros* made *philos*. The sentiments of the Old Man are echoed by the Chorus' chant:

ἐλθὲ δ' αἶψ', Ιεφθάε,
ἐλθὲ πρὸς τὴν πατρίδα,
ἐλθὲ πρὸς φίλους φίλος,
ἐλθὲ σωτὴρ τῆς χθονός. [ll. 387–90]

[Come quickly Jephthah,
Come to your country,
Come, a friend to your friends,
Come, savior of our land!]

The Chorus' invocation of Jephthah as a *philos* to his *philoi* and as the savior of his country reveals a deft blending of Greek and Christian ethics.

The Chorus' prayer sets the stage for Jephthah's return in the next scene, which includes not just a physical return to Gilead but also the reintegration of Jephthah as a *philos* to his *philoi*. Upon entering he greets the elders and Chorus, "ἄψορρος ἔρχομαι πατρὸς πρὸς δώματα. / ὦ μοῦ φίλοι, χαίρετε. χθονὸς μεθέξομαι / πάλιν μεθ' ὑμῶν" (ll. 413–15 ["I have come back to my father's home. / Hello, my friends. Once again, I am a shareholder / in our land"]). Yet again modeling good behavior, Jephthah comes back not with spite or demands, but a revived sense of self and community. To the Old Man who had demanded his recall Jephthah says, "πρὸς πόλιν σπεύδω, γέρον. / γονεῖς ποθῶ βλέπων λίαν καὶ τοὺς φίλους" (ll. 456–7 ["I hasten to the city, old man. / I miss seeing the faces of my family and friends"]). The Old Man's response—"γένοιτο τοῦτο· στεῖχε πρὸς φίλους φίλος" (l. 462 ["So it shall be. A friend returning to friends!"])—validates Jephthah's reclamation of the role of friend to his friends, a position which will bring success and prosperity to Gilead's clan. As a *philos*, Jephthah readily and effectively steps into the role of commander of the militia and, as such, he bears witness to God's role in his reintegration. Christopherson here makes an overt connection between a successful monarch and the support of the Christian God. Though there is no evidence to suggest that Henry read *Jephthah*, these words subtly encourage his temperate Catholic leanings and legislation in the years leading up to 1544. The more likely readers of Christopherson's script, his students at Cambridge, would here see the moderate and Christian instruction of a king who is on the path toward reuniting with Christ's Roman Church.

Jephthah's line: "ἑτοιμός εἰμι, καὶ βοηθός θεός" (l. 433 ["I am ready, and God is my ally"]), further echoes the playwright's own praise of Henry VIII as God's agent. In the introduction in the Trinity manuscript, Christopherson boasts of Henry's recent military victories:

> Hoc modo Invictissimus Rex noster edomat Scotos foedifragos. Sic insolentes comprimit Gallos manu Dei potentis. [...] Fugiat Scotus, Gallusque fugiat ocyus. Henricus Octavus Deo pugnat Duce. [ll. 40–41, 48–9]

> [In this let our most invincible King subdue the treaty-breaking Scots. Thus he suppresses the insolent Gauls with the hand of powerful God. [...] Let the Scot run, and let the Gaul flee. Henry VIII fights with God as his general.]

A similar sentiment appears in Trinity's dedicatory epistle:

> Hoc Invictissimus Rex noster in omni expeditione bellica perpetuo factitavit. Nam non ipse solum preces ad Deum sedulo fudit, sed omnibus suis ut idem diligenter praestarent, mandavit. [ll. 81–4]

> [This our most invincible King promised forever in every martial expedition. For not only does he himself pour out prayers to God alone, but he also commands all of his troops to do the same diligently.]

In these passages Christopherson courageously advises the king, reminding the monarch of the value of scripture and theological fidelity. The playwright was likely emboldened by the Act for the Advancement of True Religion of 1543 and by Henry's inconsistent stance on the Reformation and England's separation from Rome. While no recorded response or reaction from Henry to the playwright exists, Christopherson dedicated his Latin version of *Jephthah* to the monarch.[43] Clearly Christopherson's didacticism was aimed at others beyond the immediate academic community.

Christopherson makes a bold dramaturgical move midway through the play, after Jephthah's reintegration. Whereas Jephthah had been the primary didactic model of Christian behavior, he makes several significant mistakes in the second half of the play, beginning with the oath to perform a human sacrifice to God as payment for victory over Ammon. Jephthah's unnamed daughter—here "Bath-Jephthah" for lack of a proper name—presents the play's other important ethical model. Given her age and role as an obedient child, this character probably addressed Christopherson's Cambridge students more directly than the Israelite Judge. In his dedicatory epistle to the Trinity manuscript, Christopherson spells out her role in the play explicitly, "Si liberi parentibus obsequi recusent, proponant sibi filiam Iephte ad imitandum, quae patris verbo morem gerens mortem alacri animo oppetiit" (ll. 70–73 ["If children refuse to obey parents, let them study the daughter of Jephthah for imitation, who, complying with the word of her father, sought death with a quick spirit"]).

Christopherson stresses the friend/enemy theme less in this scene than in the play's first half, but does not abandon it altogether. When Jephthah informs his daughter of his intention to fulfill his vow he says, "ὦ φιλτάτη, χρὴ μ' αἱματοῦν δέρην σέθεν" (l. 793 ["Oh dearest friend, it is necessary for me to bloody your throat"]). His use of the term "dearest friend" picks up on the theme that the earlier action had developed and reminds spectators and readers of the obligation friends have to their friends. Bath-Jephthah at first balks at his pronouncement, but soon acquiesces when she realizes that she's fulfilling a vow to God. She instructs Jephthah, "λῆγε στοναχεῖν, ἐμοῦ πάτερ· χαῖρον λέγεις [...] πείθεσθαι γὰρ εἴθισμαι Θεῷ." (ll. 802, 804 ["Stop crying my father. I rejoice at what you've told me. [...] I am accustomed to obey God"]). Her quick and ready support of her parent, even when that parent has acted wrongly, aims to teach Christopherson's Cambridge students a valuable lesson. Christopherson reveals a concern for fostering nationalism in youth, as Bath-Jephthah also remains faithful to her nation, even to an apparently illogical extreme when she says, "καὶ μὴν νομίζω νῦν με κάρτ' εὐδαίμονα, / ἐὰν τύχοιμι θῦμα πατρίδος πέρι" (ll. 872–3 ["I declare myself most fortunate / if I might offer my body as sacrifice for my country"]). In her patriotic constancy, Bath-Jephthah ignores that her father has already won the war with the Ammonites. She plays the role of good daughter, dying to protect her land and her *philoi*. She also shows obedience to God when upon her final exit she prays to Him:

ἐλπὶς γὰρ ἐπὶ σέθεν μόνου σωτηρίας.
σὺ νυμφίος, σὺ τέκνα μοι, καὶ σὺ πατήρ·
σὺ φῶς, σὺ βίος εἷς, καὶ σὺ πάντων ἐν μέρει.
ἐν χειρὶ σοῦ πέλω· σὺ πράττε τό σοι δοκοῦν. [ll. 925–8]

[You are my only hope of salvation.
I look to you as husband, my children, and father;
You are my light and my life, and have a share in everything that I am.

I place myself in your hands now; do with me as you wish.]

This scene, with its conservative linking of nationalism and theology, complete with specific references to Christ ("You are my light and my life"),[44] makes a passionate and convincing case to children concerning obedience to parents. In case this message is not clear enough to his students, Christopherson makes a final laudatory comment about Bath-Jephthah when a Messenger enters to tell the story of her noble sacrifice. His speech ends, "ζηλῶ τὸν ἄνδρ' ἔχοντα τέκν' εὐήκοα. / παῖς ἥδε πείθεσθαι λόγῳ πατρὸς θέλειν·" (ll. 1153–4 ["I am happy for the man whose children are so inclined to listen to their parents. / Such a child wants to follow her father's every word"]). This persuasive line praises and positively reinforces Bath-Jephthah's obedient sacrifice just as it invokes the more significant sacrifice that defines the New Testament, namely Christ's sacrifice for humanity.

Ten years after writing *Jephthah*, Christopherson would again turn his attention to the moral and theological education of children. His tract *An exhortation* cites examples of the disastrous effects of adolescent disobedience. In 1554, he satirizes the outlawed Protestant movement in England and the potential theological divide between generations, thereby offering a converse model to Bath-Jephthah. One spoiled Lutheran child mocks his Catholic parents, saying:

> My father is an old doting foole, and will fast upon fryday, and my mother goeth alwayes mumblinge on her beades. But you shall se me of another sort, I warrant you. For I will never folowe no such superstitiuse folye, nor walke in the Papisticall pathes of my parents.[45]

Here Christopherson repeats the moral message of the scene in *Jephthah*. Good children would be wise to follow Bath-Jephthah's example, even if they may not understand their parents' adherence to Catholicism. Christopherson may have been attempting to answer Protestant playwrights, his academic and theological *ekhthroi*, as childrearing and good behavior were popular themes in Reformation plays.[46]

John Christopherson may not be celebrated or widely remembered for his talent in Greek composition—*The Dictionary of National Biography* cites at least three contemporaries who mocked his abilities in the language, one of whom called his style "impure and full of barbarisms"[47]—but his play provides an unusual exemplum of the role of theater and Classics in humanist pedagogy. Few other dramas of this period offer such a rich variety of didactic goals, as Christopherson tried to address the moral behavior of his students, their linguistic skills, as well as their knowledge of the formal elements of classical tragedy. Though no official record of a formal production of *Jephthah* exists, there is no reason to assume that it was never performed, particularly since St. John's and Trinity, the two colleges with which Christopherson was affiliated, required "annual production of plays" in the years immediately following the text's composition.[48] Moreover, playscripts like this one, with such an elementary level of language, can be performed in any variety of informal settings. Christopherson may have seen his pedagogical mission as a practical and urgent one, given that many of his students at Cambridge would become statesmen or clergy.[49]

To encourage students to remain faithful to God and country must have been a crucial and challenging task, given the complex relationship between England, the Tudor monarchs, and Rome. The play carefully addresses Catholics who remained loyal to Rome after England's split in 1534 and whose hopes were bolstered by Henry's seeming return to Catholic doctrine with the Act of Six Articles in 1539 and the Act for the Advancement of True Religion in 1543. The experiences of the Israelite Judge foreshadow Christopherson's own difficult vow to God *vis-à-vis* Catholicism, which would be tested three years after he wrote *Jephthah,* when Edward's anti-Catholic stance forced scholars like him into continental exile. He would of course reunite with his Catholic *philoi* and achieve esteemed ecclesiastical positions under Mary's leadership. Yet, unlike Jephthah, Christopherson would once again become an *ekhthros* to his nation and die in captivity under the Elizabethan religious settlement.[50]

Notes

1 Quoted in John R. Elliott, Jr., "Plays, Players and Playwrights in Renaissance Oxford," in *From Page to Performance: Essays in Early English Drama*, ed. John A. Alford (East Lansing: Michigan State University Press, 1995), 180. The letter comes from the Corpus Christi archives, MS. 352, pp. 41–65. See also Frederick S. Boas, *University Drama in the Tudor Age* (Oxford: Oxford University Press, 1914), 166. The epigraph can be found in Elie Wiesel, *Sages and Dreamers: Biblical, Talmudic, and Hasidic Portraits and Legends* (New York: Summit, 1991), 35.

2 Elliott, "Plays, Players and Playwrights," 180.

3 Paul Whitfield White, *Theater and Reformation: Protestantism, Patronage and Playing in Tudor England* (Cambridge: Cambridge University Press, 1993), 101.

4 Alan H. Nelson, "Cambridge University Drama in the 1580s," in *The Elizabethan Theatre 11*, ed. A.L. Magnusson and C.E. McGee (Port Credit: P.D. Meany, 1990), 20.

5 On Thomas Legge, see Boas, *University Drama*, 112; and on Nicholas Udall, see Marie Axton, *Three Tudor Classical Interludes* (Cambridge: D.S. Brewer, 1982), 3.

6 Alan H. Nelson, "Contexts for Early English Drama: The Universities," in *Contexts for Early English Drama*, ed. Marianne G. Briscoe and John C. Coldewey (Bloomington: Indiana University Press, 1989), 141.

7 Nelson, "Contexts," 141.

8 Quoted in Arthur Tilley, "Greek Studies in England in the Early Sixteenth Century," *The English Historical Review* 53 (1938): 224.

9 Tilley, "Greek Studies," 221.

10 Tilley, "Greek Studies," 234.

11 Tilley, "Greek Studies," 234–5.

12 For Christopherson's *Jephthah* as the only extant academic drama composed in Greek, see Boas, *University Drama*, 43. Other play texts in Greek may now be lost or awaiting discovery.

13 G.C. Moore Smith, *College Plays Performed in the University of Cambridge* (Cambridge: Cambridge University Press, 1923), 102, 107.

14 Nelson, "Contexts," 143.

15 The epistles praise King Henry VIII as "Invictissimus rex noster" ("Our most invincible king"), an epithet more appropriate in 1544 than in the following year, when England and Henry faced a series of military setbacks. See Boas, *University Drama*, 47; and Francis Howard Fobes, ed. and trans., *Jephthah By John Christopherson* (Newark: University of Delaware Press, 1928), 8.

16 Christopher Upton, prep., *John Christopherson IEPHTE, William Goldingham HERODES* (Hildesheim: Georg Olms Verlag, 1988), 3.

17 Upton, *John Christopherson*, 2.

18 The manuscript in Greek at Trinity is shelfmark MS. 0.1.37, that at St. John's MS. 284.H.19, and the Latin manuscript at the Bodleian is MS Tanner 466.

19 Fobes, *Jephthah*, 4.

20 Quoted in H.C. Porter, *Reformation and Reaction in Tudor Cambridge* (Hamden: Archon, 1958), 54.

21 *Dictionary of National Biography*, s.v. John Christopherson.

22 Alan H. Nelson, "Drama in the 1520s: Cambridge University," *Research Opportunities in Renaissance Drama* 31 (1992): 333.

23 Gregory Nagy, *The Best of the Achaeans: Concepts of the Hero in Archaic Greek Poetry*, rev. edn. (Baltimore: Johns Hopkins University Press, 1999), 52–3.

24 Mary Whitlock Blundell, *Helping Friends and Harming Enemies: A Study in Sophocles and Greek Ethics* (Cambridge: Cambridge University Press, 1989), 1.

25 John Christopherson, *An exhortation to all menne to take hede and beware of rebellion* (London: by John Cawood, 1554), sig. Niiiv.

26 All translations from Latin and Greek are my own from Fobes's edition. Subsequent citations of *Jephthah* will appear parenthetically in the text. The Latin text of the dedicatory epistle to William Parr, Earl of Essex, can be found in Fobes, 19–23.

27 The debate over religious identity in Reformation England may have made the Book of Judges appealing to Christopherson, especially given his ardent Catholicism. The narratives in the Book of Judges all have a strong sense of selfhood and otherness, a point underscored by religious practice. When the Israelites worship Yahweh, they are portrayed as whole, obedient, and good, yet each separate narrative in Judges begins with an assertion of Israel's collapse into religious otherness. For example, the Jephthah narrative begins, "The Israelites again did what was evil in the sight of the Lord, worshipping the Baals and the Astartes, the gods of Aram, the gods of Sidon, the gods of

Moab, the gods of the Ammonites, and the gods of the Philistines. Thus they abandoned the Lord, and did not worship him. So the anger of the Lord was kindled against Israel, and he sold them into the hand of the Philistines and into the hand of the Ammonites, and they crushed and oppressed the Israelites that year" (10.6–8, cited in Victor H. Matthews, *Judges & Ruth* [Cambridge: Cambridge University Press, 2004], 114). For more on this cycle, see Matthews, 8–9.

28 Fobes, *Jephthah*, 2. For the influence of this myth on other early modern writers, particularly those on the continent, see Anna Linton, "Sacrificed or Spared? The Fate of Jephthah's Daughter in Early Modern Theological and Literary Texts," *German Life and Letters* 57 (2004): 237–55.

29 William Shakespeare, *Hamlet*, ed. Harold Jenkins (London: Methuen, 1982), 2.2.406.

30 Upton, *John Christopherson*, 3.

31 Neither Christopherson nor his source, the anonymous author(s) of Judges 11, explain the state of Jephthah's inheritance from his father Gilead. Since the brothers argue with Jephthah over his claim to their father's property, we may assume that Gilead has died recently or, at the very least, is near death. For a discussion of inheritance laws in the ancient Near East, see Matthews, *Judges & Ruth*, 117.

32 For Socrates as the first to advocate the treating of enemies like friends, see Plato, *Crito*, in *Four Texts on Socrates*, trans. Thomas G. West and Grace Starry West, rev. edn. (Ithaca: Cornell University Press, 1998), 49a–d.

33 Matthew 5.38, New International Version.

34 While in this scene Jephthah plays the Christ figure, his daughter will fulfill the role after he makes his foolish vow.

35 Boas, *University Drama*, 14.

36 Eamon Duffy, *The Stripping of the Altars: Traditional Religion in England 1400–1580* (New Haven: Yale University Press, 1992), 432–3.

37 John Guy, *Tudor England* (Oxford: Oxford University Press, 1988), 195–6.

38 Michael Lloyd, *The Agon in Euripides* (Oxford: Clarendon, 1992), 1.

39 Euripides, *Bacchae*, ed. E.R. Dodds, 2d edn. (Oxford: Clarendon, 1960), ll. 269–71.

40 Sophocles, *Oedipus Rex*, ed. R.D. Dawe (Cambridge: Cambridge University Press, 1982), l. 616.

41 Euripides, *Bacchae*, ll. 328–9.

42 In the dedicatory letter to William Parr in the Trinity College manuscript of *Jephthah*, Christopherson advocates a course of education that honors both classical literature as well as scripture: "Et licet philosophiae caeterarumque atrium cognition nonnihil faciat, ad expeditiorem in sacris literis progressionem: non tamen in ea nimis multos annos debemus conterere, ne dum illic plurimum ponamus laboris, in istis quae Religionem nostrum et fidem continent, rudes et ignari reperiamur. Utrunque igitur studii genus sic temperavi, ut nec in Philosophia imperitus viderer, quod quidem nonnullam inscitiam indicaret,

nec in Verbo Dei negligens et dissolutus, quod permagnam argueret impietam" (ll. 26–36 ["And one can say that knowledge of philosophy and of the other arts should do some good, as a means of understanding sacred literature more quickly: nevertheless, we ought not to consume too many years in philosophy, lest, while we make much labor there, we are discovered to be rude and ignorant in those things which hold together our Religion and faith. Therefore I have attempted each type of study, so that I might seem neither untried in Philosophy, which indeed would indicate some ignorance on my part, nor negligent and lazy in the Word of God, which reveals enormous impiety"]).

43 Upton, *John Christopherson*, 3.
44 Cf. John 1.4 and 14.6, New International Version.
45 Quoted in Boas, *University Drama*, 44.
46 White, *Theater and Reformation*, 113–14; see also Boas, *University Drama*, 44.
47 *The Dictionary of National Biography*, s.v. John Christopherson.
48 Nelson, "Drama in the 1580s," 20.
49 Elliott, "Plays, Players and Playwrights," 180.
50 I would like to thank Paul Whitfield White, Victor Scherb, Jonathan Walker, and Edward Tabri for their valuable assistance with this essay at its various stages.

CHAPTER 3

The Spectre of the Shrew and the Lash of the Rod: Gendering Pedagogy in *The Disobedient Child*

Ursula Potter

Grammar schools in early Elizabethan England had few problems filling their classes with boys from the lower ranks and the middling sort, but they were less successful in attracting boys from wealthier and gentle families. Richard Mulcaster, headmaster of Merchant Taylors' School and an ardent supporter of public education, wrote at length on the problem of over-enrollments from lower class families and under-enrollments from the wealthier sort. He argued that poorer parents should consider the good of the commonwealth before their own ambitions and "thinke that it is not best to have their children bookish, notwithstanding their owne desire."[1] Wealthy parents, on the other hand, were admonished for shunning grammar schools in favour of private tuition. "Why is private teaching so much used?" asks Mulcaster, and his answer deems emulation of the gentry to be the cause: "riche men which being no gentlemen, but growing to wealth by what meanes soever, will counterfeit gentlemen in the education of their children."[2] A number of Tudor interludes deal precisely with the gentry's resistance to public schooling, and none more astutely and thoughtfully than *The Disobedient Child*, a 1560s play that displays all the hallmarks of grammar school origins.

As the play proceeds to rebut arguments used against public schools, it exposes some unexpected areas of contest in the field of Tudor education as well as in the wider domain of humanist pedagogical theory. Two particular issues are of interest here. First, the traditional gender prejudice that marks humanist treatises and that privileges fathers over mothers in the education of sons is strikingly reconsidered in this play. Second, the dramatist reveals conflict within humanist debate generally, but applicable specifically to Desiderius Erasmus on the role of corporal punishment. There is a wry irony in the fact that the playwright adopts Erasmus's own favoured mode of pedagogy—comedies—to challenge the great humanist on two issues close to every schoolboy's heart.

Schools had a difficult time trying to persuade wealthy parents of the benefits of a school education; they had to contend with class prejudices, of course, but also with entrenched reservations over the sedentary nature of schooling itself. A grammar school curriculum with its singular focus on literacy and book-learning was considered neither healthy nor appropriate for the sons of the leisured classes. As one 1598 conduct book, the *Courtiers Academie*, tells its readers, writing was a "mechanicall art" acquired for the purpose of monetary remuneration and therefore "impertinent to a civil man."[3] This must have been a particularly galling social prejudice for schoolmasters and educators. Erasmus and Juan Luis Vives devised school exercises in which to vent their indignation: "The crowd of our nobility [...] think it is a fine and becoming thing not to know how to form their letters," writes Vives in one of his Latin exercises, and Erasmus's colloquy "The Ignoble Knight" gives a colourful satire of an ignorant aristocrat.[4] Elizabethan dramatists followed suit: "I once did hold it, as our statists do, / A baseness to write fair and labour'd much / How to forget that learning," confesses Hamlet, the scholar prince, while one conniving character in *The Second Maiden's Tragedy* (1611) panders to his swaggering, illiterate young target: "you scorn to be a scholar, you were born better."[5] Nor were university students necessarily exempt from similar criticism, as Jacobean satirists took to mocking the self-styled gentleman casually attending university to study arms and books of honour.[6]

Drama and Performance Skills in the Grammar School Curriculum

Where the grammar school curriculum could appeal to the leisured classes, however, was in its enthusiastic embrace of oratory, in particular the rhetorical skills of *actio* and *pronunciatio*, those essential marks of *civilitas* so highly esteemed by Tudor court society, and which, despite some diffidence over the propriety of acting skills, were universally taught in grammar schools. In 1560, when the Headmaster of Eton conceded that the art of acting was a "trifling" one, he nonetheless had no doubts that "when it comes to teaching the action of oratory and the gestures and movements of the body, nothing else accomplishes these aims to so high a degree."[7] Erasmus, who was likewise an enthusiastic supporter of comedies as a pedagogical tool, did more than anyone else to bring the dramatic mode into English classrooms. In a recent essay on performance skills taught in Tudor classrooms (memorizing, voice training, role playing, and action), I have argued that this feature of sixteenth-century schooling is crucial to our understanding of the development of Elizabethan drama. It may have been similarly crucial to the economic success of many grammar schools in Elizabethan England. School drama offered schools a public forum in which they could demonstrate their students' skills, entertain the public, and persuade the gentry and wealthier classes of their merits.[8]

Several schools became famous for their drama, attracting not only large audiences but also enrollments from sons of the aristocracy and gentry; well known examples include St. Paul's, Merchant Taylors', Eton, Westminster, Shrewsbury, and Winchester, but many lesser-known provincial schools also staged performances. Some enshrined drama in their statutes, such as the 1566 regulations for King Edward VI's Grammar School at Norwich, which dictate that every year "the High Master was to choose a learned dialogue or a comedy or two to be presented by the boys to the Corporation." The Corporation agreed to bear the cost of costumes, indicating the expected level of performance.[9] Other schools associated with drama include Canterbury, Hitchen, Sandwich, Corfe, Salisbury, Ipswich, Wells, Louth, Ludlow, Beverley, and Kettering, and undoubtedly many more remain to be identified.[10] Elizabethan England could boast more than three hundred grammar schools across the country (and hundreds of non-grammar schools), most of which adhered to a curriculum dominated by classical drama and permeated with the Tudor obsession for oratorical skills. Comedies and colloquies were the conventional training tools, and the staging of plays was an entirely appropriate feature of Tudor pedagogy, as the school plays themselves are often at pains to make clear. In *Damon and Pithias* (circa 1564–68), for example, a play written for the Children of the Chapel, the prologue reminds the audience of the dramatic decorum of "speeches well pronounste, with action lively framed."[11] School plays typically preface their performances with claims of "honest exercise" or "honest intent" to assert a pedagogical context for the play and to avoid censorship rules imposed on popular theatres.[12] Yet school drama was much more than just a vehicle for displaying scholars' talents. It was also a promotional strategy for the schools and, as this essay will show, it offered schools one of the few means they had of directly engaging with the local community in the debate on public versus private education.

Before looking at the debate itself, it is worth defining the nature of school drama. School drama encompasses dramatic material written for performance by school-aged boys. School statutes tell us that the usual age for boys to enter grammar school was around ten or eleven, subject also to the boy having some elementary knowledge of Latin; most would have left three or four years later with a basic Latin-based education. In practice, however, many schools took boys as young as seven (the "petties") and provided the preparatory classes themselves. Whether the boy players were grammar-school boys or choristers, such as the Children of the Chapel, they all came under the auspices of a school and under the influence of a grammar school curriculum. What such plays have to say about parents and schools is therefore peculiarly informed by contemporary school culture. Plays written for child actors generally display certain generic features: comedies dominate the genre with satire and irony; displays of wit and eloquence are common, as is the use of puns and of bawdy—often in the mouth of the youngest and smallest player; self-referential comments on an actor's youth, size, or acting ability may highlight the disparity between the child actor and the part performed, creating a dual consciousness in the audience, and further conducive to parody and satirical comment, while songs, music, and several female parts are a feature of plays for choristers (such as in John Phillip's *Patient and Meek Grissil* [circa 1559–60]).[13] As a general rule, these are plays written in the vernacular for performance by the younger boys and accessible to mixed provincial and urban audiences.[14]

Dramatists writing for schoolboy performances usually had close affiliations with schools; they were familiar with the textbooks, school culture, and publicly circulating treatises on education, as well as contemporary pedagogical debates. Some were schoolmasters themselves, such as Richard Edwards, author of *Damon and Pithias*, and Nicholas Udall, headmaster of Eton, or Thomas Ashton, headmaster of Shrewsbury; others, such as John Redford at St. Paul's, were choirmasters. Although their plays were predominantly vehicles for the promotion of particular schools, these dramatists also saw themselves as negotiators in a broader public debate on education and parenting. Their plays typically address issues of education through the motif of "spare the rod and spoil the child" and frequently employ plotlines based on the prodigal son story, as for example *Nice Wanton* and *Misogonus*. As Darryll Grantley has shown, these mid-sixteenth-century plays are just as concerned with the socio-economic consequences of being ill-educated as they are with prevailing moral and religious debates. Grantley's work, which provides a useful introduction to the pedagogical and humanist contexts out of which this genre arose, is a good starting point for a close examination of some of the domestic issues that occupied the dramatists.[15] *The Disobedient Child* is of particular interest because it offers some striking insights into the problems schools faced in persuading parents of the merits of grammar schools over private education. The playwright is not just addressing resistance by parents; he is also engaging with the origins of this resistance, which are to be found in the prevailing humanist treatises on education, many of which were critical of public schools for the poor quality of schoolmasters. In this case, however, the two key issues addressed by the play, that of school cruelty and that of paternal behaviour, can be traced to a popular treatise by Erasmus, *A Declamation on the Subject of Early Liberal Education for Children* (1529).[16] As the play addresses the theories of Erasmus, it becomes clear that the field of humanist pedagogy was itself a contested terrain and that within the grammar school culture Erasmian theory and pedagogical practice were often markedly at odds with each other.

Erasmus on Parenting and Punishment

Unlike most other educators, Erasmus rejects the use of fear and corporal punishment as disciplinary measures and makes it clear he associates these tactics with public schools:

> We must choose, therefore, between a private tutor and a public school. A public school, of course, is the more common as well as the more economical solution; it is much easier for one schoolmaster to frighten a whole class into submission than to instruct one pupil according to liberal principles.[17]

He was not alone in his criticism. The risk of excessive severity in punishing students was a concern, and school governors looked for means to curb abuses. At some schools an inscription on classroom walls was a visible reminder: "*sit doctor piger ad poenas ad praemia velox et doleat quoties cogitur esse ferox*" ("let the master be slow to punish and swift to praise and let him grieve as often as he is compelled to be stern").[18] Others tried to define acceptable discipline in their statutes, such as at Bruton School in Dorset, where the schoolmaster shall be "alway discrete in correction of his scolers and in especiall that he shall not stryke any of his scolers beyng obedient upon the hedde ne on the fface with rodde ne with palmer."[19] In 1618, Bruton's schoolmaster ignored these admirable prohibitions, causing parents to complain that he gave one boy "three blows with his fist on the left ear [...] and then caused his points to be untied and then gave him four unreasonable jerks with his rod."[20] Without doubt, parents were aware of much anecdotal evidence of abuse, and those seeking authoritative advice from Erasmus on public schools would have found little to encourage them to think otherwise. Erasmus is more vocal than any other author on the subject of corporal discipline and colours his pedagogical writings with numerous anecdotes of cruelty, usually concerning boarders: "As long as the boy lived at the schoolmaster's house, no day would go by but that he would be beaten at least once or twice." Private tutors were of less hazard "because the teacher live[s] under the watchful eye of the parents."[21] In contrast, Mulcaster reflects the voice of support for public schools, "whatsoever inconveniences do grow in *common* schools" asserts Mulcaster, "yet the *private* is much worse, and hatcheth moe odde ills."[22]

In place of the familiar "spare the rod and spoil the child" adage, Erasmus proffered his own paradigm for childrearing:

> Our rod should be kind words of guidance; words of reproof are sometimes needed, but they should be filled with gentleness rather than any bitterness. These should be our instruments of discipline; only in this way can our children be properly raised at home and attain moral wisdom.[23]

A phrase in Robert Whittinton's *Vulgaria* appears to concur with Erasmus: "The gentell exhortacyons of my mayster allured my mynde merueylously. ey? & made me more diligent than all his austeryte coude do," but the possibility of irony in such a statement, given its intended use by schoolboys, should not be ignored.[24] School textbooks usually adopted the stern approach, as advocated here in the popular poem *The Zodiake of Life*:

> Thou that intendest for to keep a child in virtuousness,
> Now use to chide, and now the rod, and plain the way expresse,
> By which they may their feet direct: in no wise favour show,
> And ever angry: let them not the love of Fathers know.[25]

Pedagogical authors turned to Ecclesiasticus for their authority: "laugh not with [your son], lest thou weep with him also [...] Give him no liberty in his youth, and excuse not his folly," writes Thomas Becon in a paraphrase of the biblical text.[26] The educators all offered paradigms of paternal behaviour which privileged reason and emotional control as masculine virtues, accepting that "the severitie of the father may be somwhat mittigated by the levity of the mother," as one treatise put it.[27] Those who failed to adhere to such virtues were accused of effeminacy. *The Disobedient Child* endorses this claim as it vividly dramatises the effeminisation of both the gentle-natured father and his cockered or pampered son.

Thomas Ingelend and *The Disobedient Child*

Little is known about *The Disobedient Child* (circa 1559–70) apart from its identification as a version of Ravisius Textor's Latin play *Juvenis, Pater, Uxor*.[28] Even less is known about its author, Thomas Ingelend or Ingelond, who, like many Renaissance playwrights, was a university man, "late student in Cambridge" according to the undated title page. *Annals of English Drama* dates the play between 1559 and 1570, although an earlier dating is possible.[29] The play has been tentatively identified as the work entered by Thomas Colwell in the Stationer's Register in 1569–70 entitled "an enterlude for boyes to handle and to passe time at christinmas."[30] This is a play that has been noted as suitable for performance by a school, most likely a provincial boarding school.[31] References to regional religious issues and to "other great towns beside this same" (66) indicate a regional context for performance in comparatively small towns.[32] The audience is variously addressed as "masters," "children," "parents," "young men and children" (59, 83, and 89). Two references in the play suggest a boarding school context: one is that the allegations of cruelty stem from "those [boys] truly most of all other: / Which for a certain time have remained / In the house and prison of a schoolmaster" (48), and the other is the belated assertion by the father that had he many more children he would not suffer "one of them all at home with me to tarry" (55).

The play has many of the hallmarks of school drama, such as self-referential material drawing attention to the player's youth and size (51), frequent references to classical authors and characters, and Latin puns (59), although use of Latin is kept to a minimum and usually accompanied by a translation or paraphrase in English. This may be in deference to the audience, but it is also consistent with Janette Dillon's theory that the use of Latin in vernacular drama at this period in the Reformation held negative papist associations and was therefore used sparingly.[33] Satire, parody, and farce colour the first half of the play, which is marked by lively dialogue and domestic action; in the concluding scenes the humour diminishes as lengthy soliloquies on the themes of education and obedience are incorporated, together with a recapitulation of the plot. This is another convention of school drama, perhaps devised to capture audience attention early and to moralise later, similar to the format used by the anonymous writer of *Nice Wanton*. Thus the opening scenes are geared towards domestic realism, humour, and a context with which the audience can readily identify.

In this version of the prodigal son story, the young protagonist refuses to go to school and announces that he will marry, indicating that he is at least fourteen, the legal age for contracting marriage for boys and therefore past the years of puberty.[34] His gentle and concerned father, after lengthy efforts to persuade him at first to go to school and, failing that, to undertake some gainful employment, finally disinherits his only child. The boy marries, and his wife turns out to be a virago who beats him and forces him into labouring and household work in a clear reversal of domestic roles. The boy repents of his disobedience to his father, accepts that he is worthy of God's curse, and returns to his father in the hope of a rescue. The advice he receives is effectively that "as he had brewed, that so he should bake" (68), and he resigns himself to a bleak future with a shrewish wife. The ending is equally bleak for the father, who has no other child to comfort him, and there is no prospect of future happiness for the son. In a direct allusion to the traditional forgiving father of the biblical story, this father tells his son "I am not he that will thee retain" (88). This variation allows the play to present the audience with the domestic consequences of sparing the rod, rather than the usual criminal consequences common to other prodigal son plays.[35] The play's outcome argues rather more rationally that the social and economic consequences of an ill-educated and undisciplined son will be the squandering of patrimony and the rise of matriarchal control.

The prologue opens the drama by specifying, "In the city of London there was a rich man." The "rich man" tag is repeated throughout the play, drawing attention to the particular dangers of wealth on a child's upbringing. Similarly, "London" would have had special meaning for provincial schoolboys familiar with Whittinton's *Vulgaria*, where it signifies an indulgent lifestyle: "In this great cytees as in London / yorke / perusy / and suche where best maner shold be: the chydre be so nysely / and wantonly brought up, that (comenly) they can lytle good."[36] The play fully endorses this perception, which sees city families as more likely to spoil their children than their rural counterparts.

The father's sensitive characterisation is markedly different to similar interludes. This is no *senex iratus* of comedy but, rather, a figure for sympathy, whose grief and dignity dominate the opening and closing scenes of the play. His failings as a parent are anticipated in the prologue: he loves his son "most tenderly" and moved him earnestly "now and then, / That he would give his mind to study" (46). His counseling techniques are unhurried and mild, and the modal "would give" expresses not insistence but hope. His arguments are based on philosophies of education, such as his advice to his son that "by knowledge, science and learning, / Is at the last gotten a pleasant life" (46). He plays the older counselor role common to prodigal son drama, and the weaknesses of such counsel are hinted at early in the play.[37] Opposing his father's gentle and considered approach is the rude behaviour of his son, who "did turn to a mock and open derision / Most wickedly with an unshamefast face" (46). As the scene builds, it becomes increasingly evident that where the father fails is not in the theory but in the exercise of his authority.

Given the prologue's description of the boy's "open derision," the audience is presented with a potentially comic image of a son apparently ingenuously looking to his father for advice: "Father, I beseech you, father, show me the way, / What thing I were best to take in hand" (46). For the schoolboy performers, and those fathers in the audience who had some basic Latin schooling, this would bring to mind "The Father's Little Talk with his Boy," a popular elementary Latin exercise in which a son eagerly accepts his father's advice for school: "I will go, father, with all the pleasure in the world!"[38] In Ingelend's play it is comically clear that the son has no intention of listening to his father's advice, least of all of going to school, and that his request for advice is merely a tactic to bring his father round to agreeing to his marriage.

This first scene consists of approximately three hundred lines of dialogue between father and child on the subject of schooling, with no other characters on stage and no stage directions for action (as there are in following scenes). At the outset there are obvious possibilities for satirical humour as the two young boy players act out the parent-child debate over schooling:

SON: What, the school! nay, father, nay!
Go to the school is not the best way.
FATHER: Say what thou list, for I cannot invent
A way more commodious to my judgment. [47]

This is followed with an ironic refiguring of "who spares the rod, hates the child":

SON: It is well known how that ye have loved
Me hereto fore at all times most tenderly;
But now (me-think) ye have plainly showed
Certain tokens of hatred. [47]

As the dialogue progresses, however, the humour recedes in the face of an increasing sense of frustration being built up by the dramatist. The boy's repeated rudeness to his father continues unchecked as he disputes his father's authority: "It is not true, father, which you do say, / The contrary thereof is proved always" (48). His disobedience progresses to swearing, to outright defiance "I will not obey ye therein, to be plain" (50), and ends with contempt: "Ye speak worse and worse" and "Father it is but a folly with you to strive" (51–2). He dismisses his father and strides off stage, leaving his devastated father alone: "Room, I say; room, let me be gone / My father, if he list, shall tarry alone" (54). Such a call for "Room" is common to the traditional Vice figure of Tudor interludes, thus it has the effect of villainizing the son by association for the audience; it also serves as a reminder that the play was not written for a dedicated theatre space but indicates players demarcating space in a public or school hall or other location.[39]

The son's resistance to schooling is based on two arguments, the first being the gentleman's contempt for book learning: "Methought the book was not fit gear / For my tender fingers to have handled" (84), and here he parrots a familiar line of reasoning:

Even as to a great man, wealthy and rich,
Service and bondage is a hard thing,
So to a boy, both dainty and nice,
Learning and study is greatly displeasing. [48]

It is clear that the father himself is not averse to public schooling, or to his son mixing with other boys (46). This is a notable shift from the more usual prodigal son play, such as *Misogonus*, where a wealthy but ignorant father shows nothing but disdain for academic learning: "I am able to keep him gentleman wise; / I esteem not grammar and these Latin lessons; / Let them study such which of meaner sort rise."[40] The boy's second argument is the common notion of schools as places of "pain and woe, grief and misery" (47). This was another image perpetuated through school translation exercises, such as in the following student lament, in which a new pupil yearns for the comforts of home, from a late fifteenth-century *vulgaria*:

I was wont to lie still abed till it was forth days, delighting myself in
sleep and ease. [...] But now the world runneth upon another wheel.
For now at five of the clock by the moonlight I must go to my book
and let sleep and sloth alone. And if our master hap to awake us, he
bringeth a rod instead of a candle.[41]

The book and the rod are the two inseparable symbols of schooling in this quotation, as they are in *The Disobedient Child*. For the father, schooling is symbolised by the authority of the book; for the son it is the authority of the rod.

Bringing the familiar epithets of "prisons" and "tyrants" into play in the boy's hyperbole, Ingelend invites his audience to mock such popular usage.[42] The boy claims schoolboys undergo horrific punishments, being "whipped and scourged, and beat like a stone" both day and night (48), and he goes into detail on the horrors committed against schoolboys "Till death be almost seen in their countenance" (49). When his father refuses to believe such treatment could possibly be given to "children of honest condition," the son relates the story of "an honest man's son hereby buried, / Which through many stripes was dead and cold" (49), again going into gory detail:

Men say that of this man, his bloody master,
Who like a lion most commonly frowned,

Being hanged up by the heels together,
Was belly and buttocks grievously whipped;
And last of all (which to speak I tremble),
That his head to the wall he had often crushed. [50]

According to Alan R. Young, this is a much-expanded version of a mere detail in the source play by Textor, leading him to conjecture that the author "may have some childhood experience of his own in mind."[43] It is more likely that the writings of Erasmus have prompted some of the thematic material here. The frowning of schoolmasters was consistent with the stern visage approved by some authors, but it was a bone of contention with Erasmus. There are teachers, he writes, whose "expression is always forbidding, their speech is invariably morose [...] they are unable to say anything in a pleasant manner, and they can hardly manage to return a smile." More significantly, Erasmus relates two incidents of barbarity with elements similar to the above dramatic image: one where boys were used as battering rams, and another in which a twelve-year-old schoolboy was sent home from school in a desperate condition, having suffered a punishment that included being stripped and "raised aloft by ropes slung underneath his arms, [...] And while he hung there, he was savagely beaten on all sides until he nearly died; [...] Shortly after the punishment, he fell ill, and both his body and his mind were in great danger."[44] The images used by Ingelend appear to represent a conflation of these anecdotes from Erasmus, and the dramatist may well have expected his audience to make the same connections.

No other pedagogical author was as outspoken as Erasmus on the subject of cruelty in schools. He draws on his own experiences, we are told, but he also offers much anecdotal evidence. He writes of diseased and immoral schoolmasters, of regular floggings of innocent boys, and of acts of depravity by schoolmasters and by older boys.[45] To the expert rhetorician, such detail may be understood for what it is, that is, "in keeping with the rhetorical principle of *copia*, the argument is expounded in great, often digressive details, supported by a wealth of illustrations, anecdotes, and proverbial sayings."[46] As far as the general public is concerned, however, the formalities of rhetorical decorum may be lost in the oral or fragmented transmission, and the bias against schoolmasters is beyond doubt. It is unusual in a school play to devote so much attention to anecdotes of brutality by schoolmasters. The dramatist is pointing out that such anecdotal evidence is used as fuel in the arguments against schools, and boarding schools in particular.

Supporting this understanding is the considerable weight *The Disobedient Child* gives to the value of personal experience versus rumour, such as "What trial thereof hast thou taken, / That the school of thee is so ill bespoken?" (48), or "And this by experience he shall prove true" (69; see also 69, 76, 84, 85). The son uses only second-hand anecdotal evidence: "At other boys' hands I have it learned," and "As unto me it was then reported" (48; see also 49). His father rejects such tales as false, claiming no schoolmaster could be so fierce or so cruel (49). Whether the boy has been falsely persuaded or not is another matter. It seems more likely he is following a policy of consciously using hearsay and hyperbole to manipulate his own father since, towards the end of the play when in desperate need of his father's help, he tells the audience he will approach his father "without craft or wile" (85). The father himself offers no personal experiences of school to counter the boy's charges, and this would be in line with the play's ultimate purpose of persuading a still resistant sector of the community of the value of public schooling. All the arguments against schooling have come from the unreliable mouth of the son, and the play clearly draws attention to the dangers of hearsay and other unreliable forms of authority.

While his son has been getting progressively ruder, the father has continued in the same patient and measured vein with which he was characterised at the outset. His *modus operandi* is along the lines proposed by Erasmus, who suggests that when words of reproof are necessary, they should be filled with gentleness rather than bitterness.[47] The father reasons with the language of theory and with abstractions verging on platitudes, such as claims that school will "prove so profitable," it "maketh a man live so happily," and "A marvellous pleasure it bringeth unto us / As a reward for such painstaking" (46–7). He concludes with another argument also found in *De pueris*: "a man without knowledge (as I have read) / May well be compared to one that is dead" (47).[48] His faith in the written word is repeatedly emphasised: "Yet for because the scriptures declare" (51), and "As the book saith" (87). At the end of the play the audience is again reminded that the father's advice is based upon textual authority: "You heard that by sentences ancient and old, / He stirred his son as he best thought" (90). Such "sentences" hold little weight with a disrespectful son who dismisses them as lies from "busy brains" and as "spiteful speech" (63–5).

In the face of the failure of textual authority to persuade his son, the father falls back on his role as counselor, "I would wish thee [...] not for such tales my counsel to forsake" (50; see also 53, 54), and finally on assumptions of paternal authority: "by thy father's will and intercession" (50; see also 51, 53). Shocked at his son's intention to marry, he counsels firmly against it, to which his son responds "I trust ye will not me otherwise compel" (53). And indeed this father does not compel his son. Here again the play may be echoing Erasmian theory that compulsion was the tool of masters, not fathers:

> The old man in the comic play [Micio in *Adelphi*] was right to believe
> that there is an immense difference between a father and a master. A
> master can exert his authority only through compulsion, but a father
> who appeals to his son's sense of decency and liberality can gradually
> build up in him a spontaneous capacity for moral conduct which is
> untainted by any motive of fear.[49]

Erasmus is, of course, attacking schoolmasters, and he does so by contrasting them with an approved father image taken from Terence. In *The Anatomy of Melancholy*, Robert Burton lights on the same Terentian father, as an exemplum not of gentle persuasion but of foolish mildness in indulgent fathers who "Micio-like, with too much liberty and too great allowance [...] feed their children's humours."[50] The usual approach was to suggest, as Roger Ascham does, that if fathers were stricter, schoolmasters would not need to resort to the rod so often.[51]

By the end of the extended opening scene, a sense of frustration has been achieved by Ingelend, qualifying audience sympathy for the father by the desire for decisive, disciplinary action towards the disobedient boy. The scene ends with the father alone on stage, delivering a long soliloquy in which he recognises the error of his ways as a parent. His speech serves as a gesture towards audience frustrations. His language, tone, and reasoning have changed: no longer measured or couched in modals, his tone has become one of plaint, and he draws his authority not from abstract theories or philosophy but from personal, domestic experience. This is where the measured, wise paternal voice takes on more maternal tones, as he bemoans that had he many more children he would not keep a single one of them "at home with me to tarry; / They should not be kept thus under my wing" (55).

"Under the wing" was a biblical term (Matthew 23.37) often used in a religious context for God's divine love. In secular use it draws on the familiar image of a mother bird protecting her children, as in Whittinton's *Vulgaria* under his discussion of the difference between a child brought up in the country and a "chylde brought up at home / under ye moders wynges in the mydle of the cyte."[52] The sympathetic portrayal of the father in *The Disobedient Child* necessarily requires him to demonstrate qualities—or failings, as they may be perceived— more conventionally associated with mothers. There is, of course, no mother in this play, or any mention of nurses or other women in the household. (Prodigal son plays tend to depict a sole father as the guilty parent following the biblical story. Even the obvious exception, *Nice Wanton*, undercuts its focus on the mother by making it clear that behind her there is a father who plays no role in his children's schooling.) In *The Disobedient Child* all the affection and pampering has come from the father. His self-recriminations echo much that is more familiar in terms of maternal images. In a lengthy soliloquy addressed "to every man that is a father," he identifies familiar parental errors: spoiling children with dainty foods, rich clothing, kissing and cuddling them, and parental pride wanting them to appear "tricksy, gallant, and clean" (55). Left alone once the son has departed, he is reduced to tears (56), and when he learns of his son's marriage, he expresses his grief in culturally feminine terms:

> Into my chamber I went again,
> And there a great while I bitterly weeped:
> This news to me was so great pain.
> And thus with these words I began to moan,
> Lamenting and mourning myself all alone. [68]

In another prodigal son play, George Gascoigne's *The Glasse of Governement* (1575), the dramatist also canvasses this issue of the acceptable expression of grief in fathers. As one father grieves openly over the loss of his son, the other father chides him. It is right to care for your child, he reasons, "but this womanlike tendernes in you deserveth reprehention."[53] Both playwrights are questioning cultural representations of masculinity as dispassionate and controlled. The pathos Ingelend allows in *The Disobedient Child* affirms that paternal love is grounded in the heart, not in the head, as the text itself acknowledges (69). This does not, however, exonerate him of responsibility. His lack of discipline comes into sharp focus when his son's wife exerts her own form of discipline. When the new bride discovers her young husband has made no "careful provision" (75) for their future, her methods are swift and physical, as stage directions make clear: "*Here the Wife must strike her Husband handsomely about the shoulders with something*" (75–6). For the first time in the play, in a clear reversal of gender roles, a figure of authority takes the stage and the son sets to work—base manual and domestic work.[54]

Shrews and the Personification of Discipline

The son marries not just for lust but also in order to escape being a "slave" to any sort of work, with a probable pun on "slavery" as the term applied to grammar scholars and boarders.[55] As soon as the betrothal rites are completed, his relief is evident: "Now I am safe, now I am glad, / Now I do live, now I do reign" (62). Before long, however, the wife turns to the practicalities of how her husband proposes to make provision for the two of them, which, as she points out, is not her responsibility. Indeed, in the eyes of the Church, the boy's dereliction is most serious: "To be short, this sentence of St Paul shall for ever and ever abide true, yea, and that unto the condemnation of all sluggish and negligent husbands, and such like: 'if any man do not provide for such as belong unto him, he hath denied the faith, and is worse than an infidel.'"[56] As the young wife sets about questioning her husband, her mode of address changes from the respectful "you" to the authoritarian "thee," indicating a change of relationship. The boy who had treated his father with such contempt, and who had swaggered off stage in defiance, finds in his wife an authority of a different mettle. In language more suited to the masculine tongue, "By Christ, it were best wish might and main / To fall to some work, I swear a great oath!" (75), she continues to berate the young man for his "sluggishness" and answering back. Line by line her role becomes that of the parent and his of the child. The decisive action which the father had failed to exercise, and the boy had never learned to respect, is applied by a young woman—played by a boy, of course, with all the comic reversals and lessons about training that this entails for an Elizabethan audience. The scene was undoubtedly intended to be played as a farce, with the boy staggering on stage under a bundle of faggots as his wife scolds him. Explicit stage directions require her frequently and violently to cudgel her husband (77, 78) and suggest an element of melodrama expected in performance, for example: "*Here her Husband must lie along on the ground, as though he were sore beaten and wounded*" (79).

A sense of comic relief and poetic justice pervades this scene. The dramatist has allowed no occasion for the audience to develop any sympathy for the boy, and the wife becomes the personification of the discipline the child should have had from the father, and most certainly would have had from a schoolmaster. With a comic literalness, the dramatist is bringing into play a Renaissance commonplace, that is, the equation of a wife with the rod of discipline, Mulcaster's "Lady *birchely*."[57] Critics like Viviana Comensoli and Alan Young, who have taken this shrewish wife at face value, have overlooked the pedagogical contexts.[58] Rather than being "far more severe than any schoolmaster," she is in fact a partner in the school of discipline.[59] The shrewish wife as the schoolmaster's rod is a euphemism with which schoolboys were already familiar from their *vulgaria*:

> I maryed my mayster's doughter to daye full soore agayn my wyll.
> My thynketh her so roughe and soore a huswyfe yt I cared not & she
> were brend in the hote coles. She embraseth or enhaunseth me so yt the prynt of her
> stykketh upon my buttokkes a good whyle after.[60]

As "embraseth" suggests, a wife symbolises both punishment and reward, as does the schoolmaster's rod of the pain of study for the pleasure of knowledge. In a discussion of homoeroticism in Elizabethan schools, Alan Stewart has argued that this metaphorical analogy of wives with school discipline reflects sexual exploitation by schoolmasters.[61] Such a homoerotic reading of the shrewish wife is unlikely in *The Disobedient Child*, given the play's public purpose of persuading parents of the benefits of public schools. Rather, on the issue of sexual abuse, the play suggests attractive adolescent sons are at a greater risk in an unsupervised environment than at school. In addition, the sexual punning, which is so common to drama written for child performers, is surprisingly absent here, perhaps in deference to the school's desire to disassociate their young players from a culture of sexual awareness.

The dramatic climax in the play comes when the boy threatens to kill his wife with a knife. The text again offers opportunities for comic stage action as his undaunted wife berates him for his audacity: "By Cock's bones! I will make thy skin to rattle, / And the brains in thy skull more deeply to settle," followed by the stage direction: "*Here the Wife must lay on load upon her Husband*" (77). Verbally and physically overcome, the defiant boy reverts to a child, a "foolish calf" (77), lying prostrate on the floor before metamorphosing into a complaining, weeping housewife as he is set to the laundry and housework (78–9). For those familiar with Ovid's *Heroides*, as most schoolboys would have been, this scene brings to mind the domestic labours to which the mythological Omphale set the enslaved Hercules.[62] The scene culminates in a parody of the wife as "master" of the house instructing her husband as "mistress" not to move out of doors during his/her absence (79). A woman's place was indoors, as authors such as Juan Luis Vives and Thomas Becon repeatedly insisted.[63] The reversal of gender roles, already evident in the feminisation of the father, is staged once again as the consequences of a poor education.

The play is not unique in presenting a female scold as the necessary corrective to faulty male judgement. In another school play from the same period, *July and Julian*, an authoritarian and controlling mother is accused of being a shrew, but the play values her as a strict parent and a supporter of schools.[64] This is another play with a negligent father in the background, but this time he is characterised by drunkenness, illiteracy, and faulty judgment, and were it not for his wife's discipline, his children would be delinquents. Again, a school dramatist uses his medium to engage with pedagogical debate in general and with gender stereotypes in particular. In *The Disobedient Child* the only other female figure is also represented as a shrew, but once again the negative connotations are belied by her maturity and competence. Included in the *dramatis personae* are two cooks, one male and one female (for which there is no precedent in the source text by Textor).[65] Outwardly, the Woman-Cook, named Blanche, is a shrew with a sharp-tipped nose and called "blab-it-out" by her male companion. Yet he is named Long-tongue, a synonym for a "babbling gossip," and he indeed turns out to be the talkative, nagging one, while she proves hard working and intelligent. The audience learns that she has had some schooling: "in times past I went to school, / And of my Latin primer I took assay" (59). Long-tongue, addressing himself to the audience, responds with the familiar reasoning found in pedagogical treatises that girls rarely remembered much of what they learned:[66]

> Masters, this woman did take such assay,
> And then in those days so applied her book,
> That one word thereof she carried not away,
> But then of a scholar was made a cook.
> I dare say she knoweth not how her primer began,
> Which of her master she learned then. [59]

It goes without saying that Blanche proves him wrong, and she quotes a phrase taken from Psalm 51 and found in the English primer, "*Domine labia aperies*," as proof, thus opening the way for his ignorance in misunderstanding her Latin (59).[67] This choice quotation, "Lord, open my lips" for a "blab-it-out" cook is another instance of the play's ironic humour. Cooks, it seems, were proverbially loose-tongued. In a colloquy by Erasmus, a female cook is represented by two men as a loose-tongued "blab of a cook," but the context makes it clear that they respect her authority.[68] Given that these colloquies were standard texts in grammar schools, there can be little doubt that the dramatist is indulging in some intertextual irony. In Janette Dillon's analysis of language in this play, the cook's use of Latin, together with her plain vernacular speech, positions her as an authoritative spokeswoman for the virtues of education.[69] The male cook's accusations of shrew serve merely to highlight his own position of subjection.

Time and again *The Disobedient Child* draws attention to the female shrew (often in relation to marriage) and the dramatic treatment suggests the play is invoking misogyny as a trope for masculine failure. Only when the father first hears of his son's plans to marry does his patience finally explode: "Why, foolish idiot, thou goest about a wife, / Which is a burthen and yoke all thy life" (53), and the wise, measured tone turns heated as he realises he has failed, and women become the butt of his acrimony. He discourses bitterly and at length on the effort and expense fathers go to in order to feed and support crying children and a brawling, scolding wife (68). He concludes his speech with hostile classical precedents on marriage (69). Following this scene, the dramatist brings the young couple on stage. Still entranced with each other, they too draw on classical precedents in their eulogies on marriage, but the precedents they choose are comically inappropriate, such as Socrates, Aristotle, and the Cynic philosopher Crates of Thebes—hardly role models for this prodigal son's expectations of marriage. Crates preached a harsh gospel of voluntary poverty and independence, spending years wandering in poverty with his wife, and was an outspoken critic of parents who failed to educate their children, as Erasmus himself notes.[70] For the initiated, therefore, Ingelend is not only indulging in irony but also drawing attention to the role of classical authors in perpetuating misogyny. When the chastened young husband begs his father to rescue him from his violent wife, his father comforts him with the advice that Socrates too suffered grief and sorrow from his wife, Xantippe. The boy's reply comically exposes his ignorance: "I cannot tell what was Socrates' wife, / But mine I do know, alas, too well" (87). Had he gone to school, his Latin texts would have taught him all about Socrates' domestic problems.[71]

Critics of the play have not regarded the shrew as in any way a positive figure. Richard Helgerson attributes the misogyny evident in this and in other prodigal son plays to northern Protestant humanism, and he concludes that the intention was to remove the option of maternal charity for the prodigal son.[72] I concur with Helgerson in crediting the misogyny in the play to the humanist educational literature, but the play makes it clear that maternal charity was not the only quality for which mothers were valued; they were also capable disciplinarians. As Rebecca Bushnell has noted, however, the discipline of a shrewish woman will turn a boy into a submissive and unmanly subject, whereas the school's discipline together with the learning it imparts will turn the boy into a man.[73] This is what the play, on behalf of the school for which it was written, is ultimately offering its audience. Women may be able to train boys, exemplified in the play as training in domestic work, but women cannot train boys in the qualities of manhood.

The play puts forward one further argument for wives as trainers of men. When the son argues for marriage as the answer to his future development, he draws on prevailing wisdom that a virtuous wife could control juvenile male behaviour:

For so much as all young men for this my beauty,
As the moon the stars, I do far excel,
Therefore out of hand with all speed possibly

To have a wife, methink, would do well,
For now I am young, lively, and lusty,
And welcome besides to all men's company. [52]

Without the moral and sexual control of a wife, he contends, he is at risk of delinquent behaviour. By using imagery more usually associated with women, the boy is again being feminised, and Ingelend may be suggesting that the son is also at risk of becoming a catamite—paradoxically, precisely because he has not gone to school. The notion that a virtuous wife could transform a wild young man was not uncommon, as Esther Sowernam points out in her 1617 contribution to the pamphlet debate on women: "If [fathers] have a sonne given to spending and companiekeeping, who is of a wild and riotous disposition, such a father shall presently be counselled, helpe your sonne to a good wife, marry him, marry him, that is the only way to bring him to good order, to tame him, to bring him to be an honest man." Sowernam goes on to observe astutely that "the aunceint fathers doe herin acknowledge a greater worthinesse in women then in men."[74] The notion was popular material with dramatists. In *The London Prodigal* (1605), a relieved father tells his reprobate son "[I] applaud thy fortune in this vertuous maide / Whom heaven hath sent to thee to save thy soule."[75] *The Disobedient Child* makes a good argument for reading the boy's wife as his temporal salvation. Without her rigorous discipline, he is more likely to have ended up on the gallows or dying of the pox like other prodigals in similar plays. The drawback to a shrewish wife, as already argued, is that she renders a browbeaten husband unmanly, just as the boy's dead mother seems to have done to his father.

School Drama as the Mediation of Pedagogical Theory

The Disobedient Child stands out as one of the more carefully considered portrayals of fatherhood in sixteenth-century comedy. It rejects the Terentian comic *senex* figure, as it does the humanist ideal of the wise and firm father, portraying instead a figure of pathos, naiveté, and just as prone to the misguided expressions of love for his child more usually attributed to mothers. Ingelend is charting a careful course in his play between pedagogical theory and social practice, between empathy and criticism for Tudor parents. The play acknowledges the misogyny so prevalent in pedagogical treatises and in school textbooks by representing the women in the play as shrews, but it qualifies such cultural stereotyping by pointing out that it is precisely their shrewish qualities (assertive, articulate, rigorous) that make these women such good trainers. Equally, while the play draws favourable comparisons of shrews by analogy with schoolmasters, the dramatist is careful to restrict these women to very domestic, feminine roles and distance them from the male world of learning and economic self-sufficiency. The play is not alone in representing women so positively from the educator's perspective, as brief references to similar plays indicate, nor is it alone in putting most of the blame for failure to educate onto fathers. But it is alone in engaging so closely and so thoughtfully with the ramifications of aspects of the humanist pedagogical debate as they impacted on parental choices for their children.

We do not know what Thomas Ingelend's brief was for writing this play, but its application extends beyond any specific school to the broader pedagogical community, as its printer Thomas Colwell clearly recognised. This is school drama engaging closely with certain theories and individual voices in the humanist debate, and indeed it anticipates some of the arguments that Richard Mulcaster will later level at parents in his *Positions*. Ingelend presents a careful, nuanced analysis of the problems confronting fathers who tried to follow the advice in such texts as Erasmus's *A Declamation on the Subject of Early Liberal Education for Children*. By suggesting that such parents have been misled by aspects of humanist theory, he simultaneously respects their values and absolves them of blame, an astute move in diplomatic terms when it comes to the recruitment of sons of the wealthy to public schools, and boarding schools in particular.[76] Ingelend argues cogently for the role of schools in the intellectual development of young men and, contrary to popular opinion, for the role of schools in the development of manhood. As for his young performers, the message is loud and clear: if they wish to be master of their own households and affairs, they should value their schooling as preparation for these roles, and they should realise that it is only education that keeps boys one step ahead of the girls.

Notes

1   Richard Mulcaster, *Positions Concerning the Training Up of Children*, ed. William Barker (Toronto: University of Toronto Press, 1994), 146.34–147.02.

2   Mulcaster, *Positions*, 194.25–7; 191.31–6.

3   Quoted in Foster Watson, *The Beginnings of the Teaching of Modern Subjects in England* (London: Pitman, 1909), 268.

4   Juan Luis Vives, *Tudor School-boy Life: The Dialogues of Juan Luis Vives*, ed. and trans. Foster Watson (London: Frank Cass, 1970), 67; Desiderius Erasmus, *The Colloquies of Erasmus*, trans. Craig R. Thompson (Chicago: University of Chicago Press, 1965), 424–32.

5   William Shakespeare, *Hamlet*, ed. Harold Jenkins (London: Routledge, 1993), 5.2.33–5; Thomas Middleton, *The Second Maiden's Tragedy*, ed. Anne Lancashire (Manchester: Manchester University Press, 1978), 1.1.84.

6   John Earle, *The Autograph Manuscript of Microcosmographie* (Leeds: Scolar Press, 1966), 82–3.

7   T.H. Vail Motter, *The School Drama in England* (London: Longmans, Green and Co., 1929), 51.

8   Ursula Potter, "Performing Arts in the Tudor Classroom," in *Tudor Drama Before Shakespeare, 1485–1590: New Directions for Research, Criticism, and Pedagogy*, ed. Lloyd Kermode, Jason Scott-Warren, and Martine Van Elk

(New York: Palgrave Macmillan, 2004), 143–65.

9   Richard Harris, Paul Cattermole, and Peter Mackintosh, *A History of Norwich School* (Norwich: Friends of Norwich School, 1991), 46.

10 See Motter, *School Drama*, 22; and Paul Whitfield White, *Theatre and Reformation: Protestantism, Patronage and Playing in Tudor England* (Cambridge: Cambridge University Press, 1993), 102–5.

11 Richard Edwards, *Damon and Pithias: A Critical Old Spelling Edition*, ed. D. Jerry White (New York: Garland, 1980), Prologue, l. 23.

12 Potter, "Performing Arts," 157–8.

13 See Motter, *School Drama*, 22; Michael Shapiro, *Children of the Revels: The Boy Companies of Shakespeare's Time and Their Plays* (New York: Columbia University Press, 1977), 57–8, 106–8, 149, 235; and Martin White, *Renaissance Drama in Action: An Introduction to Aspects of Theatre Practice and Performance* (London: Routledge, 1998), 79–80.

14 Latin school drama was preferred for the senior boys and a more educated audience.

15 Darryll Grantley, *Wit's Pilgrimage: Drama and the Social Impact of Education in Early Modern England* (Aldershot: Ashgate, 2000), especially Chapter 6, "'Morrals teaching education': The issue of education in the sixteenth-century interlude," 134–67.

16 Desiderius Erasmus, *De pueris statim ac liberaliter instituendis declamatio*, in *Collected Works of Erasmus: Literary and Educational Writings 4*, 86 vols., trans. Beert C. Verstraete, ed. J.K. Sowards (Toronto: University of Toronto Press, 1978), 26.295–346.

17 Erasmus, *De pueris*, 325.

18 D.M. Sturley, *The Royal Grammar School, Guildford* (Guildford: n.p., 1980), 90.

19 F.W. Weaver, "Bruton School," *Somerset & Dorset Notes & Queries* 3 (1893): 245.

20 T.D. Tremlett, ed., *Calendar of the Manuscripts belonging to the King's School, Bruton, 1297–1826* (Dorchester: Friary, 1939), 27.

21 Erasmus, *De pueris*, 330, 322; see also his *Colloquies*, 351–3.

22 Mulcaster, *Positions*, 187.28–31, his emphasis.

23 Erasmus, *De pueris*, 332.

24 Beatrice White, ed., *The Vulgaria of John Stanbridge and the Vulgaria of Robert Whittinton* (London: Kegan Paul, Trench, Trubner & Co., Ltd., 1932), 111, ll. 24–6.

25 Marcellus Palingenius, *The Zodiake of Life*, trans. Barnabe Googe, intro. Rosamund Tuve (New York: Scholars' Facsimiles, 1947), 79.

26 Thomas Becon, *The Catechism of Thomas Becon with Other Pieces Written by him in the Reign of King Edward the Sixth*, ed. John Ayre (Cambridge: Cambridge University Press, 1844), 354. Boys were familiar with these adages, which were common components of the lower-school curriculum.

27 W.B., *The Court of good Counsell* (London: by Raph Blower, 1607), sig. G3r.

28 Alan R. Young, *The English Prodigal Son Plays: A Theatrical Fashion of the Sixteenth and Seventeenth Centuries*, ed. James Hogg (Salzburg: Universität Salzburg, 1979), 104–5. See also Janette Dillon, *Language and Stage in Medieval and Renaissance England* (Cambridge: Cambridge University Press, 1998), 237 n. 20; and Nancy Gayle Myers Allen, "A Critical Edition of Two Tudor Interludes: *Nice Wanton* and *The Disobedient Child*" (Ph.D. Thesis, Texas Tech University, 1984), xi–xii.

29 Alfred Harbage, ed., *Annals of English Drama 975–1700*, rev. by S. Schoenbaum, 3d edn. rev. by Sylvia Stoler Wagonheim (London: Routledge, 1989), 36; a line in the epilogue, "look that ye truly serve the king," suggests an earlier composition.

30 Colwell seems to have had an interest in material suitable for schools: in the 1560s he was twice licensed to publish John Phillip's *Patient and Meek Grissill*, another play dealing with the theme of obedience and suited to performance by children (*The Dictionary of National Biography*, s.v. Thomas Ingelend).

31 Ralph A. Houlbrooke, *The English Family 1450–1700* (London: Longman, 1984), 151.

32 Thomas Ingelend, *The Disobedient Child*, in *The Dramatic Writings of Richard Wever and Thomas Ingelend*, ed. John S. Farmer (London: n.p., 1905). Because there are no act, scene, or line divisions in this edition of the play, parenthetical references are to page numbers. "Great town" is a term used to indicate towns with a population of around 2000; see Peter Laslett, *The World We Have Lost* (New York: Scribner's, 1965), 56.

33 Dillon, *Language and Stage*, 104.

34 Henry Swinburne, *A Treatise of Spousals, or Matrimonial Contracts* (New York: Garland, 1985), 47.

35 E.g., *Nice Wanton* and George Gascoigne's *The Glasse of Governement*, which both end with prodigal sons on the gallows or publicly flogged.

36 White, *Vulgaria of Robert Whittinton*, 116.

37 See Richard Helgerson, *The Elizabethan Prodigals* (Berkeley: University of California Press, 1976), 17–20.

38 Vives, *Tudor School-boy Life*, 8.

39 See Peter Happé, *English Drama before Shakespeare* (London: Longman, 1999), 15.

40 *Misogonus*, in *Six Anonymous Plays*, second series, ed. John S. Farmer (London: Early English Drama Society, 1906), 140.

41 Quoted in Craig R. Thompson, *Schools in Tudor England* (Washington, DC: Folger Shakespeare Library, 1958), 5–6.

42 Epithets for "schools" and "schoolmasters"; for the pedagogical background to this usage see Ursula Potter, "The Naming of Holofernes in *Love's Labour's Lost*," *English Language Notes* 37 (2000): 13–26.

43 Young, *English Prodigal Son Plays*, 104.

44 Erasmus, *De pueris*, 324, 331, 329.

45 Erasmus, *De pueris* 326, 325, 327, 329.

46 Erasmus, *De pueris*, introduction, 229.

47 Erasmus, *De pueris*, 332.

48 "A man without education has no humanity at all," *De pueris*, 298.

49 Erasmus, *De pueris*, 328.

50 Robert Burton, *The Anatomy of Melancholy*, ed. Floyd Dell and Paul Jordan-Smith (New York: Tudor, 1938), 285.

51 Roger Ascham, *The Scholemaster, 1570*, ed. R.C. Alston (Menston: Scolar Press, 1967), 12.

52 White, *Vulgaria of Robert Whittinton*, 117–18. In the medieval Chester mystery cycle, Isaac submits to his father's sword and prays for his mother's blessing for "I come no more under her winge"; see *The Barbers Playe*, in *The Chester Mystery Cycle*, 2 vols., ed. R.M. Lumiansky and David Mills (London: Oxford University Press, 1974), 1.56–79, l. 371.

53 George Gascoigne, *The Glasse of Governement*, in *The Complete Works of George Gascoigne*, 2 vols., ed. John W. Cunliffe (Cambridge: Cambridge University Press, 1910), 2.84.

54 The exercise of authority is a recurring motif in the play. There are servants who snub their noses at a master (74), and a priest who describes a scenario of disobedience by his clerk that parallels that of the father-son conflict.

55 See Erasmus, *De pueris*, 327–9.

56 Thomas Becon quoting 1 Timothy 5.8, *Catechism*, 336.

57 Mulcaster, *Positions*, 270.6–7.

58 Viviana Comensoli, *"Household Business": Domestic Plays of Early Modern England* (Toronto: University of Toronto Press, 1996), 41.

59 Young, *English Prodigal Son Plays*, 105.

60 White, *Vulgaria of Robert Whittinton*, 87–8.

61 Alan Stewart, *Close Readers: Humanism and Sodomy in Early Modern England* (Princeton: Princeton University Press, 1997), 98, 104.

62 N.G.L. Hammond and H.H. Scullard, eds., *Oxford Classical Dictionary*, 2d edn. (Oxford: Clarendon, 1991), 752.

63 E.g., "Married women should be seen more rarely in public than unmarried women," and "I would have women confined to their homes": Juan Luis Vives, *The Education of a Christian Woman: A sixteenth-century manual*, ed. and trans. Charles Fantazzi (Chicago: University of Chicago Press, 2000), 243, 249; see also Becon, *Catechism*, 343.

64 See Ursula Potter, "Cockering Mothers and Humanist Pedagogy in Two Tudor School Plays," in *Domestic Arrangements in Early Modern England*, ed. Kari Boyd McBride (Pittsburgh: Duquesne University Press, 2002), 244–78.

65 Young, *English Prodigal Son Plays*, 105.

66 Mulcaster, *Positions*, 177.30–178.10.

67 Dillon, *Language and Stage*, 238 n. 23.

68 Erasmus, *Colloquies*, 440–1.

69 Dillon, *Language and Stage*, 131, who notes that the cook is a stock figure of earlier drama, as does Young who identifies Plautus as a source (*English*

Prodigal Son Plays, 106 n. 4). Grantley sees no direct social reference to the education of girls in this passage on the basis of their limited educational opportunities (*Wit's Pilgrimage*, 236 n. 8). However, girls attending one of the many common (public) schools, which included petty classes, would have been exposed to elementary Latin.

70 Erasmus, *De pueris*, 304.

71 See Potter, "Cockering Mothers," 253–5.

72 Helgerson, *Elizabethan Prodigals*, 36.

73 Rebecca Bushnell, *A Culture of Teaching: Early Modern Humanism in Theory and Practice* (Ithaca: Cornell University Press, 1996), 29.

74 Esther Sowernam, *Esther hath hang'd Haman [...]*, in *Half Humankind: Contexts and Texts of the Controversy about Women in England 1540–1640*, ed. Katherine Usher Henderson and Barbara F. McManus (Urbana: University of Illinois Press, 1985), 231, 114.

75 William Shakespeare [*sic*], *The London Prodigal* (London: by T.C. for Nathaniel Butter, 1605), sig. G4r.

76 By boarding schools is meant not only schools which provided facilities for boarders on their premises, but also schools where boys were lodged within the town. The important issue is the separation of the boy from his home environment.

CHAPTER 4

The Government of Performance: *Ignoramus* and the Micropolitics of Tutor-Student Relations

Emily D. Bryan

In the 1647 Folio of Beaumont and Fletcher's *Comedies and Tragedies*, James Shirley extols the virtues of the volume in his letter "To the Reader":

> [T]his being the Authentick witt that made Blackfriers an Academy, where the three howers spectacle while Beaumont and Fletcher were presented, were usually of more advantage to the hopefull young Heire, then a costly, dangerous, forraigne Travell, with the assistance of a governing Monsieur or Signior to boot; And it cannot be denied but that the young spirits of the Time [...] have from the attentive hearing of these pieces, got ground in point of wit and carriage of the most severely employed Students, while these Recreations were digested into Rules, and the very Pleasure did edifie. How many passable discoursing dining witts stand yet in good credit upon the bare stock of two or three of these single scenes.[1]

Shirley favorably compares the education a playgoer would receive in the theater to the education young men gained in traveling the continent or toiling in the classroom. As an alternative to the expense and danger of travel or the drudgery of being "severely employed Students," the plays of Beaumont and Fletcher teach in the most palatable ways, providing "digestible" lessons to the young men who would acquire "good credit" in social interactions. For Shirley, the theater was a place of edification with the power to "fashion a gentleman."[2] The success of this endeavor is evinced in the creation of "wits," who, like Holofernes the schoolmaster and Nathaniel the curate in *Love's Labor's Lost*, "have been at a great feast of languages and stolen the scraps."[3] With scraps of Beaumont and Fletcher at their disposal, the young elite male theatregoers developed social skills with more ease than they would have within the traditional humanist program that Shirley alludes to in his depiction of "severely employed" students. In making these claims, he engages in contemporary debates about humanist educational practices—the severity of schoolmasters and tutors, the efficacy of strict and tedious lessons, and the politics of tutors teaching social graces to noblemen. Not surprisingly, Shirley presents the theater as a viable alternative to academies of learning.

As a marketing ploy, Shirley's letter to the reader (presumably young men who would like to partake of the scraps, especially during a period when the theatres were closed) appealed to a privileged, all-male readership, one already acquainted with the parallels between theatrical culture and the academic world. The parallel that Shirley sets up, in other words, plays upon a set of institutional linkages that were central to the theatre and the academy alike. Though theatre history has traditionally maintained a distinction between university drama and the London playhouses, in their own time the two institutions intersected powerfully in their deployment of mimesis as a cornerstone in the education and acculturation of young elite men in early modern England.[4] In describing the historical categories of mimesis, Stephen Halliwell outlines five types: visual representation, "behavioral emulation/imitation," "impersonation, including dramatic enactment," the reproduction of sound, and "metaphysical conformity."[5] When boys or young men took to the stage in university drama, their performances signaled the collision of two categories of mimesis, those of behavioral emulation and impersonation. As a boy and a student, the actor in an academic play was already implicated in those practices of behavioral emulation that structured the development of identity, especially in the tutor-student relationship. As an actor, the student was engaged in the impersonation of a character. For student-actors, emulation and impersonation were not only processes of development within the humanist program, but they were also the substance of their experiences in the university setting. Rather than advance the broad narrative that early modern life was a theatrical one, this essay argues that academic drama provided opportunities for the community of students, tutors, and administrators to reflect on and challenge the very practices of impersonation and emulation that defined the humanist educational program.[6]

The foundational mimetic practices of the stage and the school are emphasized by the *performance of imitation* by university boys, both in their social relations and in dramatic performances. In other words, it was important for students to be seen in the act of imitating and emulating both on and off the stage. George Ruggle's Latin play *Ignoramus, or the English Lawyer* and its production at Cambridge University in 1615 present a case study for the ways that academic drama could challenge the efficacy of imitative practices. The play showcases, for instance, the dangers of empty imitation, such as the promotion of ignorance and the cultivation of immoral behavior. According to this logic, simple imitation without understanding adopts the form but not the substance of that which is imitated. Ruggle's play, then, stakes out a defensive position for a university engaged in the humanist project, with the tutors claiming that they alone are trained to instill the values and knowledge necessary to educate the elite young men of England. At the same time, the production history of the play in 1615 exposes the emotional, political, and spiritual implications of behavioral emulation in tutor-student relations at the university, revealing fissures in the humanist method of training students to follow the master, especially when abuses of power, political disappointments, and challenges to the family and the state arise.

Because a tutor's achievements at the university and in his subsequent career were inextricably tied to the success of his students and vice versa, the play and production history persistently ask: can the student become the master through imitation, and should that be the goal of students engaged in a humanist education? Tutors oversaw every detail of a student's maintenance and education, and each student would be assigned a tutor within individual colleges, which were the smaller residential units of the university. Further, tutors had the closest relationship to students of any of the college or university authorities, living with students and teaching them in the colleges. University professors and lecturers were responsible for university-wide lectures, while tutors worked in the intimate setting of individual and small-group tutorials. The micropolitics and micro-management of tutor-student relations often demonstrate local examples of macropolitical questions about the development of an elite educated class in contest with an older aristocratic order, about the right of access to education in early modern England, and about the value of education in creating a moral, intellectual, and analytical governing class.

Making Copies: Boys and Mimesis in the School and Playhouse

Imitatio has long been examined as one of the essential methods of humanist instruction.[7] Renaissance humanists debated the efficacy of imitating classical texts (Cicero primarily) as an educational program, and Erasmus argued in *Ciceronianus*, that imitation should not merely "follow" in rhetorical style but should emulate models in judgment: "we may imitate what is essential in Cicero which does not lie in words or in the surface of speech, but in facts and ideas, in power of mind and judgment."[8] The rise of printed texts and the Erasmian emphasis on a humanist method of training meant that imitation embraced more than copying Latin texts and reproducing stylistic habits. The emulation of virtuous behavior as a method of moral and educational training converged with the imitation of classical texts as a means of achieving rhetorical ability and wit. Tutors at universities and schoolmasters at grammar schools in the sixteenth and seventeenth centuries theoretically functioned as models of behavior for their students. Setting up tutors as exemplars incited a range of thorny issues, from severity of discipline to the intimacy of tutor-student relations. It also allowed tutors an inordinate potential access to power, both in personal relationships and in their roles in shaping the intellectual and political elite of the nation.[9] Richard Halpern writes about imitation in this period as a critical technique for early modern culture to interpellate subjects. He describes imitation as "a set of practices that places the subject in an imaginary relation with a governing model; it is the imaginary grasped as practice. A mimetic education installs the subject in a play of mirrors, a dialectic of imaginary capture by a dominant form."[10] Halpern's description of the Renaissance educational system importantly recognizes the production of an imaginary relation with a realized dominant model, someone such as the "governing

Monsieur" described by James Shirley above. Alan Stewart also points out that the tutor-student relationship was especially intimate and dominating in university settings, where the tutor often shared a bed with his student and functioned as the father *in absentia*.[11]

Dependent upon the imitation of dominant models, humanist pedagogy promotes mimetic activities that are structured around hierarchies of dominant and subordinate positions. Masters, whose power only existed within the confines of the university, dominated youths with aristocratic ties and eventual access to real political power. Reported in Anthony Scattergood's commonplace book (1632–40), for example, is the rivalry between one Master Hausted and his scholars writ large in the frontispiece to Hausted's play, *Rivall Friends* (1632). In Scattergood's commonplace book, Hausted is accused of "scoff[fing]" at his betters and "strik[ing]" "at the gownes [i.e., the students]."[12] For boys and even young men, these all-male associations—which were organized hierarchically and functioned within a system of imitative practices—were normative relations and, more importantly, they provided cultural access to positions of power in the government, in intellectual circles, and in religious appointments.

Just as *imitatio* was a fundamental process in the educational experiences and interpersonal relationships of the university, impersonation was a foundational principle of the early modern theater, but its influence, deployment, and effects have always been contested. The evaluation of a performance is often linked to the accomplishment of an actor's impersonation, though the criteria for a successful impersonation have varied throughout the centuries. Critics have long attempted to define and codify early modern conceptions of mimesis as an aesthetic category, especially in relation to impersonation.[13] Jonas A. Barish identifies the moral and ethical sticking points of mimesis as the basis for what he calls "the antitheatrical prejudice" in the period. Barish links Plato's distrust of the mimetic, his attack on copies as untruthful and damaging, to antitheatrical tracts of the sixteenth and seventeenth centuries.[14] In contrast, Jonathan Dollimore analyzes Renaissance literary theory to reveal that in the period there are two concepts of mimesis, an "idealist mimesis" (that poetry would show readers the way the world *should* be) versus a "realist mimesis" (an actual representation).[15] Though Dollimore writes of poetry, his question of whether impersonation is realistic or fantastic becomes especially important to university students in the performance of gender. Similarly, Phyllis Rackin astutely recognizes the challenge that gender performance poses to theories of impersonation, arguing that over several decades in the early modern period the concepts of gender and mimesis became interconnected in a fluctuating manner. She claims that, through the movement from an idealist mimesis (what she calls "fantastic imitation") to a realist mimesis (for her, "icastic imitation"), the drama reflected a shift in the representation of gender from fluid and malleable to fixed and stable.[16]

William N. West's articulation of mimetic practices in the early modern period allows for a more flexible definition of theatrical mimesis (impersonation) that can also illuminate pedagogical mimetic practices (behavioral emulation). West eschews the binary representation of mimesis as either participating in the real or as exceeding the real; instead, he attempts to carve out a space for theater "as a way of producing knowledge while deferring any definitive interpretation by turning it into the performance of an experience."[17] Theater, then, functions as a process rather than as a static artifact. In other words, endeavors either to imitate nature or to exceed nature are part of a shared experience that moves on a continuum, which is always producing knowledge. West's rendering of mimesis as the performance of an experience gives us a way of understanding the mutual properties of emulation and impersonation. What these categories of mimesis have in common is an emphasis on the action of imitation—of imitation *on display*—and they also share the insistent pursuit of hierarchical comparisons, so that the act of copying is always balancing between being better or worse than the original. In writing *Ignoramus*, George Ruggle closely examines the qualities of impersonation and emulation as a way of critiquing the humanist education he is himself responsible for administering as a tutor of Clare College, Cambridge. Moreover, the narrative of the historical events surrounding the production depicts relationships among tutors, students, and administrators, which are themselves representative of the humanist project's failures and successes in codifying imitative practices. The social performances of the students and tutors are as staged and crafted as their dramatic roles, which put the micropolitics of student-tutor relations on display within the politically sensitive arena of a performance before King James I.

Ignoramus and Imitation

Between 1614 and 1615, Cambridge University was abuzz with the prospect of a royal visitation, and so disputations and plays were selected to entertain the king. One of the dramatic productions, Ruggle's *Ignoramus*, struck the king's fancy so much that it was performed twice before him in the space of three months, first on 8 March and then again on 13 May.[18] A biting satire on English lawyers, the play mocks the common lawyers with whom James had had such difficulty. Cambridge University had also had its own share of tangles with the law, most notably in its dealings with the town of Cambridge and its recorder, a lawyer named Francis Brackyn. Ruggle's play corresponded with the sentiments of the university and the king, and so *Ignoramus* was performed before the king and members of the court at Trinity College. The hall at Trinity "accommodated 2000 spectators" during the king's visit in 1615—no small audience for non-professional actors.[19] The Latin play depicts a highly charged contemporary controversy, mocking English lawyers through the languages of "law French," barbarous Latin, and a smattering of Portuguese. In its engagement with questions of imitation and impersonation, *Ignoramus* also directly addresses the humanist program under which its writer and performers studied. It is the kind of play that only actors culled from a university community would be able to attempt.

Ruggle wrote *Ignoramus* in response to local politics, to national debates about English common law, and from within the context of his own pedagogical community. Ruggle adapted the Italian play *La Trappolaria* and, as John Sidney Hawkins writes, "[his] humor took a different direction: instead of a Thrasonical captain, his invention suggested to him the introduction of a new and original personage, an English common lawyer, whom, that he might excite in the spectators both mirth and indication, he has represented as a pedant, a dunce and a rogue."[20] Ruggle replaced a military buffoon with a pedantic one, and this "new and original" personage, the character of Ignoramus, perfectly suited the audience's taste at Cambridge. In the play, the character's greatest fault is his mangling of Latin and his constant reference to obscure legal terminology.[21] Ignoramus's entrance in act 1, scene 3, announces the mixture of languages to be parodied in the script:

> Phi, phi! Tanta pressa, tantum crowdum, ut fui paene trusus ad mortem; Habebo actionem de intrusione contra omnes et singulos. Aha, Monsieurs, voulez vous intruder par joinct tenaunt? Il est playne case, il est point droit de le bien séance.

> [Fie, fie, so much crowding and pressing that I am almost crushed to death. I will have an action of intrusion again one and all. Aha, sirs, you would intrude on me by joint tenant? The case is plain, you have no right to settle.][22]

Ignoramus, already having difficulty maneuvering through his world, can only orient himself by Latin tags or inappropriate terms of Law French. The jostling on the street becomes for Ignoramus a claim of "joint ownership," suggesting that he views the street as his property and imagines other pedestrians are making claims to his property. Everyday interactions are always framed as legal battles for Ignoramus. Even as he proposes marriage to the ingénue Rosabella, Ignoramus addresses her awkwardly: "Madame et vos mei magistri iurati, haec est actio super casum" ("Madame and gentlemen of the jury, here's an action upon the case").[23] Ignoramus's dialogue consists only of linguistic idioms misapplied and emptied of their meanings.

The Cambridge crowd and an intellectual King James could easily feel superior and mock Ignoramus's barbarous language. His very name begs the audience to scorn him, not only because it indicates his ignorance but also because his name refers to the legal term "Ignoramus," "used by the grand Enquest empaneled in the inquisition of causes criminall and publique: and written upon the bill, whereby any crime is offered to their consideration, when as they mislike their evidence, as defective or too weake to make good the presentment."[24] The hapless character's name registers a failure in court, an inability to make a case, and it is associated with things that are weak, defective, or lacking in some respect. Thus, when Ignoramus is threatened with gelding at the end of the play, this threat has already been implicit in his name throughout the action. Ruggle also invented the character Musaeus, a scholarly law clerk from university who is constantly accentuating Ignoramus's stupidity.[25] Ruggle's new characters, specifically satirizing lawyers, scholars, and actors, take advantage of the context of the performance—a university audience familiar with the king's debates with common lawyers and the university's own troubles with the law.

Like many popular plays of the period—from Shakespeare's *Comedy of Errors* to Jonson's *Volpone* and beyond—duplication, imitation, and mistaken identity drive the central, complicated plot of *Ignoramus*. Theodorus is husband to Dorothea, who is mother to four children. Before the action of the play begins, she had had two daughters (Catharina and Isabella) by her first husband, and twin boys (Antonio and Antonius) by Theodorus, her second husband; the boys are only distinguishable by a mole on one of their cheeks. The daughters from Dorothea's first marriage have been raised separately: Catharina stayed with her mother, whereas Isabella was raised by a nurse in Detford. At a very young age, Isabella was kidnapped by a Moor named Urtado. Fifteen years prior to the play's action, Theodorus had left his wife, daughter, and one of his sons in England, while he had moved to Bordeaux with his other son, Antonius (the twin without a mole). In the opening scenes of *Ignoramus*, Theodorus asks Antonius to return to England and bring his mother and siblings to Bordeaux, but Antonio is reluctant to leave because he has fallen in love with Rosabella, a ward of a Portuguese bawd named Torcol. Ignoramus, our bumbling but devious lawyer, has already negotiated to marry Rosabella (even though he only intends to keep her as a mistress). Hence Antonio enlists the help of his servant Trico and of the bookseller Cupes to outwit Ignoramus and to take Rosabella from him.

Ruggle continually deploys imitation as Trico impersonates a variety of characters: Ignoramus, Dulman (Ignoramus's clerk), and a client. Meanwhile, Trico enlists Cupes and his wife Polla to pretend to be Torcol and Rosabella. In order to confuse Theodorus and to convince him that Antonius has left Bordeaux, Rosabella pretends to be Catharina while Antonius pretends to be his twin, Antonio. Of course, soon the real Antonio and Catharina arrive in Bordeaux, and so the children are doubled for a time, until it is revealed that Rosabella is actually Isabella, the one who had been kidnapped by the Moor Urtado. Finally, Ruggle adds to the plot confusion and the theme of duplication through his characters' names: Theodorus inverted anagrammatically becomes Dorothea, Rosabella mirrors Isabella, and Antonio and Antonius can hardly be distinguished but for their endings, with the "o" in Antonio suggesting his mole.

Moreover, throughout the play, Ruggle directly challenges English common law for its absurd and empty rhetorical constructions; thus the training of the English lawyer is mocked in relation to academic training. Ignoramus is spared no indignity: he is threatened with castration by a pig-gelder and runs from the scene at the sound of a gelding horn. Like Malvolio, Ignoramus is bedeviled by Polla, Cupes, Trico, and a priest, Father Cola, who perform an exorcism on him. Yet Ignoramus's exorcism does not reveal him to be evil so much as completely trapped in his own linguistic barbarisms—after all, as Musaeus says, Ignoramus's mother was "Barbara Latina." When trying to describe his predicament and how he had intended to treat Rosabella, Ignoramus is incapable of doing so without resorting to legal jargon, which his exorcists translate into spirits:

> IGNORAMUS: Et praeter iuncturam si maritasset me, post moretem habuisset francum bancum.
> FATHER COLA: Profuge sis, Francum Bancum; separa te, Francum Bancum.

> [IGNORAMUS: And besides her Joynture, if shee had married me, I had given her *Francum Bancum* after my death.
> FATHER COLA: I conjure thee, *Francum Bancum*; hence *Francum Bancum*.][26]

Ruggle emphasizes how empty the mere repetition of these legal terms is and how easy it would be for this jargon to be turned into something much more sinister. Here, Father Cola performs an imitation of Ignoramus, which is both powerful (words as conjurers), and also demonstrates the possible moral equivocation embedded in imitation. *Francum Bancum* merely means a "Free bench," which is a widow's tenure of a leasehold in dower; yet it also suggests Francis Bacon, attorney general under King James and champion of a codified Latin legal language; and of course *Francum Bancum* also calls to mind Francis Brackyn, Ignoramus's historical counterpart, the Cambridge Recorder. Ignoramus's exorcism is a series of repetitions made devilish or suspicious because his language is so absurdly out of place. In describing what he would have given Rosabella had she only loved him, Ignoramus again supplants the language of love and heartache with legalese:

> IGNORAMUS: [...] sed si amasset me habuisset multa bona privilegia, *infangthef, outfangthef, sac, soc, tol et tem.*
> FATHER COLA: Quam multi sunt! Exite omnes, Ninantef, Nonanteff, Sac, Soc, Tol, et Tem. Exercizo omnes vos malignos spiritus.

> [IGNORAMUS: (...) if she had loved me I would have given her many priviledges, *infangthef, outfangthef, tac, toc, tol* and *tem* (*sic*).
> FATHER COLA: What a company there are! I conjure you all depart, Ninantef, Nonanteff, Tac, Toc, Tol and Tem. I exorcize all you wicked spirritts (*sic*).][27]

All the privileges that Ignoramus suggests he would give to Rosabella would divest him of the responsibilities of a landowner. Rosabella would be given the right to try felons arrested on the lord of the manor's property (*infangthef*) or she would be able, as the lord of the manor, to own serfs (*tem*).[28] The property is called "Tonguewell," ironically underscoring Ignoramus's inability to speak well. These marital gifts are ultimately empty gestures on Ignoramus's part; given his bombastic and ineptly conniving characterization, it is not plausible that Ignoramus would suddenly turn into the champion of a woman whom he so patently attempted to "buy." Of course, the vacuity of Ignoramus's terms is highlighted by Father

Cola's repetition in the exorcism. Father Cola's incantation, "Francum Bancum," turns Ignoramus's promised privileges of matrimony into "malignant spirits." The repetition and perversion of the legal terms signal not just empty rhetoric, but also the ways in which imitation exposes Ignoramus's disingenuousness. Not only are his legal terms incomprehensible, but also he never intends to enact them.

In its reliance on duplication, the play suggests that in spite of the potential dangers of mimetic behavior, imitation is the very cornerstone of social development. In other words, when Ignoramus parrots legal jargon in any context, regardless of its appropriateness, he depends upon imitation to define himself without understanding what he is imitating. Because imitation is such a critical method of subject development in the humanist program, a character like Ignoramus, who so obviously misapplies the act of imitating, warns educators of the potential dangers of the very program they are promoting. Before the exorcism, Trico says of Ignoramus, "Vel talem autem in scenam prodire nefas" ("To bring such a man upon the stage were dangerous"), to which the scholar Musaeus responds, "Totus mundus exercet histrionem" ("All the world's a stage where every man's a player").[29] Ruggle affirms the old adage through one of his university boys who plays Musaeus, emphasizing that though the university may seem removed from the theatrical culture of London, the culture of the university recognized that it shared in the mimetic practices that produced English subjects.

In depicting Ignoramus and his clerks, Ruggle presents the frustration and potential pitfalls of a master-apprentice relationship in a way that places the humanist tradition in a favorable light, but only as long as tutors and students assiduously avoid mindless imitation. Ignoramus's clerks, Dulman, Pecus (sheep), and Musaeus (the name of several classical Greek poets), illustrate the differences in university training and apprenticeships. Ignoramus is constantly critiquing Musaeus on practical grounds (e.g., his inability to ride a horse), but the play skewers Dulman and Pecus for their stupidity since they spend their lives dimly simulating Ignoramus; they are dull and sheep-like in action and in name. Musaeus recognizes the danger in Ignoramus's empty rhetoric and thoughtless repetitions: "Scientiae/Nisi Ignoramus hostis nemo est" ("For there's no greater enemy to knowledge/Then Ignoramus").[30] Musaeus's university education therefore stands as a beacon of rationality in comparison to Ignoramus's legal training. So, while the play critiques elements of the humanist method, it ultimately reaffirms the program as a superior form of training and education, providing the method is carried out in the right setting (the university) with tutors functioning as exemplary models.

Backstage *Ignoramus*

As the text of the play portrays debates over imitation, the accumulation of knowledge, and the cultivation of values, the production history of *Ignoramus* reveals those debates enacted in the micropolitics of tutor-student relations. For several students at Cambridge, *Ignoramus* represented a turning point in their lives since it inaugurated their independence from the hierarchical structure of the university, while also requiring them to work within the confines of what the administration of the university expected of them. The mimetic acts involved in producing *Ignoramus*—imitating a tutor or dominant model as well as performing a role—resemble the structured and improvisatory nature of what Pierre Bourdieu calls the *habitus*. In Bourdieu's analysis the *habitus* is "embodied history, internalized as a second nature and so forgotten as history," which produces "intentionless invention of regulated improvisation."[31] The *habitus* extends our critical understanding of mimesis to reveal a practice that produces a certain range of responses according to already socially encoded expectations. For example, although the boys who participated in the performance of *Ignoramus* came from relatively homogeneous backgrounds and were educated within the same system, there existed a range of reactions to their experiences that could be described as "regulated improvisations." Their reactions to certain events were not necessarily predictable, in other words, but they were not wholly unexpected either. Thus, while the fictional play and the actual production seem to critique the imitative practices of humanism by resisting their wholesale acceptance, they also frequently reinforce the very practices under scrutiny.

Even the history of the first performance of *Ignoramus* is embedded in a text that provides biographical models for emulation and, as such, the details of the performance were recorded decades later in a way that was especially sensitive to the social relations of these students in their maturation. Samuel Clarke, author of many historical and religious works including a series of biographical lives, recounts two different narratives about the production, one of a boy who refused to perform (Samuel Fairclough) and the other of a tutor whose student (Thomas Morgan) performed in spite of his tutor's objections. As we will see, both boys were asked to perform female roles, and thus many objections were grounded in gender impersonation as well as in anxieties about performance in general.

When Clarke published his series of biographies of eminent personages from 1660 to 1680, he aimed to provide spiritual models. The practice of collecting stories of "worthies" or "models" was an exercise in exemplarity relying on one category of mimesis, behavioral emulation. What is interesting about the stories of Fairclough and Morgan is that behavioral emulation is explicitly linked to performance, and the relationship between this category of mimesis and that of impersonation shifts throughout the two narratives, which record the same event; sometimes impersonation bolsters and strengthens acts of emulation while sometimes it undermines these acts. Part of a tradition of exemplary texts, Clarke's project finds a story to tell twice through two biographies that use the production of a play to show exemplary behavior in the rejection of performance and impersonation. The story also reveals, however, that the project of emulation is supported by the very theatricality it seems to reject. In both accounts, Clarke emphasizes the social relationships and the emulation of tutors and advisors that led Samuel Fairclough and Thomas Morgan to behave in the ways that they did.

Emulation is an explanatory model for the development of good and virtuous behavior, as Richard Baxter explains to the reader in recounting why he published Clarke's text posthumously: "When my excellent holy Friends dyed, I could have wished that the world, for imitation, had known them as I did, and that their lives had been published."[32] Baxter and Clarke imagined that others would want to model their behavior on these virtuous personages. Clarke's choice of eminent persons for imitation was dictated not only by their acts of the Puritan faith, but also by their participation within a process of imitation and subject development, as models to be imitated and as imitators themselves. Both William West's idea of imitation as a process through performance and Bourdieu's concept of "regulated improvisations" are at work together in the narratives of these boys: to gain cultural access to an intellectual and elite cadre, the boys must show themselves in the process of imitating, but they must make their own improvisatory marks upon the imitations they perform. They are obliged to perform the "unexpected" within a suitable range of expectation.

Each boy's story is repeated in one of these collections of biographical sketches that Clarke produced from 1660 to 1680. The story of Thomas Morgan is a cautionary tale about listening to a tutor's advice, as it is revealed in the biography of Doctor John Preston, written by his student Thomas Ball and reprinted by Clarke in his collection. Doctor John Preston, a well-known scholar and eventual master of Emmanuel College, Cambridge, was renowned as "the greatest pupil monger in England" and was entrusted with the education of many sons of English gentry, including Mr. Thomas Morgan.[33] Preston himself had in fact participated in the disputations before the king shortly before the performance of *Ignoramus*. And while Thomas Ball describes him as being "ambitious in nature," Preston had recently been so overawed by the performance of Master Cotton in the pulpit that he had decided that "Kings and Courts were no great things with him."[34] Thus, the king's visit coincided with a crossroads for Preston, who had just settled on theology as his life's pursuit. At this time Preston became the tutor to the orphan Thomas Morgan, and when the performance of *Ignoramus* provided an opportunity for Morgan's advancement, Preston and the guardians of the boy struggled for dominance:

[G]reat care was taken to furnish and accommodate all parts [of *Ignoramus*], with all actors answerable. Master Morgan was a comely modest gentleman, and it was believed would well become a woman's dress, and accordingly his Tutor (Master Preston sent to,) that he give way and all encouragement unto the service. He [Preston] liked not the motion, could not believe that his Friends intended he [Master Morgan] should be a player [...]. But his guardians were not so exact and scrupulous, but thought if he played the game well, he might winne more than could be hoped for elsewhere; and so Mr. Morgan was allowed by his guardians to play his part.[35]

As an orphan, Thomas Morgan's fate rested in the hands of his tutor and then, when his guardians deemed that the tutor was not acting in his best interest, in the hands of the guardians.

Flouting Preston's restrictions, Morgan played the female lead of Rosabella in *Ignoramus*, but Clarke notes that the final outcome was disappointing: "So Master Morgan was allowed by his Guardians to play his part, and afterward removed unto Oxford, and suffered to play what part he would, and so relapsed into Popery, which hath proved fatal and infortunate to him and his."[36] Because he took part in this play, the story goes, Morgan became unmoored from Cambridge and from his Puritan models of divinity, and he had to shift for himself without the good guidance of Preston.[37] From an antitheatrical standpoint, Morgan's ending seems perfectly fitting since he became aligned with the religion that had been denounced by the Puritans for its theatricality. The controversy over Morgan's participation in the play represents in part the changing identity of the university from ecclesiastical center to a place to groom young men for preferment, which prompted a variety of perceived dangers associated with such courtly grooming.

Morgan's performance of Rosabella led him to mimetic behaviors that could no longer be confined to the stage: he "suffred to play what part he would." Disregarding the conventions of the tutor-student relationship and defying the tutor's authority, Morgan found himself in a position whereby imitation and performance were no longer anchored to any moral, ethical, or spiritual model. For Preston, however, his "care" of Morgan in attempting to prevent him from becoming a "player" only increased his standing as an apt model for the youth of England:

> This faithfulness to Master Morgan, attended with so great a shadow upon himself, increased his reputation in the Countrey, so that now he was accounted the only Tutor; and being careful to read unto them, and direct their studies, he found himself abridged of his own time, and was constrained to take up time that should have been bestowed on his body.[38]

Preston's engagement with his students is presented throughout Ball's account as physically draining: his watchfulness is both a site of anxiety (the deterioration of his body) and a sign of his dedication. Since this is a biography of John Preston and not of Thomas Morgan, Preston's life is more thoroughly scrutinized than Morgan's. Indeed Morgan's decision to perform is framed more as a struggle between Preston and Morgan's guardians than as an individual act on his part.

By shirking Preston's instructions, Morgan enacts a regulated improvisation: his behavior departs from the script to emulate his tutor, yet he follows the advice of his guardians. The episode concludes with a rejection of the tutor-student relationship as Morgan's guardians "thought if he played the game well, he might winne more than could be hoped for elsewhere." Preston may have demonstrated concern for the boy's moral welfare, but his guardians were acting on behalf of the boy's political advancement. The contest over Morgan's participation in the play illustrates how emulation can go awry when the tutor-student relationship fails. It also reveals how the micropolitics of Morgan's experience with Preston engage with larger political issues concerning how best to produce an elite governing class. Preston is himself emulating humanism's doctrine by instructing his student in proper emulation, but the guardians feared that this instruction would curtail Morgan's political career. We see in Clarke's *Lives* that the process of subject development was a site of competition for academic, political, and religious interests, which were, theoretically, supposed to cohere in the objective of training scholars.

While Morgan's voice is not literally represented in Clarke's *Lives*, Samuel Fairclough—the other young man whose performance in *Ignoramus* caused contention—is given a hearing, for he explicitly refused to play "Surda," an old deaf woman. Fairclough is obviously the central figure of his biography, making his refusal to perform a critical moment in the self-creation of this Puritan clergyman. After his time at Cambridge, Fairclough enjoyed a reputation as a very scholarly and talented preacher. J.A. Granger describes Fairclough as preaching from the pulpit four times a week. Of his sermons, Granger writes: "His discourses were well digested and carefully committed to writing before they were publicly delivered. He had then his notes constantly before him; but such was the strength of his memory, that he scarce ever was seen to turn his eyes from the audience."[39] Fairclough's preaching style relied heavily on a performed presence, memorization, and audience awareness. The qualities that he would later exhibit in his sermons had probably made him a desirable candidate for performance in academic drama.

The tension between theological training at Cambridge and theatrical performance was also an issue for many other scholar-actors. In fact, the actor who played "Ignoramus, the English lawyer" was said to have "continued ever after a perfect comedian in the pulpit."[40] There is an understood alliance in both these examples between the stage performance and the sermon. This alliance, while promoted by the universities, was distasteful to scholars like John Milton who, in thinking about his days at Cambridge, writes that "in the colleges so many of the young divines, and those in next aptitude to divinity, have been seen so often upon the stage, writhing and unboning their clergy limbs, to all the antic and dishonest gestures of Trinculoes, buffoons and bawds."[41] Milton is particularly vexed in this passage by the performance of "antic" figures or comic characters. He locates his frustration in the too-supple bodies of the performers "unboning" and "writhing," as if performing somehow makes them physically too malleable, too flexible. Milton recognizes a dangerous link between theological "performances" and theatrical performances. In contrast, the representation of Fairclough as a preacher and the performance of *Ignoramus* are connected in a non-threatening way in the biography. The structures that produced Fairclough as a talented preacher—the university community, the humanist processes of emulation and imitation, the interactions of tutors or mentors and students—also produced *Ignoramus*. Fairclough's refusal to perform is couched within the very disposition of imitation that he seems to be rejecting. To interpret Fairclough's resistance, we must understand the context and institutional structures that produced him as a subject.

While Clarke's biography of Fairclough reconstructs the life of a person who was constantly looking for tutors and models to imitate, it simultaneously positions Fairclough himself as a model to emulate. For Fairclough, who was nine when his father died, the quest was for a "spiritual Father," one who would give him guidance. So insistently does the text of Fairclough's life pursue the relation between the mentor and the student that Fairclough inevitably found solace in a man named Mr. Samuel Ward, a preacher from Haverhill, Suffolk, who eventually became the master of Sidney Sussex College, Cambridge. Mr. Ward was integral to Fairclough's spiritual conversion when Fairclough, after having stolen some pears from a neighbor, felt compelled to confess his crime and sought out Mr. Ward: "he [Fairclough] opened unto him the whole *state* of his *soul* [...] Mr. Ward received him with great *affection* and *tenderness*, and proved his good Samaritan to him, pouring Wine and Oil into his wounds, answering all his questions, satisfying all his fears."[42] Fairclough's close relationship to Ward prompted his "conversion" to complete devotion to Christ. He thought of going to Ward with his problem because Ward had just preached earlier that week about the importance of making restitution. From his earliest pedagogical experiences, then, Fairclough was influenced by the performance from the pulpit and found in that performance a model for behavior.

Fairclough was apparently a *puer senex*, wise beyond his years, and, as a new student at Cambridge at the age of fourteen, Fairclough sought a tutor, vouching for his own "chearful observance of the commands of any Gentleman."[43] Yet Fairclough's ability to be subordinate and equal at the same moment is clear from his relationship with his tutor, Mr. Berry of Queen's College, who allowed Fairclough to stay with him until a place for him opened up in the college. As Clarke puts it: "He was admitted Chamber-fellow and fellow-student with his own tutor."[44] Perhaps Fairclough's own precociousness and his easy association with male mentors made him an obvious choice to become sub-tutor to Spencer Lord Compton, son of the Earl of Northampton.[45] Fairclough, in fact, achieved the position by writing a letter in Latin to the Earl of Northampton. In Clarke's biography of Fairclough, this scene represents an initiation into elite male culture. Doctor Tyndal, the master of Queen's College, asked Fairclough to write the letter, "whilst himself and the *Fellows* that were with him, and some of the *Chapter*, went to dinner in another room; where they had not fully dined, before the *Letter* was sent in *finished* as a *third course*."[46] In this narrative, Fairclough's Latin letter was a kind of command performance—a display of his ability. The letter became a "course" of the dinner, something for the men sitting with Doctor Tyndal to feast upon, analyze, and evaluate.

Thus the Latin letter is positioned as an entrée into sociability for Fairclough, much as the youths attending a play at Blackfriars might learn to discourse at dinner, as the preface to Beaumont and Fletcher's Folio suggests.[47] One of the

Fellows dining with Tyndal happened to be John Preston, who was impressed (as were the others) by

> the *manliness* of the sense, the *richness* of the fancy and the *sweetness* of the expression, the *elegancy* of the Latine and the *bravery* of the whole Texture, but Mr. Preston discerned especially the seriousness, sobriety and a seeming Piety that *breathed* in every line; and from that time he received this young man, (although somewhat his Junior) into intimate Society and Familiarity with himselfe.[48]

The Latin letter stood in for the youth himself: it functioned as an index to Fairclough's masculinity and intellectual prowess, just as it reflected an act of creation through composition and imitation. The significance of this anecdote is that the letter was a process, not an artifact, which is why Preston could feel the text "breathing" as he read it, so close was he to Fairclough's performance of imitation. For Preston, every line of the text was a breath of virtue, which persuaded Preston to allow Fairclough into his intimate company in spite of their age difference. Once again, Fairclough has propelled himself beyond a subordinate position to make himself the equal of a tutor. Throughout Fairclough's life, his ability to achieve intimacy with other men, who advanced his scholarship or shaped his spiritual being, helped to further his development and career. The letter not only won him access to Preston but also gave him the opportunity to tutor Spencer Lord Compton. Responsible for Compton's finances as well as his intellectual, moral, and spiritual education, Fairclough transformed himself into the model and standard for behavior that he looked for throughout his life. By allowing Preston, Tyndal, and others to witness his performance (offstage, if you will), Fairclough not only discloses his abilities, but he also makes their experience of his ability intimate and personal. In this example from Fairclough's life, the two categories of imitative and emulative mimesis intersect: the composition of the Latin letter is an imitative practice whereby Fairclough uses his knowledge of classical models to craft the letter, while the act of writing the letter is a behavioral emulation of the scholars dining with Dr. Tyndal.

Having gained the respect of his tutors and as a successful member of the Cambridge community, Fairclough was naturally asked to perform before King James I in the production of *Ignoramus*. Preternaturally mature, gifted in Latin, small and slight, Fairclough probably seemed perfectly suited to the role chosen for him. When Fairclough realized that he was to perform the role of a woman, however, he rejected it: "that part which was to be acted by the Sub-Tutor (who was but little and of low-stature) was that of Surda, an old woman, and it required him to be cloathed in Womans apparel, which, though it were not to be worn to deceive in the worst sense, yet it had the appearance of evil."[49] By framing the potential crossdressing as not intended to "deceive in the worst sense," Clarke's *Lives* calls to mind current literary critics' discussions of crossdressing and its relationship to Phillip Stubbes's now infamous fear that, after going to the theater, audience members might go home and "play the *Sodomits*, or worse."[50] Imagining what could be "worse" than "playing the Sodomit[e]" for Stubbes has caused much scholarly ink to be spilled; Jonathan Goldberg brilliantly delineates how critics have interpreted that phrase, from the fear of actually "being" the sodomite, to being the "sodomized," to refusing to be subordinate. As Goldberg explains, "This worse is worst not least because it also dissolves the boundary between being and playing."[51] Stubbes's antitheatrical fear resonates with Fairclough's refusal to play a woman. By using the phrase "worst sense" in relation to crossdressing and Fairclough's decision, Clarke confirms that there was a hierarchy of what was acceptable mimetic behavior and what was unacceptable or even unthinkable. Here Fairclough determines that the act of impersonating a woman would interfere with the behavioral emulation that he engaged in throughout his life. How could an aspiring religious leader and academic authority take on a role that the men whom he emulated would have condemned? Had John Preston been Fairclough's tutor, he certainly would have advised him against the impersonation.

In this case, the "worst sense" was inextricably tied to performance, but what kind of performance? Was playing the role of Surda not deceitful in the worst sense because there was no possibility of mistaking the actor for the role, or was it because this role of the old deaf woman would be an inherently undesirable one? Or is the genre of the play, a comedy, a protection against lapsing into the worst kind of deceit, in that the deceit might be more obvious and exposed than in a tragedy, which might eschew parodic mimesis? Or was it, finally, that Fairclough did not want to be signaled as actually being subordinate, in the position of the female, and that in taking on the role of Surda there could be a chance of confusing playing for being? Playing Surda, a character who is ugly and dwarfish and who is duped into thinking that the trickster servant Trico is in love with her, would have turned Fairclough into the butt of the joke. For example, Trico woos Surda with epithets Fairclough would have found difficult to hear:

O pumila, nanula, surdula, crassula, dolioriola, anicula, bibosula, barbatula, simiola.

[Oh my little peece of deformity, composed of Natures excrements, who can but admire this single-eyd, needle-nosd, maple-faced, wafter-chopt, snaggle-tooth'd, hoop-shouldred, paper-gutted, brawny-buttockt, tun-bellyed hoggs-head? Ah my little pretty, little handsome, little sweet, little bearded monkey.][52]

Surda, who is deaf, can only interpret Trico's gestures, so she laps up his insults with each kiss he offers. Because the physically demeaning language of the passage highlights Surda's masculine characteristics and animalistic traits, it is no wonder that Fairclough—slight of stature and constantly reaching beyond his years and communal standing within his social interactions—would refuse to play the role, if only to maintain his sense of dignity. In playing this character, Fairclough feared he would be embracing a subordinate role at a moment in his life when he was actively trying to transition to playing a dominant one. Impersonation, in other words, would have disturbed his process of behavioral emulation. Although Clarke's *Lives* does not explicitly link Preston's and Fairclough's opinions about the performance of *Ignoramus*, Fairclough appears nevertheless to be enacting exactly the behavior that Preston would have liked to see in his student Thomas Morgan.

In describing Fairclough's position, Clarke repeatedly resorts to a mimetic vocabulary, and he ennobles Fairclough's stance against playing the role by framing his decision in a high-minded way. The baseness of the role he depicts as "evil," not merely crass. Fairclough's refusal was the talk of the university—he directly challenged Vice-Chancellor Samuel Harsnett, who could not dissuade the youth from his decision. Presenting Fairclough's stand as courageous and triumphant, Clarke writes:

> Thus did the youth choose to lose the smiles of the Court, and to bear the frowns of the Vice-Chancellour, rather than to hazard the loss of Gods countenance or to endure the least lash of his own Conscience. He well understood the meaning of that saying, *Populous me sibilat, At mihi plaudo* ["The crowd hisses at me, but I applaud myself"]; for indeed he was always a Theatre to himself, and although he could not *Histrionem agere*, act the comedian, or [...] play the hypocrite, either with God or men or himselfe, yet he acted as one that was resolved to die and go off the stage with a well done good and faithful Servant spoken to him by the King of Kings and the great spectator and observer of all men.[53]

Fairclough's refusal to perform is a challenge to authority, as he would "lose the smiles of the Court" and "bear the frowns of the Vice-Chancellour." Further, Fairclough had to choose between his obligations to the state and the university and his obligations to God and his own conscience—and probably to others, such as John Preston, who would have been sympathetic to his position.

And yet the logic of this resistance, described by Clarke with a theatrical metaphor, makes Fairclough's antitheatrical position especially interesting: "He was always a theatre to himself" and is "one resolved to die and go off stage." Clarke depicts Fairclough's refusal as a dramatic dialogue between Fairclough and God, and God speaks to him "with a well done good and faithful Servant spoken to him by the King of Kings." Clarke rhetorically substitutes Fairclough's performance before King James with an imaginary performance before God. Or, rather, Clarke constructs Fairclough's life as a performance before God. In providing Fairclough as a spiritual model, Clarke uses performance as both the form and the content of the biography. In rejecting the theatrical impersonation, Fairclough embraced the behavioral emulation of his models, men like John Preston. While the impersonation and emulation that scholars and students practiced at Cambridge in the seventeenth century were basic processes of the humanist program, the narrative of Fairclough's life suggests that their deployment did not proceed according to predictable or codified exigencies. As in Bourdieu's description of the habitus, the boy's life was neither completely regulated nor entirely unscripted. Ruggle's *Ignoramus* challenged its Cambridge audience to recognize both the potential power (as political advancement) and the possible failure (as moral impoverishment) of these humanist practices. The play and the events surrounding it mounted a critique of and warning to humanists about a too-ready reliance upon imitation, which is evident even in Clarke's project of collecting eminent religious figures as models of virtuous lives.

In spite of his challenge to authority and his moral challenge to the theatrical performance, Fairclough was not saved by his own conscience or virtue, but rather by one of his relationships of mutual obligation at the college. Spencer Lord Compton, only playing the small part of Vince, offered to play the role of Surda as well. Compton's life was hardly adversely affected by this performance, and he was clearly not threatened by its lack of decorum. In fact, like many other actors in the production, he achieved great glory—shortly following the performance he was awarded the order of the Knight of Bath and, after an illustrious political career, Compton died a military hero. As the presumptive Earl of Northampton, Compton's status far exceeded Fairclough's, his tutor. In this particular tutor-student exchange—a literal exchange of roles—the political delicacy of the humanist project comes to the forefront. Paradoxically, Fairclough's refusal did not reaffirm his dominance over his student but, rather, made Fairclough beholden to Compton for graciously removing the university pressure on his tutor.

When Fairclough refused to perform before King James, he missed a possible opportunity for advancement. As mentioned above, the king was so enchanted with the play that he saw it twice within the span of three months; and although one cannot be sure that performing a role in this play would guarantee a place at court or a seat of power, the list of actors and their eventual positions indicate that the youths who performed eventually garnered high stations: William Lakes ("Trico") became secretary to the Lord Treasurer; John Towers ("Dulman") was the Bishop of Peterborough, 1639–49; and John Bargrave ("Torcol") was Dean of Canterbury, 1662–80. Other actors were appointed Master of Corpus Christi at Cambridge, Dean of Ely, and Secretary of State.[54] Infamous for its attack upon common lawyers, the play was printed in seven editions from 1630 to 1787, and it attracted many vituperative responses, especially from lawyers at the Inns of Court and from students at Oxford who were in competition for the king's favor.[55] *Ignoramus*'s satire also struck close to home in Cambridge by critiquing some of the underlying practices of humanist education, impersonation, and emulation, in the same way that the casting of the play ignited controversies about how the tutor-student relationship enacted those practices.

"What's Past is Prologue"

George Ruggle's use of satire and deflation through imitation repeatedly demonstrates the possible failure of impersonation and emulation to cultivate an elite, polished, and virtuous group of young men. The goal of imitative practices to copy a dominant model is impugned throughout the play in both style and content; Ignoramus and his clerks reveal the perversity of emulating an unworthy model, while the linguistic barbarisms of mangled Latin exhibit the absurdity of imitation without knowledge. Though the play's overt satirical target is the legal profession, it takes aim at larger questions about humanist methods of instruction and subject development in education, but it ultimately affirms the university's superiority in administering the humanist program. From the play's opening, Ruggle reminds the audience that they are watching an *academic* play; he displays student actors in the process of impersonation and comments upon their abilities while also creating "regulated improvisations," so that the students seem to be performing the unexpected. In two prologues, which introduced different performances, Ruggle masterfully enacts the qualities that would make humanism successful in producing scholars who were intellectually agile and sensitive to political issues. In both prologues Ruggle deflates the expectations of the audience, suggesting that the actors will be bad, or that they may not even perform at all.

In the first prologue performed before the king on 8 March 1615, the Horse Keeper and the Horse Courser attempt to restrain the Hobby Horse Davus Dromo, or Davy Drummond, from presenting the prologue.[56] By showing characters usually associated with the world of chivalry and the hunt (the Courser and the Keeper) in contest with a traditionally theatrical character (the Hobby Horse), Ruggle invites his audience to think about theatricality and pageantry, reminding spectators that they are in a venue not typically associated with playmaking. He opens the play with a commentary not on lawyers but, rather, on the ability of academics to imitate actors. The Keeper worries about the critical reception of the play, and the Hobby Horse (the self-appointed theatrical expert) tells him exactly how it will be received:

> KEEP: But what will the talk be about the play?
> HORSE: That you can see a better play at London for a groat any day,
> that here the comedians break comedy's rules.
> KEEP: And the verdict about the actors?
> HORSE: That academicians make rotten actors.
> KEEP: Which of the actors will have the biggest clique?
> HORSE: Who but Davy Drummond, the world-famous quadruped?
> KEEP: Why so?
> HORSE: A good horse always has a following.[57]

Despite an oblique reference to the law—the "*verdict* about the actors"—the prologue mainly reminds the audience that it is watching an academic play. Ruggle invites a comparison between the public theaters of London and the university drama that is about to be performed by deflating the audience's expectations and by declaring that the play does not adhere to the rules of comedy and that the university students are "rotten actors." The Hobby Horse predicts nothing less than a failed impersonation of the professional theater. Davy Drummond presents himself as the only actor who will have fans because the university actors lack theatrical sense and an understanding of comedy. Perhaps Ruggle is merely hedging his bets and lowering the audience's expectations, but by reminding them of the London theaters, Ruggle can hardly be asking the courtly audience to view this play outside the distinction between the professional acting companies in London and the present "academicians." By suggesting that the actors will "break the rules," Ruggle prepares his audience for the possibility of improvisation, and, of course, the prologue appears "improvised" as the actors argue about who will deliver it, rather than actually getting to the prologue of the play.

Ruggle's "Prologus Posterior" for the king's second visit, in contrast, suggests a complete failure of performance as a boy enters to announce that the play cannot go on. In this second prologue, Ruggle emphasizes his manifest satirical target, the lawyers, but in replacing the first prologue in this second performance, Ruggle makes the moment seem improvised:

> Boy: Trin—tran—Yield, make way. I'm the post boy, sent to you here from London to announce that *Ignoramus* is not to be acted, nor can it be. Don't stare at me, the thing is as I have said. You ask the reason? None of the lawyers will wish to lend Ignoramus his gown. For lately an injunction has been handed down, namely an injunction that only lawyers are to enjoy immunity in the theater. Therefore this screed bids you to rise to your feet and depart. Spectators, this play has been acted. Give your applause and farewell.[58]

The common lawyers, the boy suggests, have put a stop to the play before it even begins by withholding Ignoramus's costume, as if Ignoramus's gown is anything more than a costume in the first place.[59] The boy applies legal actions, "injunctions" and "immunity," to the performance, suggesting that the theater has become a courtroom. Again, Ruggle crafts the play's argument by creating unsupportable imitations; that lawyers might find immunity in the theater reveals the absurdity and lack of decorum in the comparison. In an anecdote "preserved by tradition," according to Hawkins, "When this prologue was performed before King James [...] it seems he was deceived by this passage, and, imagining a prohibition to prevent the performance of the comedy had actually been received, he grew very angry and peremptorily commanded the actors to proceed."[60]

It matters little whether or not James actually inserted himself into the performance because the very nature of the anecdote itself reveals that Ruggle's desired effect was achieved. He was able to make the audience believe that the moment was improvised, not scripted. The second opening night of *Ignoramus* began with an act that wavered between theater and reality. The play continually asks, how is it possible to distinguish the imitation from the real? At the same time the play also reminds us of the very parodic nature of the mimetic act, as "academicians make rotten actors" and Ignoramus makes a lousy lawyer, in spite of his attempted imitations. The play itself was not, in fact, a poor imitation of the repertory in the London theaters, since it thoroughly impressed its most important audience member, King James. According to other spectators, "The king said that he believed the authors and actors together had a design to make him laugh himself to death."[61] Extreme though the king's reaction might seem, the play was clearly a comic and political success, which endeared Cambridge to the king. In these prologues as in the rest of the play, and even in the lives of the actors involved, impersonation and emulation are estimable and productive when applied within the proper context of the university.

Ruggle's play offers yet another view of how mimesis is understood in the period and how university educators utilized the mimetic activities of the humanist program. This play qualifies those distinctions that critics of the period make between "realistic" and "icastic" mimesis by showing how easily one can be tricked by seemingly realistic portrayals, which either abuse the original content or are based on scurrilous content from the start. This, it seems to me, was clearly an important distinction for the educator and playwright Ruggle to make because he was involved with mimesis within both categories of emulation and impersonation. His play substantiates what the histories of Thomas Morgan and Samuel Fairclough tell us: that in deploying impersonation and emulation as pedagogical strategies humanism was only as successful as the interrelations of the tutors and students engaged in those forms of mimesis. The student who has a good master should aspire to emulate that scholar, but without an excellent model the student could be led astray. Surprisingly, in the history of Fairclough's refusal to perform, George Ruggle's voice is silent. Only the university administrators are depicted as pressuring Fairclough, and, in light of his play, it seems that Ruggle would have appreciated the student who was willing to resist authority. In the production history of *Ignoramus*, though the potential dangers of humanism that Ruggle explores in the play are apparent, the student-actors were hardly sheep-like in their engagement with authority; rather, it seems that Cambridge was in the business of producing students who largely shaped their own identities.

Ruggle's play demonstrates that the micropolitics of tutor-student relations within the humanist program had to be carefully managed to match the ideological investment of the university in creating an elite cohort of youths, who would eventually step into national positions of power in the Church, the government, the economy, and the university. Though Ruggle left Cambridge in 1619, he continued to pursue the idea that impersonation and emulation could rival succession and inheritance as strategies for cultural access, but only if practiced with judicious government and intelligent administration. After his career at Cambridge, Ruggle became a member of the Virginia Company and, until his death in 1622, was deeply involved in drafting treatises concerning the creation of a "College for Infidel Children" in Henrico, Virginia. The aim of the college was to take Native American children from their families, convert them to Christianity, and train them to be English subjects. In his will, Ruggle bequeathed one hundred pounds "towards the bringing up of the infidel's children in Virginia."[62] In removing Native American children from their families and installing them in a community of English subjects, asking them to model their behavior on the master of the college, George Thorpe, the Virginia Company hoped to apply the principles of academic and religious cultivation operating in English academies. Ruggle's experience of interrogating the very methods of humanist instruction while he was a Cambridge tutor and playwright foreshadows his later involvement in the Virginia Company. The performance of imitation therefore became an ideological tool in the process of colonization. *Ignoramus* and its production history demonstrate how carefully the academic community thought about performance and imitation, not as methods to be feared but as methods to be well-governed and even exported as a means of transmitting cultural values.

Notes

1   Francis Beaumont and John Fletcher, *Comedies and Tragedies* (London: for Humphrey Robinson and Humphrey Moseley, 1647), sig. A3r.
2   To speak of "fashioning a gentleman" invokes in recent criticism the work of Stephen Greenblatt, *Renaissance Self-Fashioning: From More to Shakespeare* (Chicago: University of Chicago Press, 1980), and other critics who emphasize role-playing and staging as a central trope of identity in the early modern period: Louis Adrian Montrose, *The Purpose of Playing: Shakespeare and the Cultural Politics of the Elizabethan Theatre* (Chicago: University of Chicago Press, 1996); Leonard Tennenhouse, *Power on Display: The Politics of Shakespeare's Genres* (New York: Methuen, 1986); and Frank Whigham, *Ambition and Privilege: The Social Tropes of Elizabethan Courtesy Theory* (Berkeley: University of California Press, 1984). Recent criticism that identifies the thematic representation of "Academies of manners" in drama of the period can be found in Ira Clark, *Comedy, Youth, Manhood in Early Modern England* (Newark: University of Delaware Press, 2003). In particular Clark's chapter "The Place of Academies of Conduct" focuses on the mechanism whereby theatrical presentation could "present dominant, contesting, and potential modes for youth to establish and assert their manhood in subtler ways than those recorded in the drama's caricatures of academies of behavior" (48).
3   William Shakespeare, *Love's Labor's Lost*, ed. H.R. Woudhuysen (Walton-on-Thames: Thomas Nelson and Sons, 1998), 5.1.35–6.
4   See E.K. Chambers, *The Elizabethan Stage*, 4 vols. (Oxford: Clarendon, 1923); Frederick Gard Fleay, *A Chronicle History of the London Stage, 1559–1642* (New York: Stechert, 1909); and Andrew Gurr, *The Shakespearian Playing Companies* (Oxford: Oxford University Press, 1995), all of whom separate or do not discuss academic drama in the context of the London commercial theaters. Those writers of the early modern period who did seem to uphold a distinction between academic drama and professional theater were antitheatrical writers

like John Northbrooke and Philip Stubbes, who tended to exclude academic or learned drama from their attacks on theatrical performance in general.

5 Stephen Halliwell, *The Aesthetics of Mimesis: Ancient Texts and Modern Problems* (Princeton: Princeton University Press, 2002), 15.

6 See Thomas Postlewait's caution against reading theatricality too broadly in the period, "Theatricality and Antitheatricality in Renaissance London," in *Theatricality*, ed. Tracy C. Davis and Thomas Postlewait (Cambridge: Cambridge University Press, 2003), 90–126.

7 Anthony Grafton and Lisa Jardine, *From Humanism to the Humanities: Education and Liberal Arts in Fifteenth- and Sixteenth-Century Europe* (Cambridge: Harvard University Press, 1986), 125. For more extended discussions of imitation and repetition as elements of early modern education see especially Mary Thomas Crane, *Framing Authority: Sayings, Self, and Society in Sixteenth-Century England* (Princeton: Princeton University Press, 1993); Jonathan Goldberg, *Writing Matter: From the Hands of the English Renaissance* (Stanford: Stanford University Press, 1990); and Alan Stewart, *Close Readers: Humanism and Sodomy in Early Modern England* (Princeton: Princeton University Press, 1997). Cf. Cicero, *De Oratore*, 3 vols., ed. Augustus S. Wilkins (Oxford: Oxford University Press, 1881), 2.315; Cicero discusses the care the orator must take in imitation and also the use of imitation by actors.

8 Desiderius Erasmus, *Ciceronianus*, trans. Izora Scott, in Izora Scott, *Controversies Over the Imitation of Cicero as a Model for Style and Some Phases of their Influence on the Schools of the Renaissance* (New York: Teacher's College, Columbia University, 1910), 129.

9 On the position of the humanist tutor or schoolmaster in relation to his student, see Rebecca Bushnell, *A Culture of Teaching: Early Modern Humanism in Theory and Practice* (Ithaca: Cornell University Press, 1996), 23–72.

10 Richard Halpern, *The Poetics of Primitive Accumulation: English Renaissance Culture and the Genealogy of Capital* (Ithaca: Cornell University Press, 1991), 29. Halpern defines Louis Althusser's concept of "interpellation" as when "the subject comes both to recognize himself within and to depend upon a dominant specular image" (29).

11 Stewart, *Close Readers*, 86–91. Wendy Wall describes the domestic nature of university relationships in her analysis of *Gammer Gurton's Needle* at Oxford in the sixteenth century; see her "'Household Stuff': The Sexual Politics of Domesticity and the Advent of English Comedy," *English Literary History* 65 (1998): 1–45.

12 "Commonplace Book of Anthony Scattergood," Cambridge, 1632–40, 12 [British Library, Additional MS. 44963, Scattergood Collections, vol. XXXII]. See also Alan Stewart on humanism and the nobility in *Close Readers*, xxxiv–xliv.

13 See the commentary by Thomas Postlewait and Tracy C. Davis on this problematic: "Theatricality: An Introduction," in *Theatricality*, ed. Davis and

Postlewait, 4–10. See also Halliwell, *The Aesthetics of Mimesis*, 344–81, who points out that "the many intertwined conceptual and terminological twists in Renaissance mimeticism [...] become lost to view if we misguidedly look for doctrinal purity or orthodoxy in this area" (347).

14 Jonas A. Barish, *The Antitheatrical Prejudice* (Berkeley: University of California Press, 1981), 26–7, 80–130.

15 Jonathan Dollimore, *Radical Tragedy: Religion, Ideology, and Power in the Drama of Shakespeare and His Contemporaries*, 2d edn. (Durham: Duke University Press, 1993), 82.

16 Phyllis Rackin, "Androgyny, Mimesis, and the Marriage of the Boy Heroine on the English Renaissance Stage," *PMLA* 102 (1987): 29.

17 William N. West, *Theatres and Encyclopedias in Early Modern Europe* (Cambridge: Cambridge University Press, 2002), 142. See also Eric Leonidas's contribution to this volume.

18 J. Bass Mullinger, *The University of Cambridge* (Cambridge: Cambridge University Press, 1873), 517, 44.

19 Alan H. Nelson, *Early Cambridge Theatres: College, University, and Town Stages, 1464–1720* (Cambridge: Cambridge University Press, 1994), 43.

20 There are several facsimiles and translations of the play. The most comprehensive edition and the only printed version with notes and editorial commentary was prepared in the eighteenth century: George Ruggle, *Ignoramus*, ed. John Sidney Hawkins (London, 1787); the quotation from Hawkins above appears at xviii. E.F.J. Tucker "prepared and introduced" a facsimile of one of the seven manuscript versions of the play, Bodleian Library, MS. Douce 43: George Ruggle, *Ignoramus*, ed. E.F.J. Tucker (Hildesheim: Georg Olms Verlag, 1987). In 1662, R.C. (probably Robert Codrington) produced a translation of the play: *Ignoramus [...] Translated into English by R.C.* (London, 1662); and in 1678 Edward Ravenscroft authored a translation and adaptation of the play titled: *Ignoramus: Or, the English Lawyer: A Comedy* (London: W. Feales, 1736). Professor Dana F. Sutton has posted an online Latin edition with an English translation of the play: George Ruggle, *Ignoramus (1615)*, ed. and trans. Dana F. Sutton, *The Philological Museum*, 5 September 2000, University of Birmingham <http://www.philological.bham.ac.uk/ruggle/>. In discussing the play, I will be referring primarily to through-line numbers in Sutton's online edition and translation, but also to Hawkins's edition and notes and to R.C.'s translation (colloquial but perhaps not exact). As Hawkins notes, translations of the play have not been very successful, which he attributes to "the want of skill in forensic phraseology, the barbarisms of law Latin, and the colloquial jargon of common lawyers" (10). In fact, much of the humor of the play does

not translate into English because it is about the very confusion of the Latin language and common law French.

21 On the critique of common law language, see E.F.J. Tucker, "Ruggle's *Ignoramus* and Humanistic Criticism of the Language of the Common Law," *Renaissance Quarterly* 30 (1977): 341–50.

22 Sutton, *Ignoramus*, ll. 3164–7 (Latin); ll. 224–7 (English). All subsequent through-line references will be given in this order.

23 Sutton, *Ignoramus*, ll. 335–6; ll. 407–8.

24 John Cowell, *The Interpreter* (Cambridge: by Iohn Legate, 1607), sig. Nn3r. Cowell's book was a very important reference for Ruggle; see Hawkins, *Ignoramus*, xvi.

25 In his edition, Tucker suggests that this character's purpose was to "dramatize the educational differences between the programs at the Inns of Court and Chancery and the universities of Oxford and Cambridge" (*Ignoramus*, 9).

26 Sutton, *Ignoramus*, ll. 2483–5; ll. 2756–8.

27 Sutton, *Ignoramus*, ll. 2486–9; ll. 2759–63. Sutton's note to these lines defines these terms: "*Infangthef*: the right of the lord of the manor to try felons apprehended on his property. *Outfangthef*: the right of the lord to try felons apprehended on their own property. *Sac*: a privilege touching the correction of trespasses within the manor. *Soc*: a power of jurisdiction. *Tol*: the right to buy and sell within the boundaries of the manor. *Tem*: the power of the lord of the manor to have serfs" (l. 2487n).

28 See Hawkins's commentary to this scene.

29 Hawkins, *Ignoramus*, 109.

30 Sutton, *Ignoramus*, ll. 951–2; ll. 1103–4.

31 Pierre Bourdieu, *The Logic of Practice*, trans. Richard Nice (Stanford: Stanford University Press, 1990), 56–7.

32 Samuel Clarke, *The Lives of Sundry Eminent Persons in This Later Age in Two Parts. I. Of Divines. II Of Nobility and Gentry of Both Sexes* (London: 1683), sig. a3r; this text contains "The Life of Samuel Fairclough." The narrative about Thomas Morgan was written by Thomas Ball in "The Life of Doctor Preston," which appears in Samuel Clarke, *The Lives of Two and Twenty Eminent Divines* (London, 1660).

33 Quoted in Mark H. Curtis, *Oxford and Cambridge in Transition, 1558–1642: An Essay on Changing Relations Between the English Universities and English Society* (Oxford: Clarendon, 1959), 80; Clarke, *The Lives of Two and Twenty Eminent Divines*, sig. Aa2r.

34 Clarke, *The Lives of Two and Twenty Eminent Divines*, sig. Z2v.

35 Clarke, *The Lives of Two and Twenty Eminent Divines*, sig. Aa2r.

36 Clarke, *The Lives of Two and Twenty Eminent Divines*, sig. Aa2r.

37 I have not been able to discover exactly what happened to Thomas Morgan after Oxford. As we will see, however, playing a part in *Ignoramus* did not preclude

any of the other actors from achieving great political, military, religious, or academic success. In fact, it probably helped.

38 Clarke, *The Lives of Two and Twenty Eminent Divines*, sig. Aa2v.

39 J.A. Granger, *A Biographical History of England*, 4 vols., 2d edn. (London: 1775), 3.39–40. Fairclough was eventually ejected from the pulpit for Non-Conformity in 1662. For more history of Fairclough's life see Thomas William Davids, *Annals of Evangelical Nonconformity in the County of Essex* (London: Jackson, Walford, & Hodder, 1863); and *The Dictionary of National Biography*, s.v. Samuel Fairclough.

40 John Walker, *The Sufferings of the Clergy During the Great Rebellion, Part II* (Oxford: John Henry and James Parker, 1862), 226.

41 John Milton, *Apology for Smectymnuus*, in *Areopagitica and Other Prose Works*, ed. C.E. Vaughan (London: J.M. Dent, 1927), 119.

42 Clarke, *The Lives of Sundry Eminent Persons*, sig. X2r.

43 Clarke, *The Lives of Sundry Eminent Persons*, sig. X2r.

44 Clarke, *The Lives of Sundry Eminent Persons*, sig. X2r.

45 Spencer Compton, 1601–43, became the Earl of Northampton and was killed at the Battle of Hopton Heath. Compton would have been about 13 at the time of *Ignoramus*'s premiere, while Fairclough would have been just 20 years old. See *The Dictionary of National Biography*, s.v. Spencer Compton.

46 Clarke, *The Lives of Sundry Eminent Persons*, sig. X2r.

47 See also Walter J. Ong's chapter on puberty, rites of initiation, Latin training, and violence in the Renaissance: "Latin Language Study as a Renaissance Puberty Rite," in *Rhetoric, Romance and Technology: Studies in the Interaction of Expression and Culture* (Ithaca: Cornell University Press, 1971), 113–41. The scene staged by Tyndal and Fairclough does not contain overt gestures of violence, but as we will see it is certainly engaged in a testing of masculinity.

48 Clarke, *The Lives of Sundry Eminent Persons*, sigs. X2r–v, my emphasis.

49 Clarke, *The Lives of Sundry Eminent Persons*, sig. X2v.

50 Phillip Stubbes, *The Anatomie of Abuses* (London: by Richard Iones, 1583), sigs. N8r–v.

51 Jonathan Goldberg, *Sodometries: Renaissance Texts, Modern Sexualities* (Stanford: Stanford University Press, 1992), 118. For his analysis of other critics' readings of Stubbes, see 118–22.

52 Sutton, *Ignoramus*, ll. 426–7; ll. 515–19 (with creative flair in the translation).

53 Clarke, *The Lives of Sundry Eminent Persons*, sigs. X2v–X3r.

54 This cast list is from one of the manuscript copies of the play owned by Archbishop William Sancroft, George Ruggle, "Ignoramus," [Bodleian Library, Rawlinson MS. D1361]. The MS. is dated 1629, so that the cast list reflects positions achieved by these actors fourteen or fifteen years after the performance. I am not suggesting that this performance led to immediate

promotion, but rather that their participation in the play was clearly not a stumbling block to their careers.

55 For a complete list of the responses to the play, see Hawkins, *Ignoramus*, xxxvii–xxxviii.

56 According to Hawkins, David Droman or Drummond was King James's jester and he is dressed as a hobby-horse to invoke the May Day mummers' costume (*Ignoramus*, 9 n. 1).

57 Sutton, *Ignoramus*, "Prologus Prior," ll. 70–80; "First Prologue," ll. 76–84.

58 Sutton, *Ignoramus*, "Prologus Posterior," ll. 1–9; "Second Prologue," ll. 1–7.

59 See Ann Rosalind Jones and Peter Stallybrass on the importance of costume on the Renaissance stage, which sometimes even dictated repertory, *Renaissance Clothing and the Materials of Memory* (Cambridge: Cambridge University Press, 2000), 175–206.

60 Hawkins, *Ignoramus*, 19.

61 Henry Stoddard Ruggles, "The Lineage of George Ruggle, a Member of the Virginia Company," *William and Mary College Quarterly Historical Magazine* 5 (1896–97): 203–4.

62 John Ferrar and Doctor Jebb, *Nicholas Ferrar. Two Lives by his Brother John and Doctor Jebb*, ed. J.E.B. Mayor (Cambridge: Cambridge University Press, 1855), 12–13 n. 3. For more on the College of Infidel Children, the Virginia Company, and George Ruggle, see my "In the Company of Boys: The Place of the Boy Actor in Early Modern English Culture" (Ph.D. Thesis, Northwestern University, 2005), 238–90.

CHAPTER 5

Theatrical Experiment and the Production of Knowledge in the Gray's Inn Revels

Eric Leonidas

Fearing the likelihood that Hal will be "horribly chid" when he finally returns to face his father King Henry IV, Falstaff pleads with the prince to "practice an answer." At that point, Shakespeare's scripted history play seems to devolve into a "play extempore," one in which performances by Falstaff and Hal illustrate competing ideas of drama.[1] Their improvised play is at once "merry sport" as well as an activity intended to develop specific rhetorical skills and confidence in preparation for an actual social performance. The festive Falstaff endorses the pedagogical view of academic drama. At grammar schools and universities, students had long been encouraged, even required, to perform plays in Latin and English for general "profit" and, more specifically, to "become better accustomed to proper action and pronunciation."[2] Hal is urged to undertake just such preparation to defend himself before his irate father. Of course, Falstaff quickly undermines his own pretensions by gloriously mocking the high ceremony and stilted oratory associated with academic drama. He chooses to burlesque in particular the extreme artifice and moral didacticism of euphuistic speech. In *1 Henry IV* generally, a sense of the "real" emerges when the extemporaneous and immediate displaces the scripted. Falstaff's inimitability, for instance, paradoxically grows out of his protean appropriation of high and low forms of speech; for his part, Hal substitutes a merchant's calculating use of factors and credit for more conventional expressions of authority, such as the chivalrous rhetoric of Hotspur or Henry IV's miserly care of his own image.[3]

Still, in the "play extempore," Hal revives a pedagogical possibility for academic drama from within Falstaff's dismissive critique that yet draws on the knight's preference for the immediately present and instinctive over abstract ideals or received assumptions. Hal's idea of playing suggests less the demonstration of learnedness intended by rote actions and careful enunciation than the purposeful deployment of knowledge gained through experience. Rather than cultivate the formal qualities of practiced academic productions, Hal pursues the improvisational and experiential talents developed in revelry, thus turning Falstaff's habitual vein to deliberate cultivation. Hal's preference for practicing a full social role, in addition, reflects changing priorities within some forms of academic theater, especially at the Inns of Court near the turn of the seventeenth century. The organized festivities of Inns students certainly incorporated the traditional rhetorical practices of the academic drama performed at other educational institutions. But the young lawyers starkly changed the comparative emphasis from recitation to response and brought into their productions a large swath of material life.[4] Inns revelers broadened the forms of communication to include clothing, pageantry, deportment, and of course improvisations, just as they varied the circumstances under which typical rhetorical skills were to be practiced. The often lavish festivities undertaken in extended revels at the Inns, Douglas Lanier observes, amounted to "a kind of cultural dress rehearsal, in which the revelers strove to (re)produce, often before an audience of actual notables, the ceremonial texture of courtly society, its oratorical style, visual spectacle, ritualized actions, and management of diplomatic challenges."[5] At their most elaborate, however, the revels demonstrated much more than the students' readiness for court life. The sustained emphasis on what is contingent and alterable, combined with the frequent invocation of material life beyond the court, showcased the students' connections to increasingly alternative sources of prestige, profit, and power.

In these aesthetic and social performances, the students had opportunities to put their training to trial and to adjust their knowledge in response to their experiences. Such performances, moreover, offered participants a much greater benefit than merely learning to deliver a script persuasively. They became rhetorical experiments, a linguistic and performative "trying out" of social, legal, political, and economic strategies and positions, whether the ultimate purpose is to shore up existing social orders and privileges within them or to encourage change. In his interview with his father, Hal deploys the conventional prodigal's admission that he has "faulty wandered and irregular" (3.2.27), but in the end he gains real traction by couching a chivalric denunciation of Hotspur in the materialist terms of accounts management and "reckoning." Figuring the moral in colloquial economic language might recall the morality play's invocation of the spiritual in the everyday (Everyman himself must present a "reckoning"), but given the settings of Shakespeare's play, we are much more likely to connect Hal's words to his experiences in the tavern. Indeed, such layerings are common in organized revels, which drew liberally from the culture's high and low places, pursuits, and forms of speech. The *Gesta Grayorum*, the Christmas revels conducted by students at Gray's Inn in 1594–95, forms a particularly rich record of just such a mix, calling equally on the participants' academic skills and on their broader social experience (much of which also issued in the satire, epigram, and innovative love poetry popular among Inns residents). The students of Gray's themselves came increasingly from families of diverse social places and occupations, including traders, merchants, professionals, and artisans.[6] In addition, given the situation of the Inns in London, the presence of mercantile, financial, manufacturing, and other materialist discourses in the revels reflects the day-to-day circulation of the students. In incorporating so wide a variety of rhetorical and dramatic performances, then, the Gray's revels catch theater in the act of structuring social life. No less importantly, the revels present and legitimize theater as social experiment—as the construction of an artificial environment within which to test conventional practices and assumptions, to assay new forms, and from which to draw knowledge.

In general, Christmas revels at the Inns of Court were elaborate if traditional entertainments staged by the gentlemen at the various Inns, typically extending from just before Christmas until February. They comprised a variety of ceremonies, most significantly the selection of a prince and court, the soliciting of funds to support the revels, the establishment of the prince's authority and laws, and a succession of orations and presentations to the prince, including masques, plays, processions, and other pageantry.[7] The *Gesta Grayorum* gives us an account of what must have been an especially sumptuous period of revels: preparations began in early December 1594, and various costly events and ceremonies took place until Shrovetide in early March, when the festivities concluded with a masque before the queen. Indeed, in the epistle that precedes the account the stationer claims that the gentlemen revelers left a "Memory of those Actions" for the express purpose of providing an example for future ages.[8] The text includes the names of some ninety participants, probably more than half of all the Inner Barristers residing at Gray's.[9]

The Gray's account brags that due to the house's tradition for large revels and, as a result of plague, the conspicuous absence of these for some years, barristers high and low supported reviving the Christmas games. One Henry Helmes of Norfolk was selected as "Prince of Purpoole" (named after the parish of Portpool, in which Gray's was located) and given lodgings, a presence chamber, and numerous "Officers of State, of the Law, and of the House-hold" (2). The account decrees that the substance of the revels was to consist of "witty Inventions" rather than "chargeable Expences." Nevertheless, a sizable sum was raised among residents, members of the Inns of Chancery associated with Gray's, and various "friends," which extended all the way up to William Cecil, Lord Burghley, at that time Elizabeth's Chancellor and Treasurer. Finally, a fulsome invitation was extended to members of the Inner Temple to send an "ambassador," who would offer counsel and serve as a "Minister of Correspondence" between the two Inns. In all, the revelers had embarked on a series of institutional procedures and rhetorical presentations that, in their self-conscious formality, would serve as the defining elements of the ensuing sports. There was to be a great deal of exaggeration, burlesque, and parody throughout, but there was also to be significant contact with the governing bodies of city and state. The compiler of the *Gesta* asserts that the chief intent of the Prince's rules was the creation of "credit" (2), both social esteem and the political influence that attends it.[10]

Given the expense, sheer size of participation, and the elevated social status of the revelers, the law sports at Gray's can hardly be considered popular carnival. They were, rather, a version of humanist theater, an attempt by the residents to define and project a practicable social reality that of course featured themselves.[11] In assuming the elevated positions of those senior members who governed Gray's, Paul Raffield argues, the junior members "presented archetypes from an ideal society, and so offered a glimpse of the Utopian state, one not subject to the uncertainties that existed beyond the wall of the Inn."[12] Yet what is particularly remarkable about the *Gesta* is the degree to which the revelers insisted on representing and reflecting upon the unpredictable and contingent world beyond the confines of Gray's. Such a predilection had become a mark of the Inn's education, where students were introduced "to a far wider range of informal cultural and intellectual pursuits than the two universities—isolated in their provincial market towns—were able or willing to provide."[13] If the forms of power and order practiced in the revels were to have any validity, they would have to be tested upon the social body they were intended to regulate. Since the disorderly social body was introduced into the revels in key moments as theater, the students at Gray's effectively staged an attempt to subsume and order one type of drama within another. The struggle with social experience was figured as a struggle with theater.

During the prince's investiture on the first night, the students confronted the material limits of performance itself. Not content to assume conventional dramatic license, the performers established for themselves a sense of the real to which their revels would adhere. After a series of ceremonies, including the arrival of the prince's champion, the blazoning of his coat of arms, and a catalogue of his prominent title-holders and the value of their annual tributes, a parliament was summoned. The parliamentary body never convened, however, lacking "some special Officers [...] without whose Presence it could not be performed" (14). The state of Purpoole, with all of its holdings, offices, and codes, might be an elaborate fantasy, but it is one intentionally beholden to limits. The same dynamic takes place in the "pardon" the Prince extends to his subjects. Opening a space of license and play, Purpoole's solicitor proclaims a "general and free Pardon of all Dangers, Pains, Penalties, Forfetures, or Offences," whether of commission or omission, to "all and every publick Person and Persons, whether they be strangers or Naturals" (15). But the solicitor continues with a series of exceptions that in fact amounts to every conceivable slight to the Prince's dignity or interests and would seem to include everyone. Not covered by the pardon, for example, are those who hunt, fish, chase women (or fail to chase women), overlook the king during financial speculations, or take too great or too little advantage of national resources. Utopia or not, within the Kingdom of Purpoole the idea of limitlessness is itself a joke.

Engagement with the world outside of the Inn takes place on a variety of theatrical levels. At the highest, the revelers invoke a "Warrant of Experience" as evidence of good relations between Gray's and the Inner Temple, and they ask that an ambassador from the rival Inn join the revels and serve as an intermediary. His arrival is to be greeted with pageantry and ceremony, which in the event looks more popular than elite, as the "good" inventions and sports planned forcibly give way to the "vain Representations and Shews" of common players (23). After a theatrical court proceeding (to which I will return) the revelers stage a "Masque of Amity," featuring a number of classical allegories of friendship and climaxing in the entry of Graius and Templarius, "lovingly, Arm in Arm" (26). But just as theater is capable of providing, ordering, and reflecting upon experience within Gray's, so the barristers were encouraged to seek its advantages outside the walls. Having instituted an Order of Knighthood of the Helmet to honor his nobility and recognize the "Deserts of Strangers," the Prince publishes strict "Rules of Arms, and Civil Government" (27). What follows is largely a parody, often bawdy, of "courtly" conduct and a satire of the social pursuits of the young barristers. Much of it mocks the physical and linguistic affectations that are repeatedly attacked in the epigrams, verse satire, and humors comedy of the 1590s and subsequent decade.

Yet even as the "Rules" suggest the corrupting influence of material London, they share the tacit defense of social circulation found in those more conventional literary forms. Acknowledging the financial entanglement of Inns residents with nearby merchants and traders, as well as the increasingly mercantile background of many of the students, the Order's knights are commanded to be "much in the Books of the worshipful Citizens of the principal City" (29). Likewise, the knights are admonished not to pawn a "Collar of Knighthood" for £100, upon penalty of discharge from the Order. However, should anyone redeem a collar so impawned, at the full sum, he is entitled to the knighthood, for "it is holden for a certain Rule, that the Knighthood followeth the Collar, and not the Collar the Knighthood" (31). The article, of course, skewers the purchase of titles, but like other articles addressing the pursuit of wards, subsidies, monopolies, and place, it also recognizes the inevitable pull of material life on men who reside at a particular point of overlap among political, civic, legal, scholarly, and economic activity.

The most interesting article that the Prince institutes for his Order speaks to the intersection of text and experience in the young barristers' education:

> *Item*, Every Knight of this Order shall endeavour to add Conference and Experience by Reading; and therefore shall not only read and peruse *Guizo*, the *French* Academy, *Galiatto* the Courtier, *Plutarch*, the *Arcadia*, and the Neoterical Writers, from time to time; but also frequent the Theatre, and such like places of Experience; and resort the better sort of Ord'naries for Conference, whereby they may not only become accomplished with Civil Conversations, and able to govern a Table with Discourse; but also sufficient, if need be, to make Epigrams, Emblems, and other Devices appertaining to His Honour's learned Revels. [29–31]

First, by invoking "Conference and Experience," the article plays on the humanist assumption that texts themselves can be sites of practical learning if they challenge their readers to make sense out of formal and rhetorical complication.[14] (The *Gesta* probably mistakes or deliberately corrupts "*Galiatto*" for Lyly's *Gallathea* and "*Guizo*" for Stephano Guazzo's *Civil Conversation*.) But the "item" also recognizes, only half-jokingly, that texts need to be tested against experience. This assumption, too, is a humanist commonplace, but here the "experience" that serves as touchstone does not constitute generally held truths but, rather, the specific and changing instances of belief, behavior, and speech to be observed in ordinary social encounters.[15] Like Shakespeare's Hal, who considers his experience among the riff-raff to be both conventional prodigal antics to be disavowed and a source of valuable rhetoric to hoard, the article laughs off the barristers' "conference and experience" as valuable only to the revels, even as the revels constantly call attention to the social and political utility of theatrical experience. Civil conversation at table, moreover, was deeply respected in the structuring of social life at the Inns and was increasingly a catalyst among legal, political, scholarly, and scientific innovators.[16]

The various uses of "experience" throughout the *Gesta* suggest the evolving meanings of the term and, more specifically, the emerging status accorded knowledge gained in particular and unusual circumstances. Before the seventeenth century, "experience" typically conveyed the Aristotelian sense of a collective appreciation of the way things are, what is universally acknowledged to be true. Rather than an individual's sensory impressions of material or social phenomena, formulated as an objective account—what is coming to be known in the period as experiment—"experience" indicated the sum of collective knowledge of the world, no matter how it was learned.[17] Experience was assumed to be universal, the basic facts of social and natural existence that could be assented to by any reasonable observer and that could stand as the ground from which to begin logical deduction. Experience thus underlay a largely static and fundamentally Eurocentric view of the natural world. There was, to be sure, another traditional view of experience that linked it to occult knowledge: an individual experience could record the exceptional or monstrous, thus giving a view toward nature's secret workings.[18] It was this latter meaning which would serve Francis Bacon, who would identify the unusual as particularly revealing and draw on it as a means to achieve practical utility, a movement from "miracles of Nature to miracles of art."[19]

Throughout the revels, the men of Gray's are instructed to attend to the particulars of their experience, to respond to them and incorporate them into the direction of the festivities.[20] Perhaps the best example here is the improvised consideration of the disastrous reception given to the Ambassador from the Inner Temple. Having been elaborately received by Purpoole on Innocents' Day, the Ambassador was to be entertained by some kind of witty and presumably decorous invention. At that moment, however, "there arose such a disordered Tumult and Crowd upon the Stage, that there was no Opportunity to effect that which was intended." The stage seems to have been crowded with men and women eager to involve themselves in the proceedings, leaving no room for whatever was to be performed. Ultimately the crowd forced the Ambassador and his train to leave, "discontented and displeased." Some disorder continued, and in response "it was thought good not to offer any thing of Account, saving Dancing and Revelling with Gentlewomen; and after such Sports, a Comedy of Errors (like to *Plautus* his *Menechmus*) was played by the Players." This was almost certainly Shakespeare's *Comedy of Errors*. Given that the night was believed to hold little beyond "Confusion and Errors," it was subsequently labeled *The Night of Errors*, thus indelibly marked by the substance of Shakespeare's play (21–2).[21]

Remarkably, the revelers decided not to dismiss the night but to take occasion to investigate what is at stake when their highly ceremonial and idealized theater is disrupted by the contingencies of experience. They established a commission of "*Oyer* and *Terminer*," and two nights later they held a trial very much in a form associated with canon law, the "*ex officio mero* prosecutions in the Court of High Commission."[22] The "color" of the trial reflects the confusion thematized in Shakespeare's *Comedy of Errors*: the charges insist that the abuses were not real but themselves theatrical, the result of "Sorceries and Inchantments [...] a great Witchcraft used the Night before, whereby there were great Disorders and Misdemeanours" (22–3). A particular prisoner allegedly responsible is arraigned, though he asks to answer with a petition of his innocence. The petition then wheels around on the Prince's attorney and solicitor, who are said to have "brought all this Law-stuff on purpose to blind the Eyes of his Excellency, and all the honourable Court there, going about to make them think, that those things which they all saw and preceived [*sic*] sensibly to be in very deed done, and actually performed, were nothing else but vain Illusions, Fancies, Dreams and Enchantments" (24). It is not clear from the text exactly what followed, but in general the court was "not a little offended" by the use of its proceedings to dissemble genuine confusion as enchantment, and by the hijacking of the power of petition to settle personal scores.

The upshot is that in the trial, as in *The Comedy of Errors*, what is taken for sorcery is discovered to be the reality of everyday, intractable social confusion—only that in the revels the confusion is even more intractable. In reading Shakespeare's play within the context of its performance at Gray's, Bruce R. Smith notes that *The Comedy of Errors* both indulges in an Elizabethan taste for medieval romantic idealism and ironically points to its own artificiality. Nonetheless, the play ultimately concludes with the affirmation of its romantic questor and lover.[23] It thus manages to explain away the confusions of social experience as temporary, a mistaken impression of sorcery and lunacy, even as it opens the possibility of the genuinely (and productively) miraculous. The trial that amounts to the play's "reception," however, effectively validates its initial picture of social existence as beguiling and chaotic. And unlike the play, with its release from the rigors of law, the court at Gray's insists that theater recognize and accommodate the difficulties of experience. Those who would have written off the Night of Errors as theater in a false or meaningless sense—"vain Representations and Shews"—are commanded to the Tower, while the man accused of building the stage and scaffolds, and generally inflating the audience's expectations, is pardoned. The theatrical court takes seriously the shock and disorder of particular experience, addressing it head-on as real and in need of acknowledgment while rebuking those who would minimize it. The court's insight thus results from a theatrical reflection upon the unscripted, and theater itself becomes a means of producing knowledge.

As central as theater also is to the subsequent effort to repair the breach with the Inner Temple, which includes the *Masque of Amity* and the celebration of the Order of the Helmet, the Gray's revelers remain ever self-conscious of the indeterminate nature of their ongoing experiment. Along with the *Masque of Amity*, the Order, the attendance of some of Elizabeth's court, an elaborate apology to the Ambassador by Purpoole, and finally various songs and dances, the night of 31 January also featured a more obviously political performance. Six lords from the Prince's Privy Council offer speeches on kingly conduct. The six orations are rhetorically elaborate, as is so much of the language in the formal speeches of the *Gesta*, but given the habitual expression of Elizabethan courtiers there is little in the counsel to indicate deliberate hyperbole or satire. Philip J. Finkelpearl believes that the orations were intended as "exercises in the high-flown, traditional rhetoric which the dramatic situation suggested."[24] Nor should the fact that the speeches flatly contradict one another be taken to mean all of them cannot be serious. They are, again, dramatic performances, demonstrations of and practice in the cross-currents that experience presents. Furthermore, in their combined demand that experience prompt consideration and investigation, the speeches reflect the mind of their author, Francis Bacon.[25]

In regarding the orations as exercises, we should avoid wholly reducing them to the scholarly exercise of *argumentum in utramque partem*. In the first place, the advice offered is not toward "any particular Action of Our State, but in general, of the Scope and end whereunto you think it most for our Honour, and the Happiness of Our State, that Our Government be rightly bent and directed" (32). The counselors are instructed neither to try to ingratiate themselves with the Prince nor to impress him with singular rhetoric; rather, they should offer a philosophy of state. The exercise neatly ensures a deliberative process rather than a defined outcome, much in the way that Joel Altman believes Elizabethan theater required audiences to evaluate conflicting phenomena.[26] It is also notable that the setting puts emphasis on the council and its variegated view of state rather than on the Prince and his consolidated authority. The counselors are placed at a table "set in the midst of the Stage, before the Prince's Seat" (31). Given the layout of the hall, Margaret Knapp and Michal Kobialka point out, the stage must have been centrally located and was almost certainly the same stage upon which the common players performed their *Comedy of Errors*.[27]

The six speeches promote, in turn, the benefits of war, the study of philosophy, the pursuit of "buildings and foundations," the amassing of wealth, the practice of virtue, and the indulgence in "pastimes and sports." Though pushing the prince in different directions, the counsels are obviously not mutually exclusive. In any case, the Prince's response reasonably introduces temporality over a strict and static dedication to one particular occupation. He admits the advice to be weighty and in need of a period of reflection; he also insists that the last case, in favor of playing, "fitteth the time," suggesting that the other ideas will find their place in time as well (41–2). This is all the more remarkable considering that the second speech, in favor of philosophy, so clearly anticipates the program Bacon advances throughout the *Novum Organum* and, most succinctly, in *The New Atlantis*. The counselor in the *Gesta* who argues for philosophy urges "four principal Works and Monuments": a library consisting of all "Books of worth," past and present; a "wonderful Garden" containing an impossible variety of plants, natural or cultivated, and surrounded by an equally expansive zoo, so that the Prince might have, "in Small Compass, a Model of Universal Nature made private"; a cabinet of curiosities, artificial and natural; and finally a "Still-house so furnished with Mills, Instruments, Furnaces and Vessels, as may be a Palace fit for a Philosopher's Stone" (35).

In fact, such works would seemingly subsume the points in the other speeches, cataloguing them not only as ideas in the library of possibilities, the first "work" described, but also enacting them as effects of the other three, in the forms of an extended empire, an eternal foundation, limitless wealth, an expression of wisdom and order, and a source of incalculable delight. Julian Martin has suggested that what Bacon here has in mind are institutions and that Bacon's response to the epistemological problems raised in the sixteenth century is typically institutional.[28] I would argue that the Gray's revels themselves support such an approach, though on a small scale. They attempt to create a theatrical world, orderly and ceremonial in nature, that yet can reflect what the revelers experience, advance what they know, and incorporate what they learn. If they are not themselves an institution, they certainly envision new aspects of experience that institutions might command.

It is little wonder, then, that the revelers worked so assiduously to prolong their reign and advance their credit. Faced with the beginning of the law term and the removal of stage and scaffolds from the hall by Gray's readers and governors, Purpoole takes to sea, so to speak. The students claim that the Prince has journeyed to Russia, and they set about staging a "return" in the form of an elaborate two-day ceremony. The loss of the hall was a major inconvenience, yet, as the author of the *Gesta* explains, the result was a successfully improvised response to necessity, an elevation of "rather what was performed, than intended" (53). The Prince's officers were summoned to Blackwall, just east of Greenwich, and then together the court rode down the Thames in fifteen barges, "bravely furnished with Standards, Pendants, Flags and Streamers," carrying musicians and trumpeters, and occasionally firing off shot. The company passed by Greenwich, extending apologies for not staying for the queen, and then proceeded from the Tower to Paul's, passing through a number of mercantile districts, and finally on to Gray's. In all, a ceremony that was intended to mark the Prince's absolute power over his far-flung provinces instead established the civic identity of a governor obviously beloved by the laborers, artisans, and merchants who populated the neighborhoods he visited and who, apparently, "thronged and filled" the streets.

If the Prince's reception suggests a basis of power and concern alternative to Elizabeth's, then a sumptuous masque staged before the queen at Whitehall two days later seemingly performs the opposite point. In the device, which marks the end of the revels, the Prince and his court are freed from a kind of material captivity by the superior influence of the queen. Nonetheless, if the masque ultimately institutes a return to the everyday order, it also suggests the vitality and utility of the students' experience outside of it. Written by Francis Davison, the *Masque of Proteus* is typically described as a conventionally iconic celebration of the cult of Gloriana, introducing the vague possibility of competing political pursuits but ultimately subsuming them in a universal love for Elizabeth.[29] Richard C. McCoy, however, has argued that instead of complete deference to Elizabeth the masque offers a "chivalric compromise, in which courtly pageantry simultaneously glorifies the exalted status and martial honour of these 'lords of liberty' while paying tribute to the queen."[30] McCoy cites Davison's connections to Essex and believes *Proteus* together with the "fighting at Barriers" that followed the performance provided Elizabeth a courtly reminder of the interests at court of Essex and his followers. In fact, the masque is less a compromise than a kind of truce: it accords to Elizabeth her traditional if exhausted images and associations but reserves to the Gray's gentlemen a competing realm of knowledge, practice, and power.

Following a hymn by Thomas Campion, the masque proper begins with an odd exchange between Proteus and an esquire to Purpoole. Esquire is surprised that Proteus enjoys music, for he had always assumed sea-gods were similar to fish, who take such small delight in song that philosophers doubt they can hear at all. This is, then, a masque drolly aware of its own theatrical license from the start. Proteus responds with a jibe at philosophical method:

Twas great Discourse of Reason, to regard
The dreaming Guess of a Philosopher,
That never held his idle buzzing head
Under the Water half an Hour's space,
More than that famous old received History
Of good Arion, by a Dolphin saved. [58–9]

Proteus advances the authority of experience against traditional natural philosophy, though such experience can be the province of "received" texts. The exchange would seem to have little relevance ("let that pass," Esquire says, and moves on), but the opposition between dreams and real knowledge runs throughout the masque. Its center is a bargain Proteus has struck after being restrained by Purpoole. In the retelling by the Esquire, who is described as an "Eye-witness" (61), Proteus' shape-shifting offers a series of challenges to the Prince that reflects his experience as a courtier more than a chivalric hero. Besides a physically intimidating serpent, Proteus becomes a "goodly Lady, passing fair," whom the Prince embraces "straiter in that feigned shape." Proteus also takes the shape of a rich casket of jewels, which the Prince scorns, and finally a picture of the Prince's own knights, wounded and distressed. Purpoole dismisses this, too, as a piece of empty theater. Having subdued Proteus, the Prince likewise rejects "huge Treasures, Ladies Loves, / Honour and Fame, and famous Victories," valuing only what can be obtained by "Sweat or Pain, Labour or Danger" (62). The Prince is a materialist, insisting on something of utility as his reward. His preference surely reflects the inclinations of the men of Gray's who, as law students, seek actual influence, which they can exercise less by place than by the control of economic and social resources that the legal courts afford. Proteus recognizes as much and promises the Prince "Th' Adamantine Rock" (62), situated under the Arctic pole, which as the lodestone creates magnetic north.

What Proteus is offering, then, is not something of inherent value but a tool. The rock controls iron, which to Proteus is more vital than gold, despite the attempt of "factious men" to displace iron and seat "Rebellious Gold in his usurped Throne." The rock is neither symbol nor magic; its own "touch," moreover, displaces the mysterious power of monarchs by offering command of navigation:

Thus hath this Load-stone, by his powerful Touch,
Made the Iron-Needle, Load-Star of the World,
A *Mercury*, to paint the gainest way
In watry Wilderness, and desert Sands. [63]

The result has been the discovery of that "new found World, / Whose Golden Mines Iron found out and conquer'd" (63–4). There is surely irony in Proteus' celebration of the age of iron before that of gold, and he further stipulates what he believes to be impossible: Purpoole can take possession of the stone only if he demonstrates a superior force. The Prince takes the challenge, as the Esquire relates, and even offers to enter into the rock as hostage, fully confident in what quickly transpires. Elizabeth, seated in the audience, is identified as the true power: "Excellent Queen, and true Adamant of Hearts." As a symbol of virtue and peace, she commands her courtiers' love, and from their love "their Motion springs" (64). Cynthia also displaces Neptune as true sovereign of the "heavenly Tides," and Britain itself becomes the true "rock" impervious to conflicting force (65). Acknowledging his defeat, Proteus opens the rock. The Prince and seven knights issue forth to dance, sumptuously dressed and accompanied by eight "pigmies" bearing escutcheons.

But while the masque extols the symbolic superiority of Elizabeth, it reserves to the gentlemen masquers power over a world beneath the ideal projections of sovereign and nation, the world apart from theater—or at least from courtly theater. Having rejected Proteus' shows in the first place, the men nevertheless enter from the adamant into the theatrical space of the masque. In the end, however, they return: "being done, they took their Order again, and with a new Strain, went all into the Rock" (66). That is, having met Proteus' conditions by deploying Elizabeth as icon, the Prince takes command of a material source of power, retreating for now from the theatrical space of courtly politics to what experience suggests is a more promising realm. Unlike the Hal of *1 Henry IV*, the Prince of Purpoole, whatever the value of his experience, has no hopes of one day holding the scepter. As a result, the attitudes of these characters toward first-hand knowledge of the material and social worlds differ. Shakespeare's Hal recognizes the potential power of experience, but as future sovereign he hopes to use the language of tapsters, drinkers, and thieves to forge an ideology of English fraternity, as he ultimately does among his "working day" warriors in *Henry V*. The men of Gray's, by contrast, attempt to put their experience of law, trade, finance, the natural world, and general social negotiation into the language of the court, if not always into the court's pattern of values. Over the course of their revels, the students suggest by turns that a knowledge founded on immediate encounters with the physical and social worlds might serve their monarch or, as in *Proteus*, that their experience might provide a source of prestige and profit apart from her largesse. The revels thus conclude, but in their moment the men of Gray's have held their heads under water long enough to hear a new strain, to create a knightly "order" that recognizes the utility of experience, and to project their knowledge as a legitimate source of authority in its own right.

Notes

1 *The First Part of King Henry the Fourth*, ed. Barbara Hodgdon (Boston: Bedford Books, 1997), 2.4.297–8 and 2.4.222. Subsequent citations will appear parenthetically in the text.

2 T.H. Vail Motter, *The School Drama in England* (London: Longmans, Green and Co., 1929), 86–7; quoted in Robert S. Knapp, "The Academic Drama," in *A Companion to Renaissance Drama*, ed. Arthur F. Kinney (London: Blackwell, 2002), 258.

3 On Falstaff's talent for parody and improvisation, see Hugh Grady, "Falstaff: Subjectivity between the Carnival and the Aesthetic," *Modern Language Review* 96 (2001): 609–23; on the play's economic language, see Sandra K. Fischer, "'He means to pay': Value and Metaphor in the Lancastrian Tetralogy," *Shakespeare Quarterly* 40 (1989): 149–64; and Nina Levine, "Extending Credit in the *Henry IV* Plays," *Shakespeare Quarterly* 51 (2000): 403–31.

4 For a survey of the various ways material life could shape early modern urban experience at the close of Elizabeth's reign, see the essays collected in *Material London, ca. 1600*, ed. Lena Cowen Orlin (Philadelphia: University of Pennsylvania Press, 2000); in his contribution, "London's Dominion: The Metropolis, the Market Economy, and the State," David Harris Sacks draws a sharp picture of the self-conscious shifts in social allegiances wrought by material life (*Material London*, 20–54).

5 Douglas Lanier, "'Stigmatical in Making': The Material Character of *The Comedy of Errors*," *English Literary Renaissance* 23 (1993): 104.

6 On the changing social backgrounds of Inns students, see Anne Jennalie Cook, *The Privileged Playgoers of Shakespeare's London, 1576–1642* (Princeton: Princeton University Press, 1981), 37.

7 For a description of Christmas revelry at the Inns, see Philip J. Finkelpearl, *John Marston at the Middle Temple* (Cambridge: Harvard University Press, 1969), 32–8; and A. Wigfall Green, *The Inns of Court and Early English Drama* (New Haven: Yale University Press, 1931), 56–96.

8 *Gesta Grayorum 1688*, ed. W.W. Greg (Oxford: Oxford University Press, 1914), sig. A2r. "The Epistle Dedicatory" appears within unpaginated front matter; subsequent citations to page numbers will appear parenthetically in

the text. We know very little about this initial publication of the revels, nearly 100 years after the fact. The *Gesta* was printed in quarto for W. Canning and contains no comment beyond a short dedication to Matthew Smith, comptroller of the Inner Temple. No manuscript exists. Nevertheless, given the printed text's mix of detailed description, letters, first-hand accounts, and plans for events that never came off, we can presume that the author or compiler was a participant and that he had at his disposal texts written by various contributors to the festivities. Desmond Bland provides a helpful introduction in his edition of the *Gesta Grayorum* (Liverpool: Liverpool University Press, 1968).

9 Finkelpearl, *John Marston*, 33–4.

10 On the growing prominence of credit in early modern England, see Craig Muldrew, *Economy of Obligation: The Culture of Credit and Social Relations in Early Modern England* (New York: St. Martin's Press, 1998). Theodore B. Leinwand examines theatrical representations of the social anxiety caused by the rise of credit in *Theatre, Finance, and Society in Early Modern England* (Cambridge: Cambridge University Press, 1999), 13–41.

11 For a discussion of the aims and effects of humanist drama, see Kent Cartwright, *Theatre and Humanism: English Drama in the Sixteenth Century* (Cambridge: Cambridge University Press, 1999), especially 12–20.

12 Paul Raffield, *Images and Cultures of Law in Early Modern England: Justice and Political Power, 1558–1660* (Cambridge: Cambridge University Press, 2004), 88.

13 Wilfrid R. Prest, *The Inns of Court under Elizabeth I and the Early Stuarts, 1590–1640* (Totowa: Rowman and Littlefield, 1972), 116.

14 See Victoria Kahn, *Rhetoric, Prudence and Skepticism in the Renaissance* (Ithaca: Cornell University Press, 1985).

15 For a commonplace view of the relationship between texts and experience, see Ben Jonson's imitation of Juan Luis Vives in *Timber: Or, Discoveries*, in *Ben Jonson*, 11 vols., ed. C.H. Herford, Percy Simpson, and Evelyn Simpson (Oxford: Clarendon, 1925–52), vol. 8, ll. 134–7.

16 For the changing representation of such conversation, see Jennifer Richards, *Rhetoric and Courtliness in Early Modern England* (Cambridge: Cambridge University Press, 2003).

17 See Peter Dear, *Discipline and Experience: The Mathematical Way in the Scientific Revolution* (Chicago: University of Chicago Press, 1995), 11–31; and his "Jesuit Mathematical Science and the Reconstitution of Experience in the Early Seventeenth Century," *Studies in the History and Philosophy of Science* 18 (1987): 141. For Aristotle's understanding of experience and the problem of particulars, see *Posterior Analytics*, in *The Complete Works of Aristotle*, 2 vols., ed. and trans. Jonathan Barnes (Princeton: Princeton University Press, 1984), 1.144.

18 For the medieval roots of this tradition, see Charles B. Schmitt, "Experience and Experiment: A Comparison of Zabarella's View with Galileo's in *De Motu*," *Studies in the Renaissance* 16 (1969): 86–92.

19 See aphorism 29 in book 2 of the *Novum Organum*, ed. and trans. Peter Urbach and John Gibson (Chicago: Open Court, 1994), 196–7. See also Paolo Rossi, *Francis Bacon: From Magic to Science*, trans. Sacha Rabinovitch (London: Routledge & Kegan Paul, 1968).

20 For examples of the growing weight accorded to experience by "traditional" humanists, see Cartwright, *Theatre and Humanism*, 14–17.

21 See Elizabeth Rivlin, "Theatrical Literacy in *The Comedy of Errors* and the *Gesta Grayorum*," *Critical Survey* 14 (2002): 73.

22 Raffield, *Images and Cultures*, 120.

23 Bruce R. Smith, *Ancient Scripts and Modern Experience on the English Stage, 1500–1700* (Princeton: Princeton University Press, 1988), 162–4.

24 Finkelpearl, *John Marston*, 41.

25 The speeches are ascribed to Bacon in *The Works of Francis Bacon*, 14 vols., ed. James Spedding, R.L. Ellis, and D.D. Heath (London: Longman, 1857–74), 8.341–2.

26 Joel Altman, *The Tudor Play of Mind: Rhetorical Inquiry and the Development of Elizabethan Drama* (Berkeley: University of California Press, 1978).

27 Margaret Knapp and Michal Kobialka, "Shakespeare and the Prince of Purpoole: The 1594 Production of *The Comedy of Errors* at Gray's Inn Hall," in *"The Comedy of Errors": Critical Essays*, ed. Robert S. Miola (New York: Routledge, 1997), 438.

28 Julian Martin, *Francis Bacon, the State, and the Reform of Natural Philosophy* (Cambridge: Cambridge University Press, 1992), 70–71.

29 See Stephen Orgel, *The Jonsonian Masque* (Cambridge: Harvard University Press, 1965), 17–18; and Green, *The Inns of Court*, 98–102.

30 Richard C. McCoy, "Lord of Liberty: Francis Davison and the Cult of Elizabeth," in *The Reign of Elizabeth I: Court and Culture in the Last Decade*, ed. John Guy (Cambridge: Cambridge University Press, 1995), 220.

CHAPTER 6

Fantastical Distempers:
The Psychopathology of
Early Modern Scholars

Sarah Knight

During the final decades of the sixteenth century, the Universities of Cambridge and Oxford witnessed an unprecedented explosion of satirical drama on college stages. The writers of university comedies relied on in-jokes, on a communal sense of texts enjoyed or endured as part of the academic curriculum, and also, more subtly, on shared professional and epistemological concerns facing both the student and the scholar. These erudite authors used comedy to discuss the effects that learning could have on scholars, drawing on contemporary writing on the humours, particularly those texts which discussed the emotional and intellectual repercussions of study on an individual's temperament. Through the exploration of psychopathology, university comedy and satire—rather than just offering recondite inkhorn entertainment for a college microcosm—deliberated on questions of contemporary epistemological value and on currents of institutional pedagogical reform. Both in these academic plays and in contemporary psychopathological writing, university authors discussed the social problem of graduate overproduction, linking this phenomenon explicitly with the perception that higher education was an inadequate preparation for life on graduation. At the same time, these writers represented the epistemological problem of how learning was thought to induce melancholy and dangerous fantasy. Authors who offered a discussion of such topics include Robert Burton, academic playwright and anatomist of melancholy; Thomas Tomkis, author of the Cambridge comedy *Lingua*; and the anonymous authors of the influential *Parnassus* trilogy, to name but a few.

These plays also reflected contemporary theatrical trends such as the late Elizabethan fashion for "humours" comedy, instigated by commercial London-based dramatists such as Ben Jonson. Taking Hippocratic and Galenic pathology as its foundational conceit, humours comedy rests on the idea that human personality is formed by a preponderance of a particular humour—blood, phlegm, yellow bile, or black bile—which in turn dictates both psychological temperament and physiological constitution, rendering the individual either sanguine, phlegmatic, choleric, or melancholic.[1] From Jonson's *Every Man in his Humour* (1598) onwards, many playwrights used this pathological system as a framework for dramatic characterisation. Academic drama provided an ideal forum for representing pressing issues facing the contemporary scholar, especially the impact his education had on his intellectual and social formation, as well as his prospects either within the university or upon graduation from it. The picture that emerges from these plays is complex and dark, as college dramatists link the melancholic humour in particular to the fate of scholars, debating at the same time the value and status of higher education at the end of the sixteenth and dawn of the seventeenth centuries.

When we consider psychopathological treatises, college plays, and key educational treatises such as Francis Bacon's *The Advancement of Learning* (1605) alongside each other, we gain insight into how ambivalent and, frequently, how potentially dispiriting for their writers and intended audiences these early modern representations of the epistemological and pedagogical aspects of higher education could be. These depictions of the psychopathological effects of learning engage both with the social problem of overproduction of university graduates and with the epistemological problems criticised by Bacon: according to Bacon's *Advancement*, young minds are especially susceptible to fantasy and melancholy unless effectively trained, a view we see represented in university plays such as Tomkis's *Lingua* (1607) and Barten Holyday's *Technogamia* (1617). The central problem examined in the psychopathological treatises and represented in the plays is that scholars were facing new difficulties and challenges at the turn of the seventeenth century. Consequently, academic writers argued both that psychologically dangerous influences such as the writing of poetry needed to be curbed, and that the higher educational system needed to be changed. They addressed this central problem using different methods of argumentation and representation, such as formal pedagogical critique, as we see in the *Advancement*, and as vivid onstage delineation of the problems students and graduates faced, as we see in several college plays of the 1590s and early seventeenth century, particularly in the *Parnassus* trilogy. For those philosophers and dramatists interested in the status of higher education during the early seventeenth century, the social and the epistemological seemed inextricably linked, and both appeared distinctly problematic.

The Humours on College Stages

Just as humanist academic playwrights earlier in the sixteenth century had adapted Plautus and Terence to a specifically academic setting, so later writers at Oxford and Cambridge mapped the humours onto the university world they knew. The *Parnassus* trilogy, performed at St. John's College, Cambridge, at the turn of the seventeenth century, shows how humours psychology became increasingly important in academic drama. In the Prologue to *The Second Part of the Return from Parnassus* (circa 1601), for instance, the character Defensor explains to the student audience what the play has to offer: "some humors you shall see aymed at, if not well resembled," acknowledging the debt to the London stage and implying that academic humours comedy will perhaps lack the lustre of its metropolitan counterpart.[2] Although not necessarily more complex in its characterisation, humours comedy at the universities was certainly more sophisticated in its incorporation and subsequent representation of contemporary psychological and pathological theories. Perhaps unsurprisingly, the authors of these plays were specifically interested in the aspects of humours pathology that were perceived to affect scholars. Consequently, in academic comedy written during this period, we see the theatrical representation of one aspect of humours pathology particularly relevant to the early modern universities: melancholia, described by its Jacobean anatomist Robert Burton as the "common maule" and "inseparable companion" of scholars.[3] What emerges from a consideration of these plays is an impression of increasing anxiety about the suitability of the educational system for training young men and preparing them for life, either within university precincts or outside its walls. University comedy offers a particularly interesting and complex perspective on this phenomenon of scholarly melancholia and the effect of learning on the adolescent mind. The representation of these symptoms and their causes on college stages corresponds to the widespread phenomenon of university graduates fearing both a dearth of jobs and a lack of opportunities for the appropriate deployment of their education.

This onstage representation of humours led in turn to a discussion of the problems facing contemporary scholars: a scholar's temperament, such plays suggest, results partly from his essential nature and partly from assimilation to the difficult circumstances many university men faced on graduation from the academic microcosm. The overproduction of university graduates in the late Elizabethan and the Jacobean periods, which has long been identified as an "economic problem of the church,"[4] was also of course a problem of the higher educational system and was discussed as such both by university graduates and by their contemporaries still ensconced within the academy. Crucial to this discussion was a debate over whether originality and creativity could stand the graduate in as good stead as a traditional education. Some dramatists took a sympathetic view of this phenomenon: in the *Parnassus* trilogy (circa 1598–1601), for instance, the playwrights represent how inadequately an early modern humanist education had prepared graduates for the world outside college precincts. Other dramatists, such as Holyday in his play *Technogamia*, adopt a more conservative stance, representing the imagination in their plays as directly antithetical to learning and genuine scholarship.

No clear picture emerges from these plays of how a young man's imagination might be either detrimental or valuable, yet this lack of representational clarity reveals a central uncertainty among contemporary writers and thinkers about how best to prepare a young man to enter the world outside the university. Such uncertainty suggests that no obvious solution existed either for the epistemological problem of young men ill-equipped by their education for a useful public life, or for the social problem of an excess of such young men pouring out of the universities and seeking positions. Bacon's *Advancement* represents one attempt to posit a clear solution, as we shall see, but the majority of other writers tackling the same issue—particularly authors of psychopathological treatises and of college drama—rather lament this socio-epistemological problem, however colourfully and intricately, instead of suggesting constructive and determined ways of solving it.

University playwrights such as Tomkis, Holyday, and the anonymous authors of the *Parnassus* trilogy, then, converted the contemporary commercial theatrical trend for humours comedy into erudite, allusive college plays that sought to explore the individual psychopathologies of students and scholars. Incorporated into these plays are equally significant meditations on epistemology and literary composition, unique to drama fomented in the intellectual and theatrical milieu of the universities. However inconclusive such meditations might be, through a close study of these plays we see how pertinent such questions were both to the dramatists and, we can assume, to the college audience. These university plays were not abstracted, precious entertainments far removed from the world of economic and social exigency but were, instead, vivid and urgent evocations of contemporary problems facing the scholar and, more specifically, the graduate. Dramatic representations of what was popularly thought to be the scholar's governing humour, melancholia, provided both a compelling exploration of an issue particularly pressing for members of the college audience, and an unprecedented means of depicting a fashionable strand in contemporary epistemological and medical theory.

Directly related to such representations of melancholia on the college stage is the debate over the proper role of the fantasy or imagination, which melancholia was commonly believed to fuel: this idea was derived from classical authorities and pillars of the curriculum such as Aristotle (regarding human thought and behaviour) and Quintilian (regarding the proper use of rhetoric) on φαντασία or *phantasia* (literally, in Greek and Latin, a "making visible"). This term also came to mean the mind's power to place objects before itself, or, more simply, the faculty of imagination.[5] In addition, early modern academic drama demonstrates a certain anxiety about the value of learning and the social significance of intellectual and cognitive functions, which related to the ongoing debate among students and recent graduates about how valuable a university education actually *was* in preparing its alumni for life in the real world, particularly in terms of finding professional employment. As a result, questions over the relevance of imagination and creativity in a world depicted as pragmatic and avaricious outside the university walls were debated on college stages, and the conclusions reached were frequently ambivalent, especially in the *Parnassus* trilogy, which offers a bleak account of several university students' efforts to find jobs upon graduation as well as a concerted critique of humanist educational methods.

The Psychopathology of Learning and Imagination

College dramatists drew both on contemporary psychopathological treatises and on the depiction of the humours on the commercial stage so that they could structure and deepen their representations of onstage melancholia. These treatises were the first to link melancholy with excessive fantasy, and the diagnoses of scholarly "weakness" they provide can be helpfully associated with how, in college plays, students and scholars were represented as sharply conscious of their own psychological fragility and social inadequacy. The influence of medical literature on university plays resulted in varying degrees of subtlety and profundity in treatment, and it met with differing kinds of dramatic success. In other media, although not yet in academic drama, by the end of the sixteenth century the equation of dedicated learning with melancholia had become almost commonplace, in pictorial art as well as in medical treatises.[6] One early example is Thomas Newton's *The Touchstone of Complexions* (1576). A grammar school headmaster,[7] Newton translated the Dutch physician Levinus Lemnius's *De Habitu et Constitutione Corporis* (*On the Condition and Constitution of the Body*), first published in Antwerp in 1561, and describes vividly in his translation the melancholy that particularly plagues "studentes which at vnseasonable times sit at their Bookes and Studies."[8] Newton, who had attended both Cambridge and Oxford during the 1560s, offers what would become a typical and much-discussed diagnosis of the detrimental effects of too much study:

> For through ouermuch agitation of the mynd, natural heat is extinguished, & the Spyrits aswell Animall as Vitall, attenuate and vanish away: whereby it commeth to passe, that after their vitall iuyce is exhausted, they fall into a Colde & Drye constitution.[9]

This medical theory of the attenuation of heat and vital spirits through overly zealous applications to one's books became fixed and embodied in the humours-based stereotype of the unworldly scholar, which can be located throughout early modern drama from Shakespeare's pedant Holofernes in *Love's Labour's Lost* (circa 1595) to the numerous complex variations on this theme in university plays. We can trace this character type to contemporary psychopathological treatises written by university scholars and recent graduates such as Newton, and so weigh how early modern academic writers—both in medical treatises and in plays—investigated and represented melancholia and its effects, exploring as a consequence the impact this "common maule" of scholars had on the process of literary composition and the epistemological repercussions of university life.

As well as in Newton's translation of the Latin author Lemnius, for the first time in vernacular treatises too we see a representation of the learned as being particularly prone to an excess of black bile and exhibiting its varied symptoms. A few years after *The Touchstone of Complexions* appeared, two Cambridge scholars published their treatises on a similar subject: Timothy Bright[10] published his *Treatise of Melancholie* (1586), followed by Thomas Walkington's *The*

Opticke Glasse of Humours (1607). This trend culminated in Robert Burton's *The Anatomy of Melancholy* (1621), the fullest and most searching discussion of the topic. These works and their authors have much in common: Bright, Walkington, and Burton are all careful to present their findings as the results of personal empirical observations of scholarly behaviour, a form of conduct which they expressly argue can develop within academic settings. Both Walkington and Burton, for instance, explicitly locate their discussions within their college studies, Walkington writing "from my study in Saint Iohns" and Burton "From my Studie in *Christ-Church Oxon.*"[11] In such treatises, we can view a richly detailed picture of a kind of melancholia that was of particular relevance to those embedded within institutions of higher education. Burton's *Anatomy* is particularly striking in this regard, since his discussion of one of the main symptoms of melancholy forms an important subsection of the work, "Loue of learning, study in excess, with a digression of the misery of Schollers, and why the Muses are melancholy."[12] It is no coincidence that during the same period we can identify a similar phenomenon of scholarly melancholia represented in university comedy. Scholars, both tutors and students, people early modern university comedy and, in academic humours comedies particularly, the pathologies of melancholy scholars are colourfully and searchingly portrayed.

The authors of these plays sought to turn pathological case studies into compelling characters. As a result, in these plays the more vivid, comic, or intriguingly complex symptoms of melancholia are foregrounded and, as in most college plays of the time, the dramatists use characterisation to examine ontological and epistemological issues of particular relevance to the student audience. It is axiomatic that early modern dramatists tailored their plays to fit their audiences, whether they were writing for a raucous group of spectators at an open-air theatre on the south bank of the Thames or for an ostensibly more refined crowd at one of the indoor theatres.[13] Similarly, playwrights at the universities included elements in their plays that were of particular significance for the demographic of their spectators. Various late Elizabethan debates about how and what to study, and about how and what to write, fuelled these plays, and, significantly, these debates arose from the meditations of men who had recently emerged from either Oxford or Cambridge, such as Thomas Nashe, George Puttenham, and Sir Philip Sidney.[14] As the relatively novel career of professional writer became an appealing—if precarious—option for university graduates, so the relationship between the training one received as a university student and the skills one needed as a professional writer (whether dramatist, pamphleteer, or poet) gained increasingly pressing importance. And so in university comedy at the turn of the seventeenth century we see these debates represented onstage, where abstract pathological and epistemological concepts became personified as dramatic characters. The representation of melancholia and its concomitant symptoms offered a means of exploring the importance and value of learning before a student audience, encompassing too the onstage opportunity to investigate the suitability of a learned mind to engage in profitable or significant literary production.

To see how these playwrights turned medical symptoms into theatrical characters, we need first to consider the pathological context these medical treatises offered for the representation of scholarly melancholia. One of the most problematic manifestations of melancholia was held to be an over-active imagination, "fantasy," one of the three internal senses located in the brain (along with common sense and memory), and particularly responsible for receiving and processing sensory impressions. According to Bright's *Treatise of Melancholie*, fantasy creates "obiects" that cause the thinker to act "against reason."[15] Locating the melancholic humour in the spleen, Bright argues that its "vapours anoyeth the harte and [pass] vp to the brayne," where the mind is grievously affected as the humour "counterfetteth terrible obiectes to the fantasie, and polluting both the substance, and spirits of the brayne, causeth it without externall occasion, to forge monstrous fictions, and terrible to the conceite."[16] Bright outlines the psychological symptoms of the condition, offering an intimate portrait of the melancholic's psyche. "Sometimes it falleth out that melancholie men are founde verie wittie," writes Bright, because "their spirits [...] are instruments of sharpnesse."[17] Bright paints a picture of a melancholic whose imagination is both creative and potentially debilitating. Similarly, among his taxonomy of the "conceits of Melancholy," Walkington defines a type of melancholic, "feculent and adust," that is to say, laden with impurities caused by an excess of the humour and dried up with internal heat, whose "minds also are so out of frame and distraught, that they are in bondage to many ridiculous passions, imagining that they see and feele such things, as no man els can either perceiue or touch."[18] In this particular case, Walkington's description recalls Newton's, showing how black bile can attenuate the vital spirits. These writers describe a specific set of psychological symptoms—sharp and discriminating wit, susceptibility to horrific fancies, and paranoia—which provided a theoretical basis for subsequent representations of melancholic subjectivity.

Both writers' identification of the power that fantasy exerts over the melancholic was particularly important. In medical theory, so in literary criticism: fantasy's function was discussed with similar ambivalence by late Elizabethan critics such as George Puttenham, who ruled in his *Arte of English Poesie* (1589) that fantasy was necessary for literary invention but warned that the would-be writer should not be governed by it:

> For as the euill and vicious disposition of the braine hinders the sounde iudgement and discourse of man with busie & disordered phantasies, for which cause the Greekes call him φαντάσικος [i.e., φανταστικός, phantastikos], so is that part being well affected, not onely nothing disorderly or confused with any monstruous imaginations or conceits, but very formall, and in his much multiformitie *uniforme*, that is well proportioned, and so passing cleare, that by it as by a glasse or mirrour, are represented vnto the soule all manner of bewtifull visions, whereby the inuentiue parte of the mynde is so much holpen, as without it no man could deuise any new or rare thing.[19]

Puttenham's description has much in common with Bright's description in his 1586 *Treatise of Melancholie*. Both writers argue that fantasy can be intellectually or creatively inspirational if well-ordered, and actively damaging if uncontrolled. Bright supplies a medical, humour-based explanation for why fantasy can spin out of control, arguing that melancholy produces overly vivid mental images that disorientate the perceiver, mirroring Puttenham's characterisation of an overly "fantastical" individual's thoughts becoming "disorderly or confused."

In the wake of such discussions, both medical (in the treatises of Bright and Walkington) and poetical (in Puttenham's *Arte*), the psychological and social role of an overly active imagination as a symptom of melancholia, and the influence of both of these mental states on scholarly life, became a central concern of university dramatists. The cognitive ideal, in all of these texts, was for the mind to be "*uniforme*" and "cleare" (to use Puttenham's terms): that is, for thought to be orderly, transparent, and rational, rather than dangerously motivated by unhinged fantasy. Yet it is the exceptions to this ideal that offered more substance for drama: in the medical treatises as in the college plays, scholarly life is represented as offering temptations towards the perilous soaring of the imagination, as a symptom of a specifically scholarly form of melancholy, and as a form of intellectual excess to which young men were prone.

Fantasy and Allegory in University Plays

The academic plays that treat these themes tended to be written within either an allegorical or a satirical mode. Before turning to how melancholia and fantasy were represented in satire, which was a dominant mode in late Elizabethan and Jacobean academic literary production, it is important to consider first why allegory lent itself to the representation of these themes. Allegory of course offers the opportunity for the personification of abstract concepts, and so we see fantasy (in Renaissance medical terms, an abstract cognitive faculty) start to become embodied in allegorically minded university plays. The idea for personifying the imagination arose from a contemporary poetic representation of the cognitive faculties in Book II of Edmund Spenser's epic romance *The Faerie Queene*. Within his allegory of Temperance, Spenser presents the fantasy explicitly as a force of melancholy. At the very top of Alma's House of Temperance, which represents the human body, live the three internal senses—common sense, memory, and fantasy—and the last poses a distinct threat to the "sober gouernment" of the body and mind.[20] As several university dramatists went on to do, Spenser personifies the fantasy as "Phantastes." Spenser's character inhabits a kind of phantasmagoria of the particular cognitive faculty he represents, where illusionistic images are painted on the walls of his chamber, "such as in idle fantasies do flit."[21] Crucially for future representations of the figure Phantastes within the university, Spenser expressly figures him as a young melancholic man sitting among the flies and alarming paintings: "A man of yeares yet fresh, as mote appere, / Of swarth complexion, and of crabbed hew, / That him full of melancholy did shew."[22] Spenser links fantasy not only to melancholy but also to poetic invention, representing Phantastes as essential for creativity. In his discussion of the importance of fantasy for the poet, Puttenham admits the possibility that he can retain control of his own imagination and the vividness of his ideas, but Spenser's allegory of the creative imagination offers no such safeguard. Spenser's ambivalence in his depiction of the fantasy set a precedent for literary representations of the interconnections between imagination, melancholy, and language.

A few years later, Spenser's representation of the internal senses directly influenced a play staged at Trinity College, Cambridge. In *The Faerie Queene*, after Phantastes and the other mental faculties are described, the House of Temperance is assaulted by the five senses. In the allegorical comedy LINGVA: *Or The Combat of the Tongue, And the fiue Senses For Superiority* (1607), the Cambridge playwright Thomas Tomkis expands upon Spenser's discussion of the relationship between the body, the senses, and the intellect.[23] Instead of discussing Tomkis's play in terms of humours theory, some critics have preferred to link *Lingua* either with allegories of the higher educational curriculum, with debate on contemporary psychopathology, or with Spenserian allegory.[24] Much more persuasively than these earlier readings, Carla Mazzio has argued that Tomkis shows how Lingua, the personification of the tongue and consequently of language, "disrupts the symmetries and hierarchies" of the human body.[25] Just as the senses assault Spenser's House of Temperance, Tomkis's play charts Lingua's efforts to enter the hierarchy of the senses. To distract attention from her schemes, she initiates a competition between the five external senses, while the internal senses comment on the action and seek to mediate the in-fighting that punctuates the play.

Even the settings for the play and for the epic romance are the same, for just as Alma's House of Temperance represents the human body, so *Lingua* takes place within the corporeal "Microcosmus." Similarly, Tomkis's Phantastes is clearly indebted to Spenser's creation, even in the description of Phantastes's costume and appearance: among Tomkis's characters, the college drama version of Spenser's young man with a "swarth complexion" becomes something of a dandy, making a vivid visual impact on the Jacobean college stage: "PHANTASTES. A swart complexion'd fellow but quicke-ey'd, in a white Satten dublet of one fashion, [...] and in euery place other od complements."[26] Flamboyant outfit and "od complements" aside, in Tomkis's allegory Phantastes is a simultaneously creative and disruptive force, one who exerts a subversive influence upon the mind. Throughout the play, Phantastes is linked with the cognitive and creative aspects of literary invention and, significantly, is also represented as a cause of melancholia.

Tomkis's Phantastes constantly complains that he is being asked for conceits and inventions. In this comedy tailored for student consumption, Tomkis makes explicit the link between the faculty of fantasy and student literary composition, that is, the kind of writing young university men might be supposed to engage in. In an oddly metatheatrical moment, Phantastes tells the other internal senses that a "Sophister"—an undergraduate in his second or third year of study—has visited him, asking "to borrow a faire sute of conceites [...] to appareile a shewe he had in hand."[27] By including such an obvious nod to his audience and their institutional context, Tomkis invites the student spectators to consider the role of the imagination, the "fantastical" part of the mind, within their own educational and epistemological experience. Tomkis continues to emphasise the link between Phantastes and creativity throughout the drama, as his character bemoans how all kinds of people constantly beset him, particularly poets, writers of ballads, and "Sonnet-mungers":

> PHA: Oh heauens, how haue I beene troubled these latter times with Women, Fooles, Babes, Taylers, Poets, Swaggerers, Guls, Ballad-makers, they haue almost disrobed me of all the toyes and trifles I can deuise, were it not that I pitty the poore multitude of Printers, these Sonnet-mungers should starue for conceits, for all *Phantastes*.[28]

Phantastes represents himself as a nurse of creativity, exhausted by his altruistic efforts to encourage the literary community. Through his ambivalent representation of Phantastes, however, Tomkis encourages his audience and readers to consider whether this dispenser of "Deuices, dreames"[29] (in Spenser's words) is really such a beneficial intellectual influence, which might cause us to question the impact of how such a potentially unsettling character, symbolic of a specific mental faculty, might affect young men. In Tomkis's play, fantasy is a dangerous but also an inspirational quality: Phantastes is a figure outside the university, but within the play there is a constant traffic between him and students wanting to borrow conceits. Tomkis's representation of the imagination is more sympathetic than that of many other early modern academic dramatists: he shows that imagination might be marginal to university study itself, but is nonetheless desired by students, and is strongly linked to academic experience.

In *Lingua*, two characters explicitly attribute to Phantastes the ability to cause vivid delusions and mental distress. Towards the end of act 1, the two senses Tactus (Touch) and Olfactus (Smell) argue: Tactus hopes to convince Olfactus that he (Touch) is no longer a threat in the combat of the senses, thereby lulling him into a false sense of security, and so Tactus says that he has become a melancholic, blaming Phantastes for his ailment. One of the play's gulls, Olfactus believes Tactus's story. Indebted to contemporary treatises on melancholia, Tomkis turns Tactus's performance of melancholia into a satirical burlesque of the humour's conventional symptoms. Olfactus notes "how melancholly he lookes."[30] Tactus, meanwhile, pretends to meditate upon human fragility and transformation: "Mans life is wondrous brittle," he says, "And many haue beene metamorphosed, / To stranger matters and more vncoth formes."[31] In a Hamlet-like rhetorical maneuver, Tactus moves in his speech from the general condition of humankind to his own specific case, passing quickly from "What a piece of work is man"-type considerations to a "Man delights not me" assertion, or, in Tactus's case, as a feigned melancholic, nothing in life delights him.[32] He locates the origin of his mental turmoil: "Lately I came from fine *Phantastes* house," and proceeds to describe the horrific delusions that have since plagued him. Tactus pretends to be convinced that he is made of glass: "when I beheld my fingers: / I sawe my fingers neere transform'd to glasse."[33] From Galen onwards, an overwhelming sense of physical frangibility had been seen as one of the primary symptoms of melancholia.[34] Walkington details a similar hallucination: "Ther was one possest with this humour, that tooke a strong conceit, that he was changed into an earthen vessell."[35]

In these treatises on the melancholic humour, imagined physical frailty signifies a sense of psychological vulnerability often experienced by young men in the academic plays, whether artificially (as in Tactus's charade), or more genuinely. In *Lingua*, through Tactus's cynical pastiche of melancholic symptoms, Tomkis represents at an allegorical level the damaging side-effects of an overactive mind. Olfactus identifies the negative aspects of melancholy and, perhaps most importantly, he singles out the power of the humour to detach its sufferer's thought from reality:

> See the strange working of dull mellanchollie,
> Whose drossy drying the feeble Braine,
> Corrupts the sense, deludes the Intellect.
> And in the soules faire table falsly graues,
> Whole squadrons of phantasticall *Chimeras*
> And thousand vaine immaginations [...][36]

Through Olfactus, Tomkis demonstrates an impressive grasp of Galenic pathology, filtered perhaps through contemporary vernacular treatises on the humours, using his knowledge to create a lively comic set-piece.

Yet the psychological implications of this piece of farcical pretence are more disturbing than the comedy might at first appear. *Lingua* offers a representation of how, in the melancholic's mind, "phantasticall *Chimeras*" replace accurate sense-perception and delude the intellect. Tactus's text-book melancholia is only a performance, yet following its Spenserian model, *Lingua* offers an unsettling treatment of the relationship between fantasy and the workings of the intellect. While showing fantasy in many ways as a positive force, Tomkis nonetheless chooses to preserve Spenser's ambivalence by making his Phantastes a force both of creation and of confusion. The character's proximity to the academy is emphasised, but his position is not stable, and he becomes a disruptive rather than a helpful influence on the young men and writers he advises. Through Phantastes's encounters with students and writers, Tomkis compels his audience and readers to consider the relationship between scholarship and invention in early modern epistemology. The play offers no comforting conclusions about this relationship, however, and by the end one is uncertain precisely how helpful an active fantasy and store of borrowed conceits acquired by the student writer are intended to seem.

Although ambivalent in its treatment of both learning and imagination, *Lingua* offers perhaps the most nuanced treatment of the character Phantastes that we see on college stages of the period. Later university comedies such as the anonymous Latin play *Susenbrotus*, first performed in 1615/16 by the students of Trinity College, Cambridge, offer a more cartoonish treatment of the personification of fantasy. *Susenbrotus* and the later play *Technogamia* are more conservative in their epistemological arguments, allowing no room for imagination within their view of the traditional academic curriculum, as Tomkis does. Following the tradition of earlier Cambridge plays, *Susenbrotus* contains many elements from Roman New Comedy: the clever slave, love-struck young men, and somewhat opportunistic women.[37] Alongside a conventional love plot, the play also charts the efforts of the pedantic grammarian Susenbrotus to produce a play. In the *dramatis personae*, Phantastes is explicitly described as "Poeta," and he is first introduced through the words of another character as one who "speaks poetically, sways poetically, and walks poetically."[38] When he finally appears at the beginning of act 3, Phantastes's first words are a quotation from Virgil, attesting to his learning while undermining his claim to originality.

We see a similar behaviour in the third part of the *Parnassus* trilogy when the character Phantasma can only quote Latin tags rather than invent any poetry of his own, whether in Latin or English. Phantastes's function in *Susenbrotus* seems merely to offer inappropriately fulsome quotations from Virgil and Ovid, and to behave as a caricature of a poet: sighing, languishing, scattering words over an indifferent beloved. He is no more ridiculous than most other characters in the play, but compared with Tomkis's unsettling, creative force, this later Phantastes seems flattened and more crudely drawn. Poetic invention in *Susenbrotus* is seen as a subject for mockery, not as a potentially destabilising force that is nonetheless intellectually desirable. As the seventeenth century progresses, the function of fantasy is increasingly represented on the academic stage as both damaging to intellectual endeavour, and as detrimental to the person motivated by it. Plays such as *Susenbrotus* emphasise the creative imagination as a thoroughly unstable force.

The Oxford playwright and translator Barten Holyday offers a personification of fantasy comparable to the Phantastes of *Susenbrotus*. Holyday also presents to his reader a reaction against extra-academic justifications of free-minded poetic invention. Holyday's *TEXNOΓAMIA: or The Marriages of the Arts* was first performed at Christ Church in 1617. Like the author of *Susenbrotus*, Holyday relies on masque conventions and departs from the allegorical physical setting of Spenser's House of Temperance and the "Microcosmus" of *Lingua*. By moving from the human body as a setting to the mythic "Insula Fortunata," the blessed island, Holyday shifts the play's emphasis from human psychology and physiology to a more remote and abstract place. In *Technogamia*, too, humours-based characterisation is not employed to such complex effect as it had been in Tomkis's earlier play, and the personification of the inner and external senses is not as carefully rooted in contemporary psychopathological theory. Holyday reduces the character Phantastes to a gaudy fop, whose dramatic purpose is to act merely as a foil to Common Sense, and whose representation offers very little in the way of psychological and intellectual ambivalence, as Tomkis's Phantastes had. Holyday's version wears what appears to have become the character's standard elaborate costume, in his

> branch'd veluet Ierkin with hanging sleeves button'd and loop'd, a short paire of Breeches, a greene Cloke with siluer lace, lin'd through with veluet, red-silke Stockings, party-colour'd Garter, a low-crownd Hat with broad brims, with a Peacocks feather in it, in a yellow Band, Gloues, and red Pumps.[39]

By 1617, of course, fabulous costume was a theatrical convention associated with the court masque, and Holyday's use of masque conventions was pronounced in other ways: his play begins with a static *tableau* of "a Heauen, and all the Pure *Artes* sitting on two semi-circular benches, one aboue another."[40] Masques, too, tended to end with an imposition of order, and Holyday's adherence to masque convention—in terms both of stagecraft and of harmonious thematic resolution— creates a somewhat more heavily didactic comedy, which perhaps explains why *Technogamia* was disdainfully received by Holyday's contemporaries.[41]

Holyday personifies the imaginative faculty to set up fantasy as a rival to the liberal arts and the rigours of the university curriculum; in *Lingua*, Phantastes is associated with intellectual activity and the academy through his involvement with the "Sophister" and the composition of college plays, whereas in *Technogamia*, Phantastes is presented as a subversive element who is *responsible* for contemporary scholarly degradation. He encourages scholars to dress in extravagant clothing and even persuades them to smoke.[42] To emphasise the point, and to associate the imaginative faculty both with a dubious profession and with a debilitating pathology, Phantastes is accompanied by the two characters Poeta and Melancholico. These three are opposed to the more scholarly characters within *Technogamia* representing the trivium and quadrivium: Logicus, Grammaticus, Rhetorica, and so on. Instead of the imagination being a potentially fertile intellectual function, in both Holyday's play and in *Susenbrotus*, imagination is set in direct opposition to educational values represented as both traditional and edifying. The fantasy, personified as Phantastes, directly urges students towards bad behaviour, such as smoking, considered particularly nefarious at a time when the king himself had inveighed against "the manifolde abuses of this vile custome of *Tobacco* taking."[43] Holyday, therefore, expressly identifies fantasy with subversive behaviour, conducted even after royal denunciation of such practices. Apart from *Technogamia*, Holyday devoted himself to translating the classical poetry of Anacreon and Juvenal as well as to sermonising. Considering his own literary habits, based more on imitation and on the use of biblical and classical models rather than on the exercise of creativity, it is perhaps not surprising that Holyday was less sympathetic to the value the imagination could potentially hold for a scholar.

While Tomkis's play explores a complicated relationship between fantasy, melancholia, and creativity, *Technogamia* reduces the melancholic to a one-dimensional type and Phantastes to a dandy. Through the description of the House of Temperance and the personification of the abstract senses respectively, Spenser and Tomkis both demonstrate that the use of an allegorical mode to explore contemporary psychopathological theory need not be reductive, but Holyday's play by contrast is full of episodes that render explicit the playwright's wish to represent learning and the imagination as starkly antithetical. In the first act, for instance, Poeta and Grammaticus physically fight, as do Melancholico and Logicus.[44] Tomkis represents the power of imagination within the *individual* self and, by extension, within the human mind, while Holyday's play deals only with generalized *social* functions of melancholy and fantasy. *Technogamia*'s resolution implies that fantasy is base compared to the more noble pursuit of the arts: in the play's Epilogue, the speaker suggests that the fantasy only yields a cheap trick, or "a nimble thing / To raise an Ignorant laugh." Addressing his "Ivdicious Hearers," the Epilogue imagines being challenged for having used such gimmicks:

> If any yet shall aske why he does bring
> A Hobby-horse, or such a nimble thing
> To raise an Ignorant laugh: It was his Art
> That said, This will expresse *Phantastes* part.[45]

Holyday's play debases the function of fantasy that writers such as Puttenham proposed as being able to provide "bewtifull visions" and devise "new and rare" subjects, and so *Technogamia* expressly negates the personification of the stimulating and inspiring imagination we find—albeit with some qualifications—in Spenser and Tomkis. Holyday's representation of Phantastes reflects an increasingly negative portrayal within academic drama of the value of imagination. In its place, new intellectual characteristics came to be prized, based more firmly on the other cognitive faculties, common sense and memory. Fantasy, by contrast, started to become represented as an affliction, a disease.

We can set these allegorical and obliquely satirical representations of fantasy on college stages against the psychopathological treatises from which many of their features of thought and conduct are derived; the representations of fantasy in university drama can also be usefully compared with contemporary epistemological works, such as Bacon's *Advancement of Learning*. These diverse, yet associated, forms of writing offer a multiplicity of contemporary perspectives on how early modern scholars should behave and think, and there is no clearly defined and consistent picture that emerges. This inconsistency is itself significant, stemming perhaps from a pivotal uncertainty in the psychopathological treatises in particular about whether melancholy and consequently fantasy are the signs of an active, questing intellect, or instead dangerous symptoms to be treated and eradicated. Such an uncertainty leads to a mimetic ambiguity on college stages, centring on the question of whether "Phantastes" is a disruptive force (as in *Technogamia*), a source of creativity (as in *Lingua*), or a spent force (as in *The Second Part of the Return from Parnassus*).

Satire, Scholars, and Melancholia

Allegory was popular on university stages at the time, but within drama and verse, an unprecedented number of English poets turned to satire during the 1590s to describe the academic milieu and, in particular, the effect that learning was often perceived to have on the minds of young men. Perhaps the most distinctive and flamboyant presentation of these themes can be found in the poems of the Oxford graduate John Marston, resident at the Inns of Court in London when he came to write his highly influential formal satires, the *Certaine Satyres* and *The Scourge of Villanie*, both published in 1598. Marston's poems provided valuable subject-matter for the Cambridge *Parnassus* playwrights, who represent with relentless pessimism the gradual debasement of the university graduate's mental faculties, including his skill as a writer and his ability to think creatively. Marston's personae in these two satirical works are based on careful self-fashioning as restless, intellectually brilliant melancholics: exaggerated fantasies, devouring anxieties, and an overwhelming sense of the futility of unimaginative learning pervade the poems, which are characterised by their speakers' conflicting attitudes towards the world around them, a world of shifting social surfaces. Marston transforms the conventional symptoms of a young man's melancholia into something quite new. His speakers cannot escape their governing melancholic humour.

Three years after Marston's two volumes of formal satire appeared, his satirical personae were dissected in *The Second Part of the Return from Parnassus*, a play which offers a fascinating perspective on the late Elizabethan world of letters. Just as Aristophanes satirically criticises his fellow dramatists throughout *The Frogs*, so the Parnassus playwrights mock their contemporaries and thereby conduct a subtle investigation into their writing. *The Second Part of the Return* mocks Marston's excesses even while it takes seriously his exploration of the relationship between scholarship and inventiveness. Consequently, two Marstons are presented in *The Second Part of the Return*: the malcontent "Monsier Kinsayder" and the swiftly corrupted "Furor Poeticus." Through these two types, the *Parnassus* playwrights respond to Marston's formal satires and comment upon his particular kind of literary melancholia. Literary satire in the *Parnassus* plays operates within several registers, ranging from crude to careful. At one point in *The Second Part of the Return*, the two university wits, Ingenioso and Iudicio, characterise Marston as a pissing dog: "What, Monsier Kinsayder, lifting vp your legge and pissing against the world? Put vp, man, put vp for shame."[46] Here, the playwrights present the more strident elements of Marston's malcontent personae in a deliberately reductive way; yet later in the play they attempt a more complicated critique of Marston's form of satire. In the first act, Furor Poeticus (poetic "inspiration" or "madness") is introduced as being *"rapt within contemplation."* If Monsier Kinsayder represents

Marston the snarling satirist, then Furor Poeticus symbolises the Marston who insists on "free-bred" poetic inventiveness. As we have seen, *The Second Part of the Return* has "aymed at, if not well resembled" a representation of the humours. Although the playwrights often neglect their declared theme, the character of Furor Poeticus is their most concerted treatment of humourous behavior.

At the start of the play, Furor Poeticus believes he walks among the gods, talking familiarly with the Muses and addressing Apollo as his teacher, calling him "Pedant" and "Don."[47] He is accompanied throughout the play by one "Phantasma" ("vision" or "dream"), a cognate term of "Phantasia," who quotes Latin; however, unlike the Phantastes characters in Spenser's poem and Tomkis's play, Phantasma is not a creative force, for the character cites the Latin of other authors, anticipating the Virgil- and Ovid-spouting Phantastes in *Susenbrotus*. It is typical of the cynicism of *The Second Part of the Return* that a figure which conventionally symbolises imaginative force can only quote Latin tags. Instead of encouraging Furor Poeticus in his contemplation and interaction with the Muses, moreover, Phantasma can only offer him raucous company in a disreputable area of London, Cheapside. And so when we next meet Furor Poeticus, he and the worldly Ingenioso are getting drunk. Somewhat unsteadily, Furor Poeticus quotes Marston, claiming that "that cælestiall fier within [his] brayne / That giues a liuing genius to [his] lines" along with his "intellectuall," have all become "dulled."[48] The recurrent narrative trajectory in the *Parnassus* trilogy describes the scholar's gradual moral decay and the ultimate prostitution of his learning, a pattern which Furor Poeticus follows. Ingenioso involves him in a plot to extract money from one Sir Raderick, an idiot gentleman. Poetry becomes nothing more than a means of earning: "let vs march on like aduenturous knights," says Ingenioso, "and discharge a hundredth poetical spiritts vpon them."[49]

Unlike the settings Tomkis and Holyday would go on to employ, the world of *The Second Part of the Return* is not an allegorical microcosm, and Furor Poeticus must make a living within the vicissitudes of late Elizabethan London. By the end of the trilogy, he has become completely corrupted and his language in the final scene is a degraded form of how he had spoken when we first encountered him, when he crammed his boastful speech full of references to the Muses, to Apollo, and to Mercury. His failure to find gainful employment as either a writer or an extortionist erupts in blasphemous slanders on the gods. Physically as well as intellectually tainted, Furor Poeticus describes a louse on his sleeve as "six footed Mercury": he initially wanted to write the story of the moon-goddess Cynthia and her lover Endymion, but now "siluer Cinthia" has become "my sluttish la[u]ndresse Cinthia," and Endymion her "squirting boy."[50] Slyly alluding yet again to a Marstonian conceit, the playwrights then present a debate over Furor Poeticus's fallen situation. "Is not here a true dogge that dares barke so boldly at the Mooone [*sic*]?" asks Ingenioso.[51] Philomusus, one of the scholar-protagonists in the play, diagnoses Furor Poeticus's condition, attributing the satirist's anger to poverty: "Exclayming want and needy care and carke / Would make the mildest spright to bite and barke."[52] Furor Poeticus has suffered the same fate as the other university graduates in the trilogy. Overeducated and undervalued, his initial idealism has become corrupted by exposure to the exigencies of life outside the academy. At the end of the play, the young students all fail in their hopes and expectations. Their retrospective attitudes towards their present situation are best embodied in Ingenioso's couplet: "For had not Cambridge bin to me vnkinde, / I had not turn'd to gall a milkye minde."[53]

Whether they choose an allegorical or a satirical mode, and despite the various conclusions they offer, many poets and playwrights connected with the institutions of learning at the turn of the century share a pessimism and a cynicism towards contemporary education. In *Lingua*, Tomkis identifies the importance of the imagination for the writer, but he also counsels against its potentially damaging effects, while Holyday's *Technogamia* offers a somewhat more simplistic version of a young scholar's tussles with melancholy and fantasy. The *Parnassus* playwrights, in contrast, chart the fortunes of scholars who ultimately fail in the dizzying array of careers they attempt after leaving the universities. From the 1590s onwards, literary evidence for academic disenchantment accumulates. University writers and recent graduates use a variety of genres to articulate intellectual frustration and occupational anxieties. The authors under scrutiny concentrate particularly on the figure of the intelligent young man and his response to the education he has undergone. By the first decade of the seventeenth century, their cumulative representation of academic experience seems shadowy and bleak.

Francis Bacon and the "fantastical distemper"

It was not just in satire and comedy that these grave repercussions of the early modern curriculum were critically considered. In *The Advancement of Learning* (1605), the Cambridge graduate Francis Bacon articulates similar concerns and presents an anatomy of the contemporary state of higher education, offering a theoretical discussion of many of the questions and problems that his peers had sought to examine in dramatic form. We have considered how contemporary satirists linked melancholia, learning, and illness, often in shifting, inconclusive, and ambiguous ways. Bacon was the first to resolve this particular ambiguity in terms of educational theory by outlining a new epistemological system that embeds the student or scholar firmly within a pedagogical framework intended to cure such dangerous "distempers of learning." Within the Baconian epistemological system, the causes of scholarly melancholy and excessive fantasy are eradicated, and simultaneously a persuasive argument is constructed for a new social system that values the truly learned rather than the imperfectly learned plagued by such "distempers." For Bacon, the epistemological problem—that university-taught logic, for instance, does not have any practical value—is directly related to the social problem that higher education does not carry much weight within (or is, at best, a poor preparation for) wider contemporary society.

Bacon, then, uses a medical metaphor to describe the problems he sees in the contemporary educational system, identifying at the start of the first book of the *Advancement* three "distempers of learning": the first, crucially, is described as "fantastical" learning, while the other two are characterised as "contentious" and "delicate."[54] "Fantastical" learning, for Bacon, arises from excessive credulity, rather than from the desirable alternative of rational and empirical comprehension. Bacon argues that young men are particularly prone to such intellectual ailments, and proceeds to offer an epistemological corrective to scholarly bad habits. Bacon goes on to ascribe "delicate" learning to an excessive love of *copia* and a privileging of words over matter, linking this with humanist rhetorical excess and arguing that such learning was fostered at the universities, so that the consequences have been grave. It was the humanists' mistake, Bacon avers, "almost [to] deify Cicero and Demosthenes" and the result has been that men "hunt more after words than matter."[55] Bacon's second distemper, "altercatious" learning, is caused partly by outmoded scholastic dialectics at the universities and partly by ill-advised exposure of the youth to logic before he can process it meaningfully. Bacon diagnoses as a curricular problem—the preponderance at the universities of ineffective scholastic and humanistic educational methods—that which college dramatists mainly *represent* as a social problem, and so Bacon offers epistemological and pedagogical explanations for why in his view learning needed to be advanced from its turn-of-the-century point of stasis.

Bacon compares logicians to spiders, writing that they rely on "infinite agitation of wit" to "spin out unto those laborious webs of learning."[56] This metaphor seems to have become conventional to describe the effects of learning on the academic mind: by the late 1620s, the young John Milton would figuratively chide a student embroiled in curricular intricacies for worrying too much about them. In his Third Prolusion, "An Attack on the Scholastic Philosophy," Milton states:

> the supreme result of all this earnest labour is to make you a more finished fool and cleverer contriver of conceits, and to endow you with a more expert ignorance: and no wonder, since all these problems at which you have been working in such torment and anxiety have no existence in reality at all, but like unreal ghosts and phantoms without substance obsess minds already disordered and empty of all true wisdom.[57]

To some extent, the scenario Milton creates is firmly embedded within a familiar humanistic criticism of scholastic method but, as the comedic and satirical examples previously discussed might suggest, it is no surprise that Milton the Cambridge student reaches the same conclusions that Francis Bacon does: namely, that demanding yet strangely "unreal" learning takes its toll on the academic mind, creating "torment and anxiety," causing melancholia and the detachment of the mind from reality, pushing it towards the realm of fantasy. For Bacon, writing a couple of decades earlier than the student Milton, the third "fantasticall" distemper of learning is the worst of all since the empiricist has no time for the deceptive if bewitching power of the imagination. Consequently, he demonizes the fantasy as a kind of lying, which "concerneth deceit or untruth, it is of all the rest the foulest."[58] *The Advancement of Learning* directly addresses problems in academic learning, and its author uses remarkably similar terminology to that favoured by contemporary college dramatists.

Bacon's epistemological agenda offers little flexibility about the incorporation of imaginative mental activity into his program of learning. Puttenham had written about what fantasy might offer the mind—"as by a glasse or mirrour, are represented vnto the soule all manner of bewtifull visions"—while Bacon distorts the same metaphor in order to describe a mind cursed rather than inspired by the "fantastical distemper." The "mind of Man," Bacon writes, is

> far from the Nature of a cleare and equall glasse, wherein the beames of things should reflect according to their true incidence; Nay, it is rather like an inchaunted glasse, full of superstition and Imposture, if it been not deliuered and reduced.[59]

The Advancement of Learning was published at a significant intermediate point between the railing satires penned by students and recent graduates during the last decades of Elizabeth's reign and the more allegorically fashioned, masque-like plays produced at the Jacobean universities. To some extent, Bacon provides answers to the questions contemporary early modern academic comedy and satire raised. Bacon characterises faults within contemporary education as "peccant humours that formed diseases," echoing the tendency of his contemporaries to equate intellectual flaws with governing humours, particularly melancholia, and its concomitant symptoms of an overactive imagination and unhealthy mental activity.[60] As a corrective for the "peccant humours" that beset contemporary scholarship, Bacon offers his "small globe of the intellectual world," evoking the "small world" of Tomkis's *Microcosmus*, the human body, which is also *Lingua*'s setting.[61]

The Advancement of Learning attacks the source of contemporary educational malaise, those institutions of learning that generated satirical criticism from their students and graduates, but Bacon also acknowledges the vulnerability and fancifulness of young men, and this, he argues, should make educators responsible for the epistemological methods they impart. Bacon's diagnosis of "peccant humours" and "distempers of learning" is in keeping with an exploration of similar themes on the university stage. Taking his argument further than contemporary psychopathological treatises do, Bacon presents as a given what writers such as Bright and Walkington offer only as a possibility: that excessive or misdirected study can adversely affect the mind. He examines how particular forms of learning can lead to the manifestation of unwanted cognitive and behavioural symptoms, such as an overly stimulated imagination, which limits the capacity for reason and for proper study, and transforms the mind into an "inchaunted glasse." Bacon's identification of faults within his contemporary academy as well as his suggestion of possible intellectual and curricular correctives directly correspond to the representation of similar themes in allegorical and satirical plays performed on contemporary university stages. Although the literary medium Bacon chooses is sharply distanced from both college comedy and formal satire, many of his conclusions mirror those represented in these other texts.

Brian Vickers has argued that Bacon "dramatises intellectual enquiry."[62] It seems equally apparent that playwrights such as Tomkis, Holyday, and the authors of the *Parnassus* trilogy literally dramatise currents of thought that we find in Bacon's theories of knowledge and of higher education, exploring through comedy and satire how contemporary humours theory could be applied to the academy, and representing in complex and unprecedented ways the relationship between psychopathology and learning. Through these representations, both epistemological commentators on the early modern academy and university dramatists articulated a growing concern that a traditional humanist education was not fulfilling the demands that a changing world placed on the university graduate. Central to this concern is the vacillation we see throughout these texts over the value of the imagination: the college plays in particular repeatedly pose the question of whether imagination and creativity will help the young man on his emergence from higher education.

Imagination or fantasy did not figure within the traditional university curriculum, and the debate over its worth was new. Apart from Bacon's direct criticism of fantasy as a "distemper" in *The Advancement of Learning*, few early modern authors on scholarship provide a clear answer to the debate over fantasy. By using humours theory as a starting point for discussing the psychopathological symptoms and rigors of learning, of immersion in university life, these writers attempted to embed a late Elizabethan and Jacobean social problem—the overproduction of graduates—within an intellectual and pedagogical framework, and to relate this problem to an educational corollary, the inefficacy of contemporary pedagogy. These problems are represented on college stages in terms of the effect of education on the individual, as either a critique (as in the *Parnassus* trilogy) or a defense (as in *Technogamia*) of humanist educational methods. Representations of the humours on college stages, particularly melancholia and its impact on the scholar and student, constitute a nuanced contribution to this early modern debate over higher education, its pedagogical causes, and its social and economic effects.

Notes

I would like to thank my doctoral supervisors, Lawrence Manley and David Quint, for their advice and guidance given when this essay was in its earlier incarnation as a chapter of my PhD thesis. I am also indebted to Jayne Elisabeth Archer for many illuminating discussions of early modern psychopathological theories, and to Philip Shaw for his keen-eyed reading and invaluable suggestions.

1   See Lawrence Babb, *The Elizabethan Malady: A study of melancholia in English literature from 1580 to 1642* (East Lansing: Michigan State College Press, 1951), Chapter 1, "The Physiology and Psychology of the Renaissance,"

especially 2–3. For a discussion of the medical curriculum at the early modern English universities, and the reading and teaching of Hippocrates and Galen, see Gillian Lewis, "The Faculty of Medicine," in *The Collegiate University*, ed. James McConica (Oxford: Clarendon, 1986), 213–56, vol. 3 of *The History of the University of Oxford*, 8 vols., 1984–97.

2 *The Second Part of the Return from Parnassus*, Prologue, ll. 32–3. All quotations from the *Parnassus* trilogy are to through-line numbers in *The Three Parnassus Plays (1598–1601)*, ed. J.B. Leishman (London: Ivor Nicholson & Watson Ltd., 1949).

3 Robert Burton, *Anatomy of Melancholy*, Part 1, Section 2, Mem. 3, Subs. 15 (p. 302). Unless stated otherwise, citations are taken from *The Anatomy of Melancholy*, 6 vols., ed. Thomas C. Faulkner, Nicholas K. Kiessling, and Rhonda L. Blair, intro. J.B. Bamborough (Oxford: Clarendon, 1989–2000).

4 See Christopher Hill, *Economic Problems of the Church: From Archbishop Whitgift to the Long Parliament* (Oxford: Clarendon, 1956).

5 For discussions of *phantasia* in Platonic and Aristotelian philosophies of mind, see Hendrik Lorenz, *The Brute Within: Appetitive Desire in Plato and Aristotle* (Oxford: Clarendon, 2006); and Ned O'Gorman, "Aristotle's Phantasia in the *Rhetoric*: Lexis, Appearance, and the Epideictic Function of Discourse," *Philosophy and Rhetoric* 38 (2005): 16–40. See also Charles B. Schmitt, *John Case and Aristotelianism in Renaissance England* (Kingston: McGill-Queen's University Press, 1983).

6 See Rudolf Wittkower and Margot Wittkower, *Born Under Saturn: The Character and Conduct of Artists* (New York: Norton, 1969), 98–132, especially 102–108.

7 Gordon Braden, "Newton, Thomas (1544/5–1607)," *Oxford Dictionary of National Biography* (Oxford University Press, 2004), <http://www.oxforddnb. com/view/article/20069>.

8 See Lemnius, *De Habitu et Constitutione Corporis* (Antwerp: Apud Guilielmum Simonem, 1561): "Est enim maxima hominum ineunte vere & autumno, quibus anni temporibus is humor redundat atque effunditur, melancholicis affectibus obnoxia, præsertim qui rebus politicis aut studijs literarum atque intempestiuis lucubrationibus sunt addicti" (sigs. 127v–128r). For ownership of Lemnius's works in individual scholars' libraries at sixteenth-century Cambridge and Oxford, see Mordechai Feingold, *The mathematicians' apprenticeship: Science, universities and society in England, 1560–1640* (Cambridge: Cambridge University Press, 1984), 116–18.

9 Thomas Newton, *The Touchstone of Complexions* (London: by Thomas Marsh, 1576), sig. 136v. See Lemnius, *De Habitu et Constitutione Corporis*: "Siquidem ex immoderata mentis agitatione natiuus calore extinguitur, ac spiritus quum animalis, tum vitales attenuati euanescunt, quo fit vt exhausto vitali succo ad frigidum siccumque habitum deuergant" (sig. 128r).

10 Bright (circa 1551–1615) matriculated at Trinity College in 1561, took his B.A. in 1568, his M.B. in 1574, and his M.D. in 1576. He lectured in Cambridge

until 1584, when he took up residence in Ipswich. See Page Life, "Bright, Timothy (1549/50–1615)," *Oxford Dictionary of National Biography* (Oxford University Press, 2004), <http://www.oxforddnb.com/view/article/3424>.

11 Timothy Bright, *Treatise of Melancholie* (London: by Thomas Vautrollier, 1586), sig. *vv; Thomas Walkington, *The Optick Glasse of Humours* (London: by Iohn Windet for Martin Clerke, 1607), sig. ¶6r; Robert Burton, *The Anatomy of Melancholy* (Oxford: by Iohn Lichfield and Iames Short, for Henry Cripps, 1621) sig. Ddd 3v.

12 For a discussion of this section of the *Anatomy*, see Sarah Knight, "'He is indeed a kind of Scholler-Mountebank': Academic Liars in Jacobean Satire," in *Shell Games: Studies in Scams, Frauds, and Deceits (1300–1650)*, ed. Mark Crane, Richard Raiswell, and Margaret Reeves (Toronto: Centre for Reformation and Renaissance Studies, 2004), 75–8.

13 See Andrew Gurr, *Playgoing in Shakespeare's London*, 2d edn. (Cambridge: Cambridge University Press, 1996), 60–80.

14 Key works that address such questions are Philip Sidney, *The Defence of Poesy* (written circa 1582–83); Thomas Nashe's preface, "To the Gentleman Students of Both Universities," affixed to Robert Greene's *Menaphon* (1589); and George Puttenham's *The Arte of English Poesie* (1589).

15 Bright, *Treatise*, 102.

16 Bright, *Treatise*, 126.

17 Bright, *Treatise*, 126.

18 Walkington, *Optick Glasse*, 69.

19 George Puttenham, *The Arte of English Poesie. Contriued into three Bookes: The first of Poets and Poesie, the second of Proportion, the third of Ornament* (London: by Richard Field, 1589), sig. Diijv.

20 Edmund Spenser, *The Faerie Queene*, ed. Thomas P. Roche, Jr. (Harmondsworth: Penguin, 1987), II.ix.1.

21 Spenser, *Faerie Queene*, II.ix.49.

22 Spenser, *Faerie Queene*, II.ix.52. Compare Newton, *The Touchstone of Complexions*, sig. 69r, in which the melancholic is described as "swarte."

23 Thomas Tomkis entered Trinity College, Cambridge, in 1597 and received his B.A. in 1600, becoming a minor Fellow in 1602, and an M.A. and major Fellow in 1604.

24 See G.C. Moore Smith, *College Plays Performed in the University of Cambridge* (Cambridge: Cambridge University Press, 1923), 8: "In the first twenty years of the seventeenth century there was a curious revival of the morality-type play, in which the characters were abstract conceptions."

25 Carla Mazzio, "Sins of the Tongue," in *The Body in Parts: Fantasies of Corporeality in Early Modern Europe*, ed. David Hillman and Carla Mazzio (New York: Routledge, 1997), 53–80, especially 65. See also the forthcoming critical edition of *Lingua* edited by Carla Mazzio and Anne Lake Prescott.

26 Thomas Tomkis, LINGVA: *Or The Combat of the Tongue, And the fiue Senses For Superiority* (London: by G. Eld, for Simon Waterson, 1607), sigs. Dv–D2r.

27 Tomkis, *LINGVA*, sig. D4v.

28 Tomkis, *LINGVA*, sig. D2v.

29 Spenser, *Faerie Queene*, II.ix.51.

30 Tomkis, *LINGVA*, sig. B3v.

31 Tomkis, *LINGVA*, sig. B3v.

32 See Hamlet's speech to Rosencrantz and Guildenstern, *Hamlet*, ed. Ann Thompson and Neil Taylor (London: Arden Shakespeare, 2006), 2.2.261–76, in which he explains the reasons for his loss of mirth.

33 Tomkis, *LINGVA*, sig. B4r.

34 See Babb, *Elizabethan Malady*, 43.

35 Walkington, *Optick Glasse*, sig. 69v.

36 Tomkis, *LINGVA*, sig. B4r.

37 See "Introduction," in *A Comedy Called Susenbrotus*, ed. and trans. Connie McQuillen (Ann Arbor: University of Michigan Press, 1997), 22–3; for discussions of the influence of Roman New Comedy on early modern academic drama, see Frederick S. Boas, *University Drama in the Tudor Age* (New York: Benjamin Blom, 1971), 15–21, 108; and Bruce R. Smith, *Ancient Scripts and Modern Experience on the English Stage 1500–1700* (Princeton: Princeton University Press, 1988), 157–77.

38 *Susenbrotus*, 1.3 (72): because McQuillen's translation lacks line numbers, I have supplied the page number after act and scene. FORTUNIA: "Alter Phantastes poeta est qui poetice loquitur: nutat poetice et poetice ambulat."

39 Barten Holyday, *TEXNOΓAMIA: or the Marriages of the Arts* (London: by William Stansby for Iohn Parker, 1618). All quotations from *Technogamia* are to through-line numbers in Barten Holyday, *Technogamia: or the Marriages of the Arts*, ed. Sister M. Jean Carmel Cavanaugh (Washington, DC: The Catholic University of America Press, 1942), ll. 15–20. See John R. Elliott, Jr., and Alan H. Nelson (University), Alexandra F. Johnston and Diana Wyatt (City), eds., *Records of Early English Drama: Oxford*, 2 vols. (Toronto: University of Toronto Press, 2004), 2.823 for performance details (hereafter cited as *REED: Oxford*).

40 Holyday, *Technogamia*, Prologue, marginal s.d.

41 See *REED: Oxford*, "Appendix 2," 2.772–89, for contemporary satirical responses to Holyday's play; see also Anthony à Wood's *Athenæ Oxonienses*, 4 vols., ed. Philip Bliss (London: for F.C. and J. Rivington, 1813–20), 3.522: Wood describes the play as "too grave for the king, and too scholastic for the auditory."

42 See Holyday, *Technogamia*, ll. 474–5, 445–7.

43 James VI and I, *A Counterblaste to Tobacco* (London: by R.B., 1604), sig. B1r.

44 Holyday, *Technogamia*, l. 550 ff.

45 Holyday, *Technogamia*, Epilogue, ll. 10–13.

46 *Second Part of the Return*, ll. 267–8.

47 *Second Part of the Return*, ll. 450, 464.

48 *Second Part of the Return*, ll. 1301–3.
49 *Second Part of the Return*, ll. 1377–9.
50 *Second Part of the Return*, ll. 2078, 459, 2135, 2137.
51 *Second Part of the Return*, ll. 2141–2.
52 *Second Part of the Return*, ll. 2143–4.
53 *Second Part of the Return*, ll. 2180–81.
54 Francis Bacon, *The Advancement of Learning*, ed. Michael Kiernan (Oxford: Clarendon, 2000), 23.
55 Bacon, *Advancement*, 24.
56 Bacon, *Advancement*, 28.
57 John Milton, "An Attack on the Scholastic Philosophy," in *Complete Prose Works*, 8 vols., ed. Don M. Wolfe et al. (New Haven: Yale University Press, 1953–82), 1.245.
58 Bacon, *Advancement*, 28.
59 Bacon, *Advancement*, 116.
60 Bacon, *Advancement*, 31.
61 Bacon, *Advancement*, 221.
62 Brian Vickers, *Francis Bacon and Renaissance Prose* (Cambridge: Cambridge University Press, 1968), 200.

CHAPTER 7

Cambridge at Sea:
Byrsa Basilica and the
Commercialization of Knowledge

Helen Higbee

John Ricketts's *Byrsa Basilica, Seu Regale Excambium* (*The Royal Exchange*) (circa 1633) is a Latin Cambridge University play that was never printed in the period, possibly never produced, and has hardly been the subject of more than a footnote since it was translated and published by R.H. Bowers in 1939.[1] Yet the play's startling imposition of a classical framework onto a contemporary economic subject raises questions about the pedagogical uses to which Latin drama was put at the universities. In particular, the mercantile subject-matter of this academic play takes up issues that often preoccupy the popular theater and then imports them to the university, making the literary and socio-economic spheres of production interpenetrate with the production of knowledge.[2] Set in the Royal Exchange, the play takes as its model Plautine comedy and as its subject the transactions, machinations, and anxieties of London merchants, factors, mountebanks, and insurers. A Prologue, Interlocution, and Epilogue are spoken by Mercury, the god of both linguistic and manual dexterity and thus the deity of traders and thieves. Mercury's temple is the Exchange itself and, in addressing his academic audience, he makes frequent allusions to the similarities between life in the Exchange and life in the university: "ingenii pari / Acumine artes si tractentur, et lucra" (ll. 64–5 ["learning should be conducted with equal sharpness of talent as gain"]).

This mercantile setting is not merely atmospheric but is integral to the plot: in act 3, three characters engage in a lengthy discussion of the moral problems and practical merits of marine insurance, which was the main business transacted in London's Royal Exchange from its founding in 1570; the play also provides examples of the two primary "instruments" of the insurance business, the insurance policy (ll. 1104–10) and the bill of exchange (ll. 370–79),[3] and the character Rialto is based on the historical founder of the Exchange, Sir Thomas Gresham.[4] The mercantile setting of *Byrsa Basilica* and the issues it addresses were not unknown to the commercial stage, whose famous early specimens of city comedy include Thomas Heywood's *Four Prentices of London* (circa 1592) and Thomas Dekker's *The Shoemaker's Holiday* (1599), but as far as extant records show the play is an exception to the usual dramatic fare of Cambridge University in the early seventeenth century. The obscurity and peculiarity of Ricketts's play are probably the factors that have condemned it to the critical cold shoulder, the assumption being that the play was unpopular because it was peculiar, making it an anomaly of little cultural importance. But I argue that the play served three pedagogical functions: it taught student readers and performers the conventions of formal disputation, Latin grammar, and versification, like much other academic drama; it familiarized them with some of the intricacies of London business life; and it advanced a progressive viewpoint on the related debates about the merits of judicial astrology and the emerging practice of insurance. The play's impetus might partly be explained through the curricular changes taking place at the universities in the early seventeenth century, which its action draws on, inflects, and advances. In addition, by asserting the rhetorical quality of commercial culture, the play demonstrates how trade relies upon just the sort of skillful rhetoric that students acquire at university. Finally, in its casting of trade as a form of state service, *Byrsa Basilica* opens up the possibility of a nontraditional way in which scholars might serve the commonweal.

The manuscript text of this play "is unique, and [...] apparently in the same hand as the parish register of All Saints', Worcester, started in 1641 by John Ricketts, who is presumably the author of the play."[5] Very little is known of Ricketts: a John Ricketts was admitted to Emmanuel College in 1623 and, moving to Jesus College, he earned a B.A. in 1625–26 and an M.A. in 1629, then becoming rector of All Saints' Church in Worcester in 1633, the presumed date of the play.[6] The Cambridge play manuscript made it into Oxford's Bodleian Library by passing through two collections, those of Archbishop William Sancroft (1617–93) and Bishop Thomas Tanner (1674–1735). Sancroft's uncle was Master of Emmanuel College from 1628–37, and Sancroft himself was admitted to Emmanuel in 1633 and graduated B.A. in 1637, going on to become a Fellow of the college and a tutor in 1642, then College Bursar in 1644. A royalist and an antiquarian, Sancroft had amassed a huge collection of literary materials, including important documents related to the civil war. Three hundred manuscripts belonging to Sancroft came into the ownership of Thomas Tanner, an Oxford antiquarian and author. Upon his death, Tanner bequeathed to the Bodleian his entire collection of printed books and manuscripts, which had been housed in Christ Church, Oxford.[7]

Apparently, there is no mention of *Byrsa Basilica* or John Ricketts in the extant writings of either of these collectors, and the manuscript was unconnected with any other works in the Sancroft papers. Sancroft and/or his uncle may have known Ricketts at Cambridge, judging by their concurrent dates there, which might explain Sancroft's possession of the manuscript. Since internal evidence dates the play in the same year that Ricketts left Cambridge and if, according to Bowers, the manuscript was written hurriedly, perhaps it was a farewell presentation copy for his old college. Sancroft's possession of the manuscript and his long tenure at Emmanuel suggest that it remained at the university for the edification of the students rather than being taken to Worcester by the author.

The performance history of the play is equally meager. Bowers suggests that one reason why the play has so many characters (twenty) is to provide parts for a greater number of student actors.[8] But following the entry for this play in *Records of Early English Drama: Cambridge* is a note stating that, though Jesus College has been suggested, "no performances are recorded for Jesus after 1598–99 except for a possible performance of 1613–14 and a certain performance of 1622–23."[9] The mere fact that no expenditures were recorded for a production of the play, however, does not allow us to conclude that it was not studied, read aloud dramatically, or even performed privately by students; it is likely that students could stage a play without generating expenditures. G.C. Moore Smith discusses the possibility that costly stage-houses did not need to be constructed for all performances: perhaps "for the performance, structures or partitions already existing in the hall were adapted to stage purposes and obviated the need of building stage houses *ad hoc*."[10] Smith also notes that "the actors' garments were kept from year to year in a chest," and so might have been available for performance.[11] H.R. Woudhuysen points out that "copying [of parts] for college productions was undertaken by members of the university rather than by professional scribes," eliminating another expense that would have been recorded in the account books.[12] Thus, neither the history of the manuscript nor that of its performances bars us from concluding, provisionally, that it was circulated and performed at Cambridge.

Dramatic activity at Cambridge University has a very long history, the earliest recorded reference of expenditures for a performance being in the King's College accounts of 1482.[13] Frederick S. Boas explains the students' need for "ludi" of all sorts:

> It was inevitable that academic societies whose members were in residence all the year round, and who needed some outlet for high spirits at holiday times, should have taken some part in the extraordinary series of mummings and disguisings, known in different forms as the Feast of Fools, the Boy Bishop, the Christmas Prince, the Lord of Misrule and the like.[14]

Outside players were also often invited and paid to perform at King's College in the fifteenth century, and, though administrative opposition against visiting players grew from the 1570s through the '90s,[15] Shakespeare's companies visited Cambridge in 1591, 1594, and 1607.[16] In 1510–11, notes Alan H. Nelson, "King's Hall staged a comedy of *Terence*, the first known play by a classical author performed by any college in either Cambridge or Oxford."[17] The mid-sixteenth century was the apex of dramatic production at Cambridge, when the majority of plays performed there were classical in origin, though some were contemporary Latin plays based on classical models, and fewer were contemporary English plays—*Gammer Gurton's Needle* is a famous example of this last group, performed at Christ's College in 1550. Classical plays later gave way to contemporary histories and satires:

Topical satire surfaced in attacks on the mayor by Thomas Mudd in 1582–83, and in attacks on townspeople in *Club Law* at the turn of the century. *Pedantius*, a satire on the pedant Gabriel Harvey by Edward Forcett of Trinity College in 1580–81, gained a national reputation.[18]

In the Jacobean period, performances began to dwindle, though there were performances for King James I in 1614–15, and for other members of the royal family in subsequent years up to 1642, when "the puritan spirit, embodied in the harsh words of Milton, brought Cambridge drama temporarily to a halt."[19] But Ricketts must have seen at least some plays during his tenure at Cambridge.

In addition to their entertainment value, plays were of course understood to have specific educational purposes for university students. Writing and/or performing in Greek and Latin dramas grounded students in classical learning and helped prepare them for public life, as Oxford playwright William Gager writes in 1592:

> [Plays serve] to practice our own style either in prose or verse; to be well acquainted with Seneca or Plautus; honestly to embolden our path; to try their voices and confirm their memories; to frame their speech; to conform them to convenient action; to try what mettle is in every one, and of what disposition they are of; whereby never any one amongst us, that I know, was made the worse, many have been much the better.[20]

Thomas Heywood, referring to his own experiences at Cambridge, concurs in his *AN APOLOGY for Actors*:

> this is held necessary for the emboldening of their *Iunior* schollers, to arme them with audacity, against they come to bee imployed in any publicke exercise [...] It teacheth audacity to the bashfull Grammarian, beeing newly admitted into the priuate Colledge, and after matriculated and entred as a member of the Vniuersity, and makes him a bold Sophister, to argue *pro et contra*, to compose his Sillogismes [...] to reason and frame a sufficient argument to proue his questions [...].[21]

Heywood here also points out a more immediate benefit of plays: they help students prepare to meet one of the primary requirements of the university, the disputation.[22] The disputation was a formal, public argument between students on a controversial point from one of the scholastic fields of study. Required to engage in at least four disputations during their tenure, students were given the topics, given or asked to choose a position "*pro et contra*," and they then prepared syllogistic arguments to promote their side and counter-arguments to answer the opposing student. They were required to argue forcefully and with "audacity" to persuade their audience of their conviction and truthfulness, yet their speech and actions were to seem natural.[23] Watching or performing in plays such as *Byrsa Basilica* taught the student a kind of *sprezzatura*, how "to keepe a decorum in his countenance," "to fit his phrases to his action, and his action to his phrase."[24]

Written in iambic Latin and full of classical allusions, contemporary situations, and current debates, *Byrsa Basilica* would have well-suited these educational goals.

As plays like the *Parnassus* trilogy and *Club Law* demonstrate, drama written by college fellows for their students was often progressive, topical, satirical, and bitingly self-aware. Yet the subject of Ricketts's play—marine insurance—is indeed anomalous when compared to that of other Cambridge plays of the period. For instance, an Oxford play whose title hints that it might have similar subject-matter, *Mercurius Rusticans* (circa 1605–18), is about three penniless Oxford students left behind at their college on Christmas vacation; they travel to a nearby town and play a series of tricks on the ignorant villagers. Another "mercurial" Oxford drama, John Blencowe's *Mercurius Sive Literarum Lucta* (1629), is a mythological play in which Mercury and Jupiter fight a great battle. When Jupiter wins he asks the Fates to decide an appropriate punishment for Mercury; they decree that Mercury and all who follow him (i.e., scholars) will be eternal paupers. Edmund Stubbe's *Fraus Honesta* (Trinity College, Cambridge, 1618–19) is a play Ricketts may be alluding to in the Prologue: "Sit fraus honesta; quando etiam fraus est pia!" (l. 77 ["Let fraud be honest, since fraud is indeed pious!"]).[25] Set in Florence and filled with intrigues, *Fraus Honesta* is "light and lively entertainment devoid of any message or commentary."[26]

Three other plays that Ricketts may have been familiar with are *Albumazar*, a play in English by Thomas Tomkis (Trinity College, Cambridge, 1614–15), which like *Byrsa Basilica* pokes fun at judicial astrology and contains references to the Royal Exchange; *Susenbrotus* (Trinity College, Cambridge, 1615–16), which satirizes pedants; and Peter Hausted's *Senile Odium* (Queen's College, Cambridge, 1631), which is set in Frankfurt and is also full of intrigues. *Senile Odium* also ridicules quack scientists and almanac-making. Though some of these plays share the Plautine intrigues and the satire of astrologers, none shares the particular focus of *Byrsa*.[27] From its very Prologue, the play teasingly challenges the traditional social dichotomy between letters and lucre, with the figure of Mercury arguing that scholars and merchants are tricksters in league. The play's titular setting, The Royal Exchange, jars satirically with its academic context, the university, while the main character is named Rialto, a name which positions him as a nexus of exchange through whom all the other characters either profit or lose.

As Bowers says, the play "deals with the career of Sir Thomas Gresham and aspects of London commercial life in combination with the intrigue and horse-play of classical comedy."[28] But the play deals with Cambridge academic life as well because, as I suggest above, the Prologue Mercury equates it with "London commercial life":

Academici! Si duplex in duplici meo
Nomine sit numen, et munus; ingenii pari
Acumine artes si tractentur, et lucra:
Utrinque patronus, et conciliator venio.
Vobis mercatores cumque eis commendo hanc fabulam;

Nam literatam aeque mercaturam colitis:
Estote per me vel fratres fraterimi.
Quasi vos inter vos non noritis? Quid si extrusio
Nundinalis imbuitur praestigioso encomio?
Quasi non idem queritur de fucis rhetoricis?
Dialecticisque maeandris saepe veritas?
In pactorum casses speciosis obtentibus
Lactatur emptor? Quid non mathematicus
Promittit? Atque astrologus e caelo redux?
Neque medicina corpus humanum minus
Interpolat; quam nos nostra mercimonia.
Grave hoc, sibi prospicere versutias?
Sit fraus honesta; quando etiam fraus est pia!
Ridete tacti, et vicissim ignoscite! [ll. 63–78]

[Academics! If my divinity is twofold in my double name, so is my duty; learning should be conducted with equal sharpness of talent as gain: I come as a patron and promoter on both sides. I entrust merchants to you and with them this tale; for you equally cultivate learned trading. Be brothers or at least most brotherly through me. As if you are not acquainted with one another? What if a selling of the market is filled with praise full of deceit? As if the same thing were not complained about rhetorical dissimulation? Is there often truth in crooked dialectics? Is the buyer cajoled into the snares of contracts by pretended pretexts? What does a mathematician not promise? And an astrologer returned from the sky? And medicine does not dress up the body of man less than we dress up our wares. Is this harsh, to provide for oneself through cunning? Let fraud be honest, since fraud is indeed pious! Laugh, you who are touched, and in turn forgive.]

Mercury, the "twofold" god of learning and trade, links these two spheres both in himself and in his equation of rhetoric with salesmanship. Mercury's Elizabethan associations have been traced by Joseph Porter, who argues that as England moved from a barter to a market economy, the shifting textual references to this trickster figure signified the anxieties of an emerging capitalist society. For instance, in his language manual *Fruits for the French* (1593), John Eliot refers to Mercury as "the God of cunning," a term whose negative connotation dates at least to the 1580s.[29] And in his *The Third Part of the Countesse of Pembroke's Yuychurch* (1592), Abraham Fraunce "relate[s] that while 'Such as be Mercuriall' are seldom rich, they may find ways to enrich themselves out of the chests of princes, and when caught can 'smooth up al by facility of discourse.'"[30] Indeed, this Prologue exemplifies Mercury's ability to "smooth up" or rationalize the duplicitous activities of his followers, equating their business practices with those of academics.

In classical mythology, Mercury is also a liminal figure:

Appropriately, it was Hermes, god of the boundary stone, who became the Greek patron of trade [...] Hermes shared with Proteus the image of duplicity, if not multiplicity. He was known as both trickster and thief [...]. As a god, Hermes was a marginal figure known for his "skill at the oath," that is to say, his ability to manipulate the literalism that others brought to transactions bound by kinship or familial honor.[31]

His associations make him a perfect Prologue, marking the boundary between the real world and the world of the play, yet also blurring the boundary between the academy and the marketplace both in his speech and in his twofold nature. Like some of Jonson's prologues, especially that of *Bartholomew Fair*, *Byrsa Basilica*'s Prologue is a transaction of sorts with the audience: "Vobis mercatores cumque eis commendo [...] Ridete tacti, et vicissim ignoscite!" (ll. 67, 81 ["I entrust merchants to you (...) Laugh, you who are touched, and in turn forgive"]). None of the contemporary university plays I have examined uses Mercury as a Prologue figure, but Ricketts does have an ancient precedent in Plautus' *Amphitryon*, and this Mercury, too, makes a lucrative transaction with his audience:

> If you want my blessing on your businesses,
> Bargains, lucky deals in buying and selling
> [...]
> And nothing but good news, sensational
> Reports of general good for you and yours
> [...]
> Please keep still while we act this play.
> Then you can judge it fair and squarely.[32]

Here, Mercury is trading on both his power over the market and his power over words. While Plautus' Mercury goes on at length to give the argument of the play, Ricketts's divine Prologue instead foreshadows the issues that his play will raise: misrepresented goods, skillful lies, false contracts, and astrologers' promises.

Additionally, he provides a "mercantile" model for disputation, making light of rhetorical skill, perhaps hinting to students that they should not take themselves too seriously, and admitting that one must often defend points with which one disagrees, arguing *in utramque partem*. The relationship he posits is none too flattering to the "academici," and could be seen either as a jab at the "political unconscious" of Renaissance humanism—necessitating the conventional begging for pardon at the end of the Prologue—or as an instruction to students that they should indeed consider the "profits" of education, and know how to dissimulate through "crooked dialectics." This second alternative is probably too cynical to be likely, but it is significant that the very attempt to celebrate humanism and mercantilism as bedfellows must resort to satire: whether they become dialecticians, mathematicians, astrologers, or physicians, the students will all be "mercatores" ("merchants"), always selling something and always "dressing it up" through rhetoric, just as in a play. The tone is consistently playful, with Mercury insisting that fraud is pious, that by profiting through deceit the merchant is worshipping him. In other words, "Sit fraus honesta; quando etiam fraus est pia!" (l. 77 ["Let fraud be honest, since fraud is indeed pious!"]).

The Prologue is appropriately followed by numerous practical applications of its message, most significantly in the threefold deception of the Exchange's founder, Rialto. Mercury's "lepidus cliens" ("charming client") Rialto is characterized as bombastic and obtuse, the object of flattery and swindling. In act 1, upon his first entrance, Rialto becomes the victim of the parasite Cicadillo who, following the Plautine model, is defined by "his willingness to say anything or praise anyone for a meal."[33] Cicadillo uses "praise full of deceit" to get money from Rialto while simultaneously ridiculing him: "Virum magnum sequi paene est sapere!" (l. 84 ["It is almost to be wise to follow a great man!"]). Then in act 3, Rialto falls prey to Dequoy, a dishonest merchant who views the Exchange as a smorgasbord of fools. His name is fitting: when applied to a person in the early seventeenth century, this term meant "a swindler, sharper, an impostor or 'shark' who lives by his wits at the expense of his dupes."[34] Dequoy tricks Rialto out of his ring so that he may fraudulently borrow money on the surety of it. And the play ends as it began, with another wily character, Captain Mercantuccio, using "crooked dialectics" to gain Rialto's bounteous gratitude by exaggerating his difficulties in returning Rialto's ships to safe harbor.

In act 1, the monopolist Rialto, puffed up by Cicadillo's false praise, defines himself against speculators, passionately defending his business practices:

Banccae ruptores de industria, seu ficta inopia!
Regratores! Annonaeque flagellatores! Magni fures!
Impostores liberae mercaturae! Pestes reipublicae!
Non istae meae sunt virtutes: nunquam ego Mercurii in justitio
Factus sum literate Martius! Praedo authenticus!
Nunquam meum mercurium infamarunt mercium adulteria!
Nunquam monetam peregre cusam advexi vorsura criminis!
Domi non perduellis! Foras non falsarius!
Sed neque cives de me, exportatis mercibus
Illicitis; lac subductum: ver aere publico, miserum sanguinem!
Tantum mihi semper displicuit fori illa tyrannis; mercurii supplantatio.
[ll. 118–28]

[Bankrupts either on purpose or by false poverty! Degraders! Scourges of the marketplace! Great thieves! Deceivers of free trade! Pests of the republic! These are not my virtues: I never became more skilled of Mars in the holiday of Mercury! An authentic robber! Adultery of goods never dishonored my trade! I never brought money struck abroad in the conversion of a charge. I am not a public enemy at home! Not a deceiver abroad! And no citizen suffers from me with illicit goods having been exported; neither milk nor the blood of the poor was taken away by taking the public funds! That tyranny of the marketplace, the throwing down of trade is displeasing to me just as much.]

Though this tirade may owe something to Plautus, it also characterizes Rialto as perhaps "protesting too much," trying to sell his version of his past actions, "adulterated goods," to himself. He denies committing the kinds of deceptions Mercury celebrates in the Prologue, and he claims that trade should be free, unrestrained, and that attempts to control it are immoral and tyrannical. The argument made here against monopoly and restraint of trade anticipates those made against marine insurance and astrology later in the play.

Bowers argues that Rialto is characterized positively, and that "it is possible that this play, in spite of its comic tone, reflects a remembrance of the supposedly halcyon days for people in trade during the reign of Elizabeth, when Gresham was the bright star in the mercantile firmament, in contrast to the oppression of Charles I."[35] There is no mention of either Elizabeth or an Elizabethan facility of trade in the play, however, and the charming tycoon Rialto is incredibly naïve, the victim of conmen and the butt of satire. Also, if Ricketts knew enough about London mercantile life to write this play, he may have been aware that the historical Sir Thomas Gresham actually did commit the rapacious acts Rialto so vehemently disowns in the above speech:

> Thomas Gresham made a net annual profit of nearly 15 per cent between 1546 and 1551, and must have doubled his capital in those five years. Yet it is likely that [his] gain was the country's loss, for the exchange rate had been so distorted that a greater and greater volume of goods had to be exported to pay for an equal quantity of imports.[36]

Unlike his wily Elizabethan counterpart, Rialto makes only one advantageous exchange in the entire play. And, as with the distinction between Rialto's stentorious claims and Gresham's nefarious activities, this advantageous exchange distances the dramatic character from the historical figure—in this case, temporally. Rialto invites us to look at the economic situation of the 1570s through the lens of the 1630s when, in order to obtain a better deal when buying marine insurance from Doso, he commits an anachronism:

> DOSO: Dabis autem mihi decem pro centenario.
> RIALTO: Minime non—Dabo *a otto per cento* (ut loquuntur moderni mercatorum principes!) [ll. 1072–4]
>
> [DOSO: Then give me ten percent.
> RIALTO: By no means—I will give eight percent (as the modern leaders of trade say!)]

Bowers notes that, "in 1571, parliament [...] legalized payment of interest up to ten percent," but "the legal rate of interest was lowered to eight percent in 1624,"[37] so Rialto's knowledge of the historically later interest-restriction keeps him from being taken advantage of by Doso. Rialto's anachronistic response jarringly resituates the historical context of the play from the 1570s to the 1630s. By the latter period, the popular backlash against monopolism and its concomitant trade restrictions had begun, which made monopolists unsavory figures in the eyes of the London mercantile community.[38] Ricketts's satirical portrait of Rialto may be inspired by this ill feeling, as Gresham had been a merchant-prince of legendary wealth. Rialto's advocacy of free trade over the stifling monopolism of the Elizabethan period, his approval of marine insurance, and his familiarity with changes in the legal interest rate make him the epitome of the "modern" businessman. The fact that he, like anyone engaging in exchange, must beware of deception only reinforces Mercury's opening message: since all—merchants and academics alike—are deceivers, "let fraud be honest," and *caveat emptor*!

Rialto's purchase of insurance at "*otto per cento*" from Doso, the public insurer, gives the playwright an opportunity to represent the logistics and merits of marine insurance. Doso is desperate to make a sale because he believes the ships he has insured have been lost at sea: "Navium navigantim o quam altum silentium!" (l. 1049 ["Oh how profound the silence of my sailing ships!"]). Like Antonio in *The Merchant of Venice*, Doso has over-speculated and is now insolvent and hiding from creditors.[39] Doso meticulously explains to Rialto the policy conditions and why each is necessary, and then reads the policy aloud to him.[40] Rialto cheerfully accepts the terms and praises insurance policies: "Sane sine hisce assecurationibus politicis / Merces exponere infido pelago, mercatorum praesumptio est!" (ll. 1116–17 ["Indeed, it is presumption of merchants to set forth their goods on the untrustworthy sea without these assurance policies!"]). His praise introduces the debate on the morality of insurance between Doso and Dequoy, who has just entered (ll. 1125–90).

The form of the ensuing debate resembles that of the disputations which were so integral to the university curriculum:

> A complete performance had three separate stages. A participant, called the respondent, first offered an answer or interpretation of the question and advanced arguments to support it. Next, an opponent [...] stating contradictory propositions and attacking flaws in the respondent's reasoning, replied to him. The final act was determination. The moderator, or determiner [...] handed down the decision or 'determination' of the question.[41]

The question posed by Doso is "Quare non curasti assecurandas?" (l. 1126 ["Why have you not taken care of assurances?"]). Dequoy, acting as the respondent, answers that insurance is both morally wrong and practically unfeasible. He advances four arguments to support his answer: first, "Nam assecurare, quid aliud quam clavum providentiae / Caelo extorquere?" (ll. 1132–3 ["For to insure, what else is it than to wrench out the nail of providence from heaven?"]); second, "Spem pretio non emam" (l. 1136 ["I will not buy hope for a price"]); third, "Quid quod juris-consultis quibusdam videri comperi / Conventionem istam qua quis in se periculam / Sumit pretio periculi, non valere legibus?" (ll. 1140–42 ["What about the fact that I have learned that to certain lawyers this contract by which one takes up risk onto himself for the price of risk seems not to be effective by law?"]); and fourth, "Taceo infinitas fraudes; quarum ansa et origo omnium / Ab assecuratione fluunt; ambarum partium dolo" (ll. 1143–4 ["I leave unsaid countless frauds, the occasion and origin of all of which flow from assurance, from the artifice of both parties"]).

The first part of Dequoy's reasoning is reminiscent of the common argument against usury: that it is a sin to buy and sell that which belongs to God, namely, time. As Thomas Wilson states in *A Discourse Upon Usury*, "They saye tyme is precious. Hee may well saye, tyme was precious to hym that payed so deerely for it; or rather the usurer maye saye that tyme was verye precious to hym that tooke so much unto hym."[42] Dequoy's second point, that the insurer buys hope of safe arrival, was a thorny question for moralists; some accepted insurance because the insurer took on the burden of risk, but others responded that insurance was still no better than usury, which is Dequoy's first argument. As an earlier legal theorist, John Consobrinus, states in *De iustitia commutatiua* (1483):

> This [marine insurance] contract is usurious on both sides, because each one intends to place himself in gain and the other in loss [...] [Also] he [the insurer] sells for 50 pounds, what is not his own, nor can be, because it is of God alone to preserve the ship. Therefore, he does a great injustice to God.[43]

Dequoy similarly argues that insurers buy and sell providence, which belongs to the heavens, because if an insured ship is lost at sea, the shipowner does not suffer the loss. Doso responds to Dequoy's objection: "Nam sponsio illa admittitur / Quae non sapit inhonestatim; maxime quia / Solatii causa magis concipitur, quam lucri" (ll. 1173–5 ["For that promise is allowed which does not savor of dishonesty; particularly because it is taken up more with the motive of relief than of gain"]). So the insurer is merely trying to alleviate possible misfortune by sharing the risk of the venture with the shipowner and with his fellow insurers; rather than being usurious, his actions actually benefit the community as a whole by protecting its individual members.[44] A possible source for this argument is the first English parliamentary act regarding marine insurance, "An Acte concerninge matters of Assurances amongste Merchantes," passed in 1601:

> [...] by means of which policie of assurance it cometh to passe that upon the losse or perishinge of any shippe there followethe not the undoinge of any man, but the losse lighthe rather easilie upon many than heavilie upon fewe, and rather upon them that adventure not than those that doe adventure, whereby all merchantes, speciallie the younger sorte, are allured to venture more willinglie and more freely.[45]

Insurance is thus vital to the accumulation of national wealth through protected trade, which explains the government's desire to begin regulating it. Though the issue of marine insurance did not engender the level of righteous furor as in the usury debate, and the practice of insuring ships in England was well-established and well-regulated by the Crown in the 1630s, this type of argument would have been well-known to those who were familiar with the anti-usury discourse, and of practical value to those who were not.

Points three and four of Dequoy's argument above address the feasibility of marine insurance, to which Doso's response sounds very much like the earlier words of Mercury, "Fraudes oggeris. Sed, quid ab his sanctum satis / Divini, humanive?" (ll. 1178–9 ["You bring out frauds. But what, divine or human, is inviolable enough from these?"]). Instead of a moderator deciding the outcome of this debate, as in the college disputations, Dequoy gives up, saying that he was just testing Doso, and proceeds to insure two ships (ll. 1189–90), which implies that in disputations outside the university the respondent must draw his own conclusion and act upon it. All sorts of people commit fraud—not just insurers but even dialecticians, mathematicians, astrologers, and physicians—and they should thus be scrutinized individually.

Dequoy's argument is shortly followed by a discussion of fraudulent astrologers; as Dequoy reads the predictions of an almanac to Rialto, the merchant prince responds laughingly: "Si vulgus vult decipi, decipiatur—per hunc licet" (l. 1420 ["If people want to be deceived, let them be deceived—for all I care"]). Dequoy recites predictions of terrible calamities and great profits that are supposed to happen at the same time, while Rialto interjects scornful remarks. Judicial astrology here appears plain foolish, but the fact that the men who ridicule it are the ones who have just bought marine insurance points to the connections between the two spheres of prognostication for profit. Keith Thomas notes that "astrologers *were* frequently consulted on insurance problems during these early days of marine insurance," and "a skeptic observed that, if the astrologers really knew so much about the fate of ships at sea, they could have made their fortunes by dabbling in marine insurance, and advising the insurers how to collect easy profits."[46] Additionally, a similar moral argument was made against astrology as that against marine insurance and usury: in *An Admonicion against Astrology iudiciall and other Curiosities, that raigne now in the World* (1561), John Calvin's "objections center not so much upon the principles of astrology as upon the impiety of any attempt to seek out God's plans."[47] Listeners or readers of the play would have been made familiar with this religious discourse against "stealing from God" as it was employed against both marine insurance and astrology, as well as the arguments made to refute it.

Thus, from *Byrsa Basilica*, the student participants and audience members would not only have been able to practice their Latin, to deliver arguments in formal disputations, and to learn classical allusions, character-types, plotting, and verse-form, but at the same time gain knowledge of the intricate arguments for and against marine insurance. If performing the part of Doso or Dequoy, moreover, an inexperienced student would be trained in the method of disputation without having to make and support an argument of his own. Beyond these formally pedagogical merits, the play's satire would have challenged university scholars to rethink their social and moral pretenses, and more fully to appreciate the function of language in diverse types of exchange.

But to understand more generally how this hodgepodge play, with its mixture of contemporary, classical, and academic elements, functioned in the Cambridge curriculum, we need to consider both the social and the educational changes at the universities in the period. That such a play as this came out of early seventeenth-century Cambridge would stand conveniently to reason if, as has generally been noted, there was a trend in university attendance towards the middle class—in other words, towards scholars with specifically mercantile interests. But while merchants' sons did attend university in increasing numbers throughout the century, that increase turns out to have been proportionally slight. There has been disagreement among social historians such as Mark H. Curtis, Lawrence Stone, and Joan Simon regarding the proportions of members of different classes in attendance at Cambridge during this period. Curtis and Stone argue that the universities were inundated with gentles and nobles, causing shifts in entrance requirements, curriculum, and teaching methods, all of which benefited them at the cost of their social inferiors. Simon claims that an over-broad understanding of "gentleman" has led these historians to misread the data, and that actually middle class students comprised the majority. David Cressy points out, however, that both claims depend on misinterpreted information; his revised figures show that rather than there having been a staggering influx of one class or another, "it can be argued that the significant characteristic of the social composition of one Cambridge college [Caius] in the period of the educational revolution was its stability."[48] In a later essay, Cressy gives social status percentages for students of four Cambridge colleges throughout the seventeenth century; most significant here is his finding that "The clergy, professionals, gentry and their families together comprised probably no more than 5% of the English population, yet they filled more than 50% of the places at the university. Sons of tradesmen and merchants provided just 16% of the Cambridge admissions."[49] These statistics refute any simple conclusion that Ricketts's play was catering to the needs of a mercantile majority, yet they could indicate the extent to which the needs and interests of all these groups of scholars came increasingly to converge upon the London marketplace.

Curricular changes were implemented to serve these emerging needs and interests, and *Byrsa Basilica* represents a shift towards contemporary knowledge and dialectic in university curricula. The academic program in which drama played such a substantial role was characterized by a combination of scholastic and humanist elements. Which of these elements held sway depends—as in the case of the scholars' social status discussed above—on the particular historian one reads, but all would agree that the basis of the curriculum was the *trivium* (the study of language and its uses: grammar, rhetoric, and logic/dialectic), the *quadrivium* (mathematics and the fields in which math is applied: geometry, astronomy, music), and philosophy, which employs the technical training of the *trivium* and the *quadrivium* in the study of natural phenomena, human behavior, and first principles. Since this was essentially a scholastic program inherited from a medieval curriculum, some historians see early modern curricula as virtually unchanged. Kenneth Charlton, for instance, notes that although each new Tudor monarch nominally revised the university statutes, these revisions concerned religious conformity more than educational reform.[50] While there were college lectureships established in humanist subjects (Latin, Greek, rhetoric, and moral philosophy), these additions did not demonstrate a "serious attempt" to introduce a new curriculum.[51]

Yet others claim that the humanist reforms had a greater influence on the universities. Although the early sixteenth-century humanists such as Desiderius Erasmus, John Colet, Thomas Elyot, and Thomas Starkey had advocated learning for the nobility, they criticized the essentially scholastic character of the university curriculum. As Curtis notes, "influential humanists were among the severest critics of the universities."[52] These criticisms bore fruit: just as increasing numbers of the noble and wealthy were going up to Cambridge and Oxford, curricular changes were made with the goal of better training these scholars for a life of public service. Though these changes may not have been evident in the statutes or in the general outline of study, it has been argued that they are discernable in two elements of university training: the supplemental reading scholars were assigned by the more enlightened of the tutors and the way in which the *trivium* subject of logic, or dialectic, was taught.

For instance, account lists for book purchases survive which indicate that university scholars were engaged in "modern" humanist readings. Of particular interest are the dramatic texts listed in the accounts of a Cambridge tutor of the early seventeenth century, Joseph Mead (1586–1638). Included are the playwrights recommended by the humanists: Aristophanes, Euripides, Plautus, Seneca, and, the favorite, Terence.[53] And university educators, particularly the students' tutors, began to recommend readings which "served the interests and needs of young gentlemen by enlarging their knowledge of the contemporary world and its ways."[54] Additionally, Lisa Jardine argues that the undergraduate curriculum came to be dominated by dialectic, the subject most closely related to dramatic activity. Of the *trivium*, grammar was a basic entrance requirement, and scholars' study of rhetoric, also "already a familiar part of a student's academic equipment by the time he reached university," was only lightly supervised.[55] But reformist educators saw dialectic as the key to undergraduate studies, giving scholars the pre-professional training they would need to serve the state. Dialectic was broadened from merely concerning the art of formal disputation to become a key to understanding the practice of all rational thought and, in Jardine's words, "a firm grounding in the art of reasoning in all contexts, as the basis for understanding of all the curriculum subjects,"[56] including the newly introduced modern ones. In this context, *Byrsa Basilica* provides not merely an example of a formal disputation but also, more important, an example of dialectic *applied*, of "the art of reasoning" in a real-world context, that of England's economic epicenter, the Royal Exchange.

As the play's supreme practitioner of dialectic applied, the protean master-rhetorician Doso establishes himself not only as a model servant of the state but also as (perhaps only half-satirically) a model for scholars. In act 4, believing himself financially undone, Doso soliloquizes on the larger implications of his impending ruin: "A me *Assecuratore* tota pendet respublica / Mercaturae" (ll. 2158–61 ["The entire mercantile commonwealth depends on me as its insurer"]). Yet Doso's survival tactics are far from conventionally ethical: he escapes the clutches of his creditors through prevarication and ultimately by hiding behind a claim of royal protection, but, according to the terms of the play's Mercurial morality, he is an upstanding citizen. His service to the "mercantile commonwealth" is rewarded in the end with a promotion to City Wool Commissioner. The play's curious characterization of marine insurance and of overseas trade as forms of state service not only suggests obliquely an alternative to scholars' usual modes of service in clerical, political, legal, and diplomatic capacities; it might also be seen in Marxist terms as an attempt to recast the economic practices of an emergent international capitalism within the moral terms of feudalism, with the residual ideology playing catch-up to the dominant mode of production, and the university playing catch-up to the capital.

In the play's Epilogue, appropriately enough, Mercury reiterates his equation of scholarship with trade:

Academici! Non sic vobiscum portatis omnia,
Ut non hinc intueri liceat quod vobis accidat:
Nimirum incerta est studiorum quoque alea,
Militia periculosa. Nec sedentarios
Lucifugas semper pascit sua intertia.
Quoties solertiae pretium opimior locus,
Honestior conditio: bellulum salarium
Petitur: nonne omnes tunc tenduntur nervuli?
Tunc aestuoso navigatur in mari? [ll. 3146–54]

[University Men! Do not think you have everything on your side, or that there is no need to learn from this what may befall you. Surely the hazard of studies is also risky; your warfare is not free from peril, nor does their physical inertia always profit light-fleeing and sedentary scholars. How often is not a richer place, a more eminent station, a handsome salary, sought as a reward for ability? Are not then all nerves tense? Does not one sail then on a tossing sea?]

Mercury's closing image of the "hazard of studies" reveals the extent to which Cambridge is "at sea" in the 1630s, both institutionally and ideologically. *Byrsa Basilica*, then, may be viewed as one scholar's attempt to re-position the university within a culture that often perceived it as irrelevant, while at the same time educating and equipping students with non-traditional forms of academic knowledge so that they might adapt themselves to a nation in flux. No longer able to situate itself as the culturally central institution that humanism had envisioned as an ideal some century earlier, the educational system represented in *Byrsa Basilica* participates in its own brand of prognostication for profit by buying in to the futures market of capitalism and imperialism.

Notes

1 John Ricketts, *Byrsa Basilica, Seu Regale Excambium: A Latin Academic Comedy of the Early Seventeenth Century, by J. Rickets*, ed. and trans. R.H. Bowers (Louvain: C. Uystpruyst, 1939). Translations are mine unless Bowers is cited. Wherever it has seemed necessary, I have preferred to translate as literally as possible, at the cost of eloquence in places. Bowers's edition of the play, from which I quote, is divided into acts and scenes, but since the line numbers are continuous I cite passages by line number only. All subsequent citations of the play will appear parenthetically in the text. Bowers's facing-page translation has been of immense aid to me in providing my own, as have the glossaries of Latin terms in Andrew Wright, *Court-Hand Restored: Or, the Student's Assistant in Reading Old Deeds, Charters, Records, etc.* (London: H.G. Bohn, 1846), 51–62; and in *The Compleat* CLERK, *Containing the best* FORMS *Of all sorts of* PRESIDENTS, *for* CONVEYANCES *and* ASSURANCES; *and other* INSTRUMENTS *now in use and practice*, 4th edn. (London: by G. Sawbridge, T. Roycroft, and W. Rawlins, for H. Twyford, O. Blagrave, J. Place, and R. Harford, 1677), sigs. Ooo6r–Ooo8v.

2 See, for example, Theodore B. Leinwand, *Theatre, Finance, and Society in Early Modern England* (Cambridge: Cambridge University Press, 1999); and Richard Halpern, *The Poetics of Primitive Accumulation: English Renaissance Culture and the Genealogy of Capital* (Ithaca: Cornell University Press, 1991). For a critique of how literary critics read economic metaphors and themes, see Marc Shell, *The Economy of Literature* (Baltimore: Johns Hopkins University Press, 1978), 1–9.

3 For a discussion of the development of marine insurance, see Frederick Martin, *The History of Lloyd's and of Marine Insurance in Great Britain* (London: Macmillan and Co., 1876), 1–51; and Florence de Roover, "Early Examples of Marine Insurance," *Journal of Economic History* 5 (1945): 172–200; for an explanation of how different kinds of bills of exchange work and of the practice of hiding interest to avoid anti-usury laws, see Raymond de Roover, *Business, Banking, and Economic Thought in Late Medieval and Early Modern Europe*, ed. Julius Kirshner (Chicago: University of Chicago Press, 1974), 183–99.

4 Concerning Gresham and marine insurance, Martin notes that "how far he himself influenced legislation on marine insurance is not known. But it is certain, from several of his letters, that the vessels and cargoes which Gresham dispatched from Flanders and Germany to England were duly insured through the medium of Hanseatic merchants" (*History of Lloyd's*, 15–16).

5 Bowers, *Byrsa Basilica*, xi. However, there seems to be some confusion about whether it is an authorial manuscript: Bowers first states that "the numerous mistakes in the MS. render the possibility of its being holograph slight. It is surely a copy, not a first draft, since no corrections of any importance are to be found" (xi), but he goes on to affirm that the manuscript is in the same hand as the parish record, which was definitely written by Ricketts. His unsatisfying

solution to this problem is that Ricketts must have hurriedly re-copied an original which has not survived: "It follows that, unless MS. Tanner is of a strikingly similar hand [as that of the register], several pages of *Byrsa* were written most carelessly and distractedly, and were not favored with an attentive re-reading" (xxxvi). Significantly, the author of the play can be identified no more surely than can the transcriber of this manuscript. In *Sir Philip Sidney and the Circulation of Manuscripts, 1558–1640* (Oxford: Clarendon, 1996), 104, H.R. Woudhuysen discusses why an author would make or have made a fair copy of his work: "to see one's work collected, gathered up, from various sources, and put into a permanent form, perhaps by a skilled penman, must have had its own satisfactions. But the most powerful motive for these transcripts may have been to have one's work in finished and corrected form ready for publication either in manuscript among family, friends, or a more general audience, or for all in print." Manuscript circulation of plays was common at the university; Woudhuysen notes that of the 120 manuscripts of academic plays which survive, containing about 110 different dramatic works, "the majority were written for performance at Cambridge (thirty-nine with another possible thirteen) [...] Cambridge plays also circulated most widely in manuscript: the forty or so identified Cambridge plays survive in a total of about one hundred manuscript copies" (144).

6   Bowers, *Byrsa Basilica*, xiv.
7   This biographical material is taken from *The Dictionary of National Biography*, s.vv. William Sancroft and Thomas Tanner. Additionally, in 1724, Tanner bought, "apparently from the London bookseller Christopher Bateman, the greater part of the surviving papers of Archbishop Sancroft" (Ian Philip, *The Bodleian Library in the Seventeenth and Eighteenth Centuries* [Oxford: Clarendon, 1983], 81). For further discussion of the Tanner collection and the Sancroft papers, see Philip, 82–3.
8   Bowers, *Byrsa Basilica*, xix.
9   Alan H. Nelson, ed., *Records of Early English Drama: Cambridge*, 2 vols. (Toronto: University of Toronto Press, 1989), 2.935 (hereafter cited as *REED: Cambridge*).
10 G.C. Moore Smith, *College Plays Performed in the University of Cambridge* (Cambridge: Cambridge University Press, 1923), 27. See his "Appendix 2" for pictures of the hall and the chapel of Jesus College. In *Jesus College* (London: F.E. Robinson & Co., 1902), 95, Arthur Gray states, "the stage was usually in the Hall, but sometimes the plays were acted in the chapel."
11 Smith, *College Plays*, 31.
12 Woudhuysen, *Sir Philip Sidney*, 144.
13 "'Item sol. Goldying & Suthey pro expensis circa ludos in festo Natalis domini vii ij'" (Frederick S. Boas, *University Drama in the Tudor Age* [Oxford: Oxford University Press, 1914], 2). As with the London theaters, the most specific evidence of early university performances are records of the money spent on them or the items bought for them. Alan H. Nelson gives a list of other

primary sources for college dramatic activities in "Contexts for Early English Drama: The Universities," in *Contexts for Early English Drama*, ed. Marianne G. Briscoe and John C. Coldewey (Bloomington: University of Indiana Press, 1989), 139.

14 Boas, *University Drama*, 4.

15 In his chapter on "University Discipline" at Cambridge, J.R. Tanner places the administrative attitude towards playing in the context of other pastimes, such as football, dice, bowling, and bear-baiting, which were viewed as "'showes of unlawfull, hurtfull, pernicious, and unhonest games'" (*The Historical Register of the University of Cambridge* [Cambridge: Cambridge University Press, 1917], 200).

16 Frederick S. Boas, *Shakespeare and the Universities and Other Studies in Elizabethan Drama* (New York: D. Appleton and Company, 1923), 47.

17 Nelson, *REED: Cambridge*, 2.711.

18 Nelson, *REED: Cambridge*, 2.713.

19 Nelson, *REED: Cambridge*, 2.714, who follows this outline of performance history at Cambridge with an interesting section on the conditions of performance of college drama; see especially 714–22. Cf. Alan H. Nelson, "Cambridge University Drama in the 1580s," in *The Elizabethan Theatre 11*, ed. A.L. Magnusson and C.E. McGee (Port Credit: P.D. Meany, 1990), 19–31, especially 24–5.

20 Quoted in John R. Elliott, Jr., "Plays, Players and Playwrights in Renaissance Oxford," in *From Page to Performance: Essays in Early English Drama*, ed. John A. Alford (East Lansing: Michigan State University Press, 1995), 180. For the circumstances of Gager's remarks, see Linda Shenk's contribution to this volume.

21 Thomas Heywood, *AN APOLOGY for Actors* (London: by Nicholas Okes, 1612), sig. C3v.

22 For a more detailed explanation of disputations, see Mark H. Curtis, *Oxford and Cambridge in Transition, 1558–1642: An Essay on Changing Relations Between the English Universities and English Society* (Oxford: Clarendon, 1959), 88. Additionally, in *The Scholastic Curriculum at Early Seventeenth-Century Cambridge* (Cambridge: Harvard University Press, 1958), 17, William T. Costello gives several examples of disputation topics, including "the production of the rational soul involves a new creation, the origin of well-water is the sea, and an hereditary monarchy is better than an elective one," and explains the sequence of the debate. He also discusses how disputations, like the dramas, were public performances that were as entertaining as they were instructive. And, like plays, disputations were part of the entertainment for visiting monarchs, and were particularly enjoyed by King James I: see, for example, Emily D. Bryan's contribution to this volume.

23 In his *Academiarum Examen, or the examination of academies*, in *Science and Education in the Seventeenth Century: The Webster-Ward Debate*, ed. Allen G. Debus (London: Macdonald & Co., 1970), 174, John Webster criticizes this

emphasis on performance in the disputation, arguing that it teaches nothing but bad acting: "Their custome is no less ridiculous, and vicious, in their histrionical personations in the performance of their exercises, being full of childishness and scurrility [...] using so much lightness as more befits stage-players than diligent searchers of Science, by scoffing and jeering, humming and hissing, which shewes them like those animals they imitate." Webster's criticism strengthens the connection between university drama and disputation, and also hints that neither type of performance was attended in polite silence.

24 Heywood, *AN APOLOGY*, sig. C4r.

25 "Fraus pia" is a tag from Ovid, meaning "a merciful craft or deceit"; see Church of England, Diocese of Lincoln, Bishop [Thomas Cooper], *Thesaurus linguae Romanae & Britannicae tam accurate congestus, vt nihil penè in eo desyderari possit [...]* (London: by Henry Denham, 1584). The phrase is also the title of another university play, so Ricketts may have been making a double reference.

26 Thomas W. Best, "Introduction," in Edmund Stubbe, *Fraus Honesta*, prep. Thomas W. Best (Hildesheim: Georg Olms Verlag, 1987), 22.

27 For editions of these Mercury plays, see *Mercurius Rusticans: A Critical Edition*, ed. Ann J. Cotton (New York: Garland Publishing, 1988); John Blencowe, *Mercurius Sive Literarum Lucta*, prep. Heinz J. Vienken (Hildesheim: Georg Olms Verlag, 1981); Edmund Stubbe, *Fraus Honesta*, prep. Thomas W. Best (Hildesheim: Georg Olms Verlag, 1987); Thomas Tomkis, *Albumazar: A Comedy*, ed. Hugh G. Dick (Berkeley: University of California Press, 1944); *A Comedy Called Susenbrotus*, ed. and trans. Connie McQuillen (Ann Arbor: University of Michigan Press, 1997); Peter Hausted, *Senile Odium*, ed. and trans. Laurens J. Mills (Bloomington: Indiana University Press, 1949).

28 Bowers, *Byrsa Basilica*, xv.

29 Quoted in Joseph A. Porter, *Shakespeare's Mercutio: His History and Drama* (Chapel Hill: University of North Carolina Press, 1988), 80.

30 Porter, *Shakespeare's Mercutio*, 84.

31 Jean-Christophe Agnew, *Worlds Apart: The Market and the Theater in Anglo-American Thought, 1550–1750* (Cambridge: Cambridge University Press, 1986), 20. See also the forthcoming volume by Adam McKeown, *English Mercuries* (Vanderbilt University Press), which charts the relationship between the figure of Mercury and English soldiers in the period.

32 Plautus, *Amphitryon*, in *Three Plays by Plautus: Miles Gloriosus, Amphitryon, and The Prisoners*, ed. and trans. Paul Roche (New York: Mentor Books, 1968), Prologue, ll. 1–16.

33 Kathleen McCarthy, *Slaves, Masters, and the Art of Authority in Plautine Comedy* (Princeton: Princeton University Press, 2000), 202.

34 "decoy, n^2 4a," *The Oxford English Dictionary*, 2d edn. (Oxford University Press, 1989).

35 Bowers, *Byrsa Basilica*, xiv n.

36 D.M. Palliser, *The Age of Elizabeth: England Under the Later Tudors, 1547–*

1603 (London: Longman, 1983), 283. For the way in which Gresham, as the Crown's financial agent, "brought money struck abroad in the conversion of a charge" for England, see Robert Brenner, *Merchants and Revolution: Commercial Change, Political Conflict, and London's Overseas Traders, 1550–1653* (Princeton: Princeton University Press, 1993), 55–6.

37 Bowers, *Byrsa Basilica*, 205.

38 See Brenner, *Merchants and Revolution*, 87–8. This Jacobean reduction in the interest rate supports Bowers's remark about the mercantile "oppression of Charles I"; though the merchants could obtain better insurance rates, the rate of interest which they could charge when selling bills of exchange, a primary mode of investment, was lowered also. The passage additionally connects monopolists with the unsavory figures of usurers, who were also seen to commit "tyrannies of the marketplace" and whose business was equally impaired by the mandated lowering of interest. Yet another connection the passage highlights is that between monopolists and marine insurers in the Elizabethan period: "A patent had actually been passed conferring on Richard Candler 'the office of makinge and remakinge of all manner of assurances, policies, intimations [...] and other things whatsoever that hereafter shalbe made upon shippes or shippes' goodes or other merchandise or anie other thinge or thinges in the Royalle Exchange aforesaid'" (Thomas Wilson, *A Discourse Upon Usury*, ed. R.H. Tawney [New York: A.M. Kelley, 1963], 100). In other words, Candler was granted a monopoly on the writing of insurance policies.

39 See William Shakespeare, *The Merchant of Venice*, in *The Riverside Shakespeare*, ed. G. Blakemore Evans, et al. (Boston: Houghton Mifflin Company, 1974), 1.3. Marine insurance was a lucrative business in this period, and there were several ways an insurer could speculate: he could either underwrite one ship for a great deal of money, or several ships for a smaller amount (the usual and much safer practice), or illegally "subscribe several policies on one vessel for the same voyage" (Martin, *History of Lloyd's*, 24). In his complaints and concerns, Doso also resembles the miser figure in Plautine comedy; see Erich Segal, *Roman Laughter: The Comedy of Plautus* (Cambridge: Harvard University Press, 1968), 77–9.

40 This policy is very abbreviated but contains the essential elements of contemporary policies. See Bowers, *Byrsa Basilica*, 206; and William D. Winter, *A Short Sketch of the History and Principles of Marine Insurance*, 2d edn. (New York: Insurance Society of New York, 1935), 24.

41 Curtis, *Oxford and Cambridge*, 88; see his "Appendix 3" for a detailed account of a Cambridge disputation. See also Laurence Fowler and Helen Fowler, eds., *Cambridge Commemorated: An Anthology of University Life* (Cambridge: Cambridge University Press, 1984), 62.

42 Wilson, *Discourse Upon Usury*, 228; see also Phillip Stubbes, *The Anatomie of Abuses* (London: by Richard Iones, 1583), sig. K5r–L2r.

43 This work is a Latin quarto about interest, commercial law, and gambling; quoted in John T. Noonan, Jr., *The Scholastic Analysis of Usury* (Cambridge:

Harvard University Press, 1957), 203.

44 Keith Thomas discusses how the development of insurance contributed to the decline of magic and superstition in his *Religion and the Decline of Magic: Studies in Popular Beliefs in Sixteenth and Seventeenth Century England* (Letchworth: The Garden City Press Limited, 1971), 651–4. Doso's ridicule of Fortuna (ll. 1157–60) affirms the power of humanity to overcome unforeseen disasters through rationality rather than superstition.

45 Quoted in Martin, *History of Lloyd's*, 12.

46 Thomas, *Religion and the Decline of Magic*, 310.

47 Hugh G. Dick, "Introduction," in Thomas Tomkis, *Albumazar: A Comedy*, ed. Hugh G. Dick (Berkeley: University of California Press, 1944), 22. For a full discussion of this controversy, see Bernard Capp, *English Almanacs 1500–1800: Astrology and the Popular Press* (Ithaca: Cornell University Press, 1979), 131–79.

48 David Cressy, "The Social Composition of Caius College, Cambridge 1580–1640," *Past and Present* 47 (1970): 115.

49 David Cressy, "Educational Opportunity in Tudor and Stuart England," *History of Education Quarterly* 16 (1976): 312; in the introductory pages of the essay, Cressy summarizes this historical debate. Joan Simon's contributions to the argument include: "The Reformation and English Education," *Past and Present* 11 (1957): 48–65; "The Social Origins of Cambridge Students, 1603–1640," *Past and Present* 26 (1963): 58–67; and *Education and Society in Tudor England* (Cambridge: Cambridge University Press, 1966). For Lawrence Stone's contributions, see "The Educational Revolution in England, 1560–1640," *Past and Present* 28 (1964): 41–80; and "Social Mobility in England 1500–1700," *Past and Present* 33 (1966): 16–55.

50 See Kenneth Charlton, *Education in Renaissance England* (London: Routledge and Kegan Paul, 1965), 141.

51 Charlton, *Education*, 145. Curtis disagrees with Charlton about the extent of revision in the statutes: "when the statutes of both universities were revised by Edward VI's commissioners, the second generation of English humanists won a great victory by getting the whole university curriculum in the liberal arts modified according to their ideas" (*Oxford and Cambridge*, 70–71). See also Costello, *Scholastic Curriculum*, 4, 8; and Hugh Kearney, *Scholars and Gentlemen: Universities and Society in Pre-Industrial Britain, 1500–1700* (Ithaca: Cornell University Press, 1970), 77.

52 Curtis, *Oxford and Cambridge*, 65.

53 See "Appendix 1: The Book Purchases in Mead's Accounts, 1614–37," in Harris Francis Fletcher, *The Intellectual Development of John Milton*, 2 vols. (Urbana: University of Illinois Press, 1961), 2.553–622. See also Charlton, *Education*, 151.

54 Curtis, *Oxford and Cambridge*, 132. Victor Morgan discusses "the overall pattern of the 'Educational Revolution' in 16th and 17th century England" and London's role in it, noting that, "Exposed to novel educational experiences

and immersed in the delights of a scintillating capital, who can doubt that the gentry shed their provincialism and acquired a new urbanity unknown to their rustic forbears, that they became articulate participants in a more homogeneous nation, and that the universities were the main instrument in effecting this transformation?"; see Victor Morgan, "Cambridge University and 'The Country' 1560–1640," in *The University in Society*, 2 vols., ed. Lawrence Stone (Princeton: Princeton University Press, 1974), 1.183, 184.

55 Lisa Jardine, "The Place of Dialectic Teaching in Sixteenth-Century Cambridge," *Studies in the Renaissance* 21 (1974): 50.

56 Jardine, "The Place of Dialectic," 58.

CHAPTER 8

Drama in the Academies of Early America

Odai Johnson

Writing to the poet and intellectual Elizabeth Fergusson on 2 March 1781, College of Philadelphia Provost William Smith recalls a play he had seen a few nights before on campus:

> My bones are yet sore with the pressing and pounding received the other night at the College, where I was fool enough, with thousands of others, to go and see a play performed, called *Gustavus Vasa*. It was as much like a bull-bait as a play. Noise, shouting and ill Manners of every kind and denomination, was all the entertainment. There must be an amazing turn for dissipation at present in this city, by the vast crowds that resort to such places. I really think it would afford Government a great revenue, if they were to open the Theatre, and employ a Company of Comedians on public account at once.[1]

What is remarkable about Smith's account of the college production is not so much the bad manners exhibited, or the "amazing turn for dissipation" displayed, or even the vast crowds of the "thousands" who attended it. Nor, for that matter, that at the time there had been no professional theater in Philadelphia for nearly a decade. The first Continental Congress had declared the theater illegal in October of 1774 as they prepared for what looked like open war with Great Britain, reaffirming its illegality again in 1778. The professional company who developed and operated the American circuit of playhouses—the American Company—was obliged to close up their theaters and sit out the hostilities in Jamaica. And when, just months after Smith's evening at the theater, a professional company did attempt to reopen the Southwark playhouse, they were rebuffed and closed after one performance, notwithstanding the presence of both General George Washington and the French Minister in the side box.[2] What is surprising and frankly remarkable about the raucous evening in the theater in Philadelphia in 1781 is that at the time the city was still in the midst of a war against Great Britain, which raged across the recently united colonies. Independence may have been declared there, but the outcome of such a declaration was far from settled. Indeed during much of the winter and spring the British General Henry Clinton, headquartered in occupied New York, had seriously toyed with retaking Philadelphia (already once occupied and evacuated).[3] Just across the river in New Jersey, Camden Town had fallen to

General Charles Cornwallis earlier, and it would not be the first time in this war that merry-making citizens found themselves suddenly surprised in the theater by a real army within shelling distance.[4] Even in the thick of the uncertainty of ongoing military operations, and in spite of the illegal status of theater during the Revolution, student theatricals were thriving.

Nor was Smith alone in his appraisal of theater. In his autobiographical novel *The Bay Boy*, Royall Tyler—often noted as the first American playwright—confessed that his passion for the stage was greatest during his student days as an amateur in Boston (again, where there was legally no theater), a passion, he tells us, unachieved on the later professional stage.[5] That student theatricals were not only tolerated but flourished in colonial America in the face of prohibitions, antitheatrical legislation, a revolution, and *haute culture* bigotries, especially while professional theater struggled, exposes a rupture in the culture of both the theater and the academy. From the beginning of the colonial calendar of performances to the onset of the Revolutionary War, professional players came and went, particularly in the first half of the eighteenth century, but student theatricals were a continual tradition, established early and enduring late. This dramatic tradition served to keep the idea of theater alive in the cultural imagination during the long absence of professional playing companies.

Student theatricals in America had their roots in the English university productions at Oxford and Cambridge, which stretched back to the sixteenth century. Delivering plays as exercises in oratory, debate, and memory, or the writing of them from Latin models, were the standard justifications of the practice that allowed it to become established in colonial America, even in the absence of universities, and even when professional theater was itself prohibited.[6] As Provost William Smith reminds us, the quality of student drama was not always high, but the pedagogical function of academic theater created the market for professional theater. Historically, academic theater existed before, during, and after the arrival and subsequent departure of the professional players, often thriving in New England cities that were unapproachable by the professionals. I want here to explore the circumstances and reasons why academic theater succeeded when the early professional theater in America struggled so profoundly.

The acceptance of academic drama even by the theater's fiercest opponents has been noted often. Stephen Greenblatt quotes the English clergyman John Northbrooke, who published a tract against "dicing, dancing, vain plays or interludes" in 1577. Yet even the most zealous opponents of the decadence of London culture, such as Northbrooke, excepted school plays, if "suitably expurgated."[7] But nowhere was opposition against the theater stronger than in colonial America, where Quakers in Philadelphia and Puritans in New England both enacted legislation severe and early to prevent professional theater from ever being established. The colonies of Massachusetts and Philadelphia both had antitheatrical legislation in place by the close of the seventeenth century, laws which remained largely unrelaxed for the next hundred years. Yet throughout this century nowhere was the acceptance of academic drama so popular as at the colleges of those very regions who sought so vigorously to suppress the theater: Harvard, Yale, and the College of Philadelphia.

Long before the professional actors arrived in the English colonies in America, long before the colonial equivalents of Northbrooke spoke the first antitheatrical diatribes from pulpits in Boston or pushed them through the legislature in Pennsylvania, students at the oldest colleges in America were already performing plays before a receptive public, who had a pronounced distaste and distrust of theater. *Gustavus Vasa*, the play William Smith endured in Philadelphia in 1781, had been performed at Harvard as early as 1690—before there was much of an America to speak of. By the time Smith witnessed the production a century later, Harvard, Yale, Princeton, Dartmouth, William and Mary, the College of Philadelphia, and many smaller, provincial schools all had long and accepted traditions of academic performance. Indeed Smith himself had done much to promote academic theater. As Provost of the College of Philadelphia, his students regularly performed, and Smith himself even composed dialogues for the public Commencement. Thus, in his own way, Smith contributed to the crowds of whom he would later complain.[8]

The colleges were the ideal venue for the introduction of drama in America. They had an established tradition for oratorical training for the bar and the pulpit that extended back to the English Renaissance and thus, for pedagogical purposes, they were exempt from antitheatrical legislation. The first colleges in America were the last installments of the old English tradition. But unlike England, by the time the academic tradition was imported to North America, the professional theater had long been established in Great Britain. Consequently the overt fears about professional theater came as hidden cargo with the academic. The unique and uneasy partnership between pedagogy and performance meant that, in New England particularly, the academic tradition flourished in a kind of isolated ideological ecosystem, sealed off from the professional theater that was being introduced in the middle and southern colonies and well-resisted in the north. In middle colonies like Pennsylvania, which would occasionally see professional plays, two discrete ideologies toward the theater developed simultaneously. It also meant that a successful tradition of student productions inadvertently created the marketplace for the professional theater that followed.

In some colonies where the two traditions collided, the fraught relationship between the academic and professional was deeply pronounced. In Philadelphia, 1749, the first professional troupe attempted to establish itself, a troupe that would later become the Murray-Kean Company. They had a patron in William Plumstead, prominent merchant, former Grand Master of the Masons, and future mayor of Philadelphia in 1750–51, who rented the players a warehouse for performances. Though they seemed to enjoy some genteel support for a clandestine season, by January of 1750 they were called before the city council and reprimanded for their activities. But on 1 August 1749, the same year that the first professional troupe tried to make its way in Philadelphia, the prominent merchant Edward

Shippen could write to his nephew James Burd and encourage the young man's participation in student theatricals:

> You acquaint me of your acting a play the last Winter to the Satisfaction of all Spectators. I am glad the Spirit is kept up, because it is an amusement the most useful of any to Your People and I heartily wish it would spread itself to ye younger sort, I mean School Boys. For I think there is no method so proper to teach them Grace of Speech and an elegant Pronunciation and withal there is nothing that emboldens a Lad and rids him of his natural Bashfullness and fear so much as this.[9]

Why theater was encouraged pedagogically and discouraged professionally speaks as much to the theater's ideological position in the culture as to the rhetorical training it offered in the academy. Some of the most charismatic detractors in Philadelphia—such as the preacher George Whitefield—learned their delivery from actors. Thomas Sheridan's critiques of Methodists in his highly attended *Lectures on Elocution* declare as much: Sheridan claims that anyone who desires to speak well and to learn proper deportment, carriage, and gesture should adjourn to the playhouse, for concerning matters of rhetoric there is no better training than the stage.[10] In Paul Goring's phrase, graceful delivery in speech and deportment "fixed the language of gentlemen."[11] In ways that the professional theater could not achieve, academic drama exploited the oratorical training that performance offered by translating theater from an industry of dissipation into a model of gentility. Untainted by the stigma of commerce or the *infamia* of the player, students offered an exhibition of rhetorical skills that masqueraded as both theater to the public and pedagogy to the censors. In some cases, students advertised expressly that tickets were printed for *gratis* admission and that they were not tarnishing their reputations by playing for profit. In other cases, they played the game of "lectures on elocution" to line their own pockets.

Even in places where the professional theater found wide encouragement—such as in Virginia, for example, which hosted every major and minor touring company—it was nonetheless preceded by an academic tradition. When the Hallam Company of Comedians arrived in Williamsburg in 1752, the capital had known a half century of amateur theater, commencing with a 1702 performance at the newly founded College of William and Mary. Governor Francis Nicholson was present at the anonymous *Pastoral Colloquy* and later enclosed copies of the work in a letter to the Archbishop of Canterbury.[12] This was the first in a long tradition of student recitations at that institution. Indeed, the 1736 Statutes of the College of William and Mary had a proviso for the performance of plays: "And if there are any sort of Plays or Diversions in Use among them, which are not to be found extant in any printed Books, let the Master compose and dictate to his Scholars Colloquies fit for such sorts of Plays, that they may learn at all Times to speak Latin in apt and proper Terms."[13] Some years later, John Randolph recounted his days as a student at William and Mary: "The boys were in the habit of acting plays in the original language from Plautus and Terence."[14]

Indeed, so vibrant was the academic tradition that they began to schedule their recitations to capitalize on the court session in Williamsburg. In September of 1736 we find an advertised production of *Cato* by the "Young Gentlemen of the College." The production met with immediate competition from an amateur group in Williamsburg, who also performed during the same court session. The rivalry inspired the students to mount a second collegiate production that same year, Joseph Addison's *The Drummer; or The Haunted House*. For both productions the students performed off-campus in Williamsburg.[15] So accepted was this student tradition that colonies which had never seen professional theater enjoyed academic performances. Connecticut, for example, would not see a professional company until long after the Revolutionary War, but forty years earlier its collegians at Yale would annually mount a production. The same would be true for the Cambridge student body in and around Harvard, and later in the century for the students at Princeton in New Jersey.

For its part, the professional theater was not above attempts to borrow legitimacy from the academies whenever it encountered difficulties with authorities. When David Douglass and his American Company were first denied permission to perform in New York in 1758, he masqueraded his productions as a "Histrionic Academy." After being denied in Providence, Rhode Island, Douglass opened "the New School House," where the company performed "oratorical exhibitions," drawing audiences from as far away as Boston.[16] Douglass's subterfuge fooled no one, and in both cases his efforts were suppressed. But it reminds us that, while the professionals struggled to gain a foothold, academic performances were understood to be culturally accepted, and their methods were occasionally deployed in the service of profit. The extent to which student theater was accepted by the culture becomes more apparent when we rehearse two case studies from the calendar of academic performances in early America.

The Linonian Society

At the close of 1754, Lewis Hallam's Company of Comedians from London were winding down their three-year continental tour, which had included stops in Virginia, New York, Philadelphia, and Charleston, but not in New England. At the northern end of the colonies, far from the professional circuit, the students at Yale College in New Haven, Connecticut, inaugurated a society that same year for the clandestine production of plays: the Linonian Society. Neither professional nor London-trained—nor, for that matter, even legal—the Linonian Society would continue their clandestine theatrical tradition right up to the outbreak of the Revolutionary War, and quite independently of the professional circuit.

The first evidence of this tradition is a record of fines meted out when several of the students were caught and punished for their roles in the illicit production carried out in Amity, Connecticut, sometime between December 1754 and January 1755.

But the evidence also indicates that this had not been their first warning (the numbers after the students' names refer to their class standings):

> Whereas it appears that sometime last winter, Stoddard 2, Strong 2, Lyman 1, Clark, Martin, Noble 2, Smith 1, Reaves, and Wright went up to Amity, and there publicly acted a play—which is contrary to the express orders of the President heretofore several times given [...]. It is therefore considered by the President with the advice of the Tutors, that the said Lyman, Martin, Clark, Noble, Reaves and Wright to be fined 20'/Old Tenr each [...]. And whereas the said Strong voluntarily came before the president and Tutors and said that upon consideration he was sensible it was wrong, it is thereon considered that said Strong shall be finned 10/only. And whereas in order to act this play, said Stoddard and Smith dressed themselves in women's apparel which is contrary to the Laws of God, the Laws of this colony as well as the Laws of this college, it is thereupon considered that the said Stoddard and Smith be publickly admonished.[17]

Fines notwithstanding, the following year they were at it again, this time in New Haven. On 16 January 1756, the students of the Linonian Society performed again and escaped unfined. Emboldened by their success, they offered a second end-of-term production at Grosvenor's Tavern, Pomfret, for which they advertised. Incidentally, the son of the tavern owner was among the company:

> whereas it has been oftentimes declared that the Actings of Plays by the students of this College is of very bad tendency to corrupt the morals of this seminary of Religion and learning and of mankind in general, and yet it appears that Craft, Chandler 2, Pain, Sabin Grosvenor, Sumner 2, Weld and Nide in May last publickly acted a Play at the Tavern in Pomfret before a great Number of Spectators, and gave previous Notice of it in the neighboring Towns, many days before.[18]

When Harvard College commenced a rival tradition with the creation of a drama club in 1758, Yale was not to be bested, and the Linonians, too, continued their clandestine endeavors. In April of 1762 in Milford, Connecticut colony, a student named Ingersal and "a number of Scholars and others went to the Tavern and acted a Play and had a mixed dance": when caught, Ingersal was fined three shillings.[19] Records are intermittent, but the annual tradition seems to have continued right through the 1760s. Playing at many venues in surrounding towns within the vicinity of New Haven, Milford, and Pomfret, the students were in some years caught and fined, in other years not. On 2 January 1771, the drama club performed *The Conscious Lovers* and the afterpiece *The Toy Shop*. In this year one of the students was the young Nathan Hale, later captain in the Continental Army during the Revolutionary War. He was fined but to no avail, since the following year Harvard's drama club presented *The Beaux' Stratagem*. At Atwater's Tavern in New Haven in 1773, they took on the first part of Stevens's *Lecture on Heads*, followed by *The West Indian*. The play for the following year is unknown.[20]

Tales of a Wayside Inn

In some cases, what began as an academic tradition evolved into a quasi-professional theater. The case study of Nathaniel Ames, a student at Harvard College, is useful because this was, after all, Cambridge, Boston, a colony where professional theater was prohibited and remained so until well after the Revolutionary War. Nonetheless, Ames and his fellow students and alumni documented a market as well as the necessary market strategies for evading prohibitions on theater.

The diary of Nathaniel Ames tracks his career from his entrance to Harvard in 1758 at age seventeen. Among the more enthusiastic extracurricular activities of his first year is his attendance of plays and his later involvement in the production of them. His diary—omitted from most studies of the Boston stage—reveals a lively and somewhat subversive interest in theater, which spilled out beyond the halls of Harvard. On 22 June 1758, William Whitehead's *The Roman Father* (1750) was produced at the college, followed shortly afterwards by *Cato* on 3 July and again on 6 July. *Cato* was acted "to perfection," says Ames about the first performance, and in his entry for 11 July he writes that the second performance was "more perfect than before."[21]

But the students had rivals: an amateur company of Boston tradesmen also took to performing. This unknown company of artisans offered *The Revenge* on 23 March 1759 at a private house in Boston. On 13 April, the company performed *The Orphan* at How's Tavern, and a week later Ames watched them act *The Drummer* in the same venue. That these were not student productions is made clear by Ames, who notes in his diary whenever plays were "acted by ourselves," suggesting that the tradesmen were an amateur assembly availing themselves of the many wayside inns just outside Boston.[22] On 18 May, this amateur company continued their season by mounting *The Brothers*, and the following month they put on *The Recruiting Officer*. The students, for their part, carried on in Cambridge, offering *The Revenge* and a remount of *Cato* in the summer of 1759.[23] If these productions seem like ambitious undertakings, the next season's efforts were even richer, both for students and for amateurs. It is unclear from Ames's diary whether it was the Harvard students who reprised *The Revenge* in November at Bowman's tavern in Boston, but it was certainly the amateur group who assembled to perform *Cato* in December 1759. Their performances had by this time become public enough to warrant a reprint of the prohibition against theatricals, republished in *The Boston News Letter*: "At the desire of a number of the principal inhabitants of this town."[24] In spite of the proclamation, both companies continued to perform in January, March, April, and June of 1760.[25] The students earned the rebuke of the college when it began to crack down on all extracurricular activities. A wave of discipline was meted out for various offenses, including "going upon the top of the college, or cutting off the lead, tumultuous noise, [...] rudeness at meals, keeping guns, going skating, etc." One deduces that theatrical clubs fell under the same disfavor, as the last entry in Ames's diary about acting in a student production describes a

performance on 12 June 1760 of *Tancred and Sigismunda*—its third production—
"for which," he writes, "we are likely to be prosecuted."[26]

Yet in spite of the college crackdowns and the republication of the prohibition,
the interest in and productions of clandestine drama continued nearly unabated,
as did Ames's participation in them. During the confrontations with college
administrators during the spring of 1760, Ames is still being roped into
productions: "engag'd in a Play," he writes on 17 March, while also lending plays
to other students. Even after he graduated, Ames maintained his links with theater
in his native Dedham, Massachusetts, and at the many inns in the neighboring
communities of Sudbury and Roxbury. On the post road out of Boston, How's
Tavern in Sudbury, the original Wayside Inn of Longfellow fame, was a particularly
favorite venue.[27] Nor was the Sudbury Inn the only rural outlet for amateur drama
in the Boston environs. Ames and his colleagues—now graduates beyond the
censure of the college—acted a play at Battle's Inn in Roxbury during October of
1761: he writes that they were "rebuked for it by our parents." Again, the rebukes
had little impact on Ames, as a month later the company was planning another
production, this time in Dedham. Under the initiative of Ames and his colleagues,
Dedham saw occasional productions between 1762 and 1772 at inns and taverns,
presented in the "lecture" format. As he wrote in the concluding lines of one of his
prologues: "Whatever people may conjecture / You'll safely call it but an Evening
Lecture."[28]

Meanwhile at Harvard, after the departure of Ames, his underclassmen
continued their theatrical activities, so much so as to cause the governors of
Harvard to publish in 1762 a more severe prohibition targeting plays:

> Whereas the attending upon Stage-Plays, Interludes, and Theatrical Entertainments,
> tends greatly to corrupt the Morals of a people, and particularly with respect to the
> College must needs (besides corrupting their Morals) be highly detrimental to their
> learning, by taking off their minds from their studies, drawing them into such Company,
> as may be very insnaring to them, expensive to their parents, and tending to many other
> disorders; Therefore Voted, that if any undergraduate shall be an Actor in, a Spectator at,
> or any Waies concern'd in any such Stage Plays, Interludes or Theatrical Entertainment,
> in the Town of Cambridge or elsewhere, He shall for the first Offence be degraded,
> according to the Discretion of the Pres[ident] and Tut[ors] and for any repeated offence,
> shall be rusticated or Expelled.[29]

The decree dampened theatrical pursuits at Harvard, but the alumni outside its
authority were unaffected. As late as 1772, Ames was still involved in amateur
productions in Dedham, when his company mounted the farce *The Toy Shop*, for
which Ames himself wrote the Prologue:

> Here, though no Theatres our Land adorn,
> This work they left their children then unborn;
> We then, their offspring, diffident presume
> To make a present Theatre of this room.

And tho' the piece we've chose fine thoughts displays,
Tis not so striking as some other plays.
Yet, if our undertaking you approve,
Some leisure Night we'll all your passions move.
We'll make you laugh or shed the generous tear,
With plays yon virgins need not blush to hear;
Or be as solemn, let it not alarm one,
As the dull Priest who steals his weekly sermon.
Of this, whatever People may conjecture,
You'll safely call it but an Evening Lecture.[30]

Of that evening's production, Ames records in his diary that it was richly attended, performed "before a numerous audience of the most respectable inhabitants of the First Parish in Dedham both male and female." Such a market encouraged Ames to consider a larger season, as intimated in the Prologue, promising tragedies and discrete comedies for "some leisure night" at this makeshift theater. That both they and their patrons operated under the lecture format betrays their familiarity with another level of theatrical convention: the evasion of authority.

The theater that began under the aegis of pedagogical exercises escaped from the ivy halls of Harvard. The market that Ames and his company of alumni created found competition by the mid-1760s, and a second amateur company was also seeding audiences within Boston proper. From subsequent reactions, this was presumably a company of tradesmen who undertook clandestine performances in the city. On 13 March 1765, John Rowe attended one production and notes that he "Went in the evening over to Gardners to see *The Orphan* acted which was miserably performed. About 210 persons there."[31] This was a tavern performance at Gideon's on Boston Neck, and in Rowe's recording of the event there is nothing curious about well-attended plays in Boston taverns, only that this one was poorly done. Heather S. Nathans has remarked that in this entry Rowe observes no attempt at all to prohibit the production, and he is equally "undisturbed by the impropriety or illegality of witnessing" the production.[32]

Notice of the same and other amateur productions find their way into the Boston newspapers, too. In March 1767, *The Boston Evening Post* asks the rhetorical question: "Is it not surprising that such a number of lads should be encouraged to act in characters unbecoming their callings?" It then provides an answer for the reader with another question: "Does it not tend to take their minds off from their business, and instead of making them good taylors, shoemakers, &c. render them nothing more than strolling players?"[33] A rebuttal to this attack the following month in the *Boston Gazette* defends the performers, before relating the curious fate of the company:

On the 30th of last month, "The Fair Penitent" made an appearance in Boston; she then look'd very beautiful, and with her attendants made a very brilliant figure (her

Metamorphosis and all things considered); But as there was a great deal of nonsensical talk about her, and many impertinent things said of her, besides an inexplicable hypocritical fellow wrote such a [nonsense] performance in the Evening Post, that she left the town immediately (dismissing her attendants at Boston) and went to Cambridge, where a number of grand young gentlemen (who had before entered into her service) immediately waited upon her, and invited her about a mile and a half from town, where they most barbarously murder'd her before a number of grand spectators—Oh! cruel butchery—worse than "Cobblers and Bunglers."[34]

In allegorical terms, the writer describes two productions. At the first, the tradesmen—the "Cobblers and Bunglers"—were dismissed. Hence the "Fair Penitent"—either the play, the character, the "metamorphosed" boy-actor who played Lavinia, or, loosely, theater itself—transferred her talents to the students at Harvard, with whom she had played before, and who now produced a second, rival production at an inn some "mile and half" from Boston. According to the writer, the second production was far inferior than that of the tradesmen's. This, notwithstanding the severity of the legislation, the threats of expulsion, and the parental rebukes.

Though denied theatricals, Boston nonetheless provided a base of support for both theater producers and consumers, and for amateurs and professionals alike, which arose from the tradition of academic productions. When David Douglass brought his American Company to Rhode Island in 1761, he attracted Boston audiences, including Nathaniel Ames, who records a playgoing trip to Providence in August of that same year. Writing of the American Company's visit to Newport, B.W. Brown also provides a document about the Bostonians who were in the house: "News of the theatre spread to the hearth-stone of censorship—Boston; and wayward sons and daughters pleasure-bent braved a four hours drive in stagecoach to visit the world of make-believe and went away highly gratified."[35] Ames is perhaps not hyperbolic when he writes on 9 September 1761 that "Boston people flock up to Newport to see the Plays by the English Actors," and again a week later: "Many people go from Boston to Newport to see the Plays."[36] The following summer Douglass and the American Company returned to New England, this time Providence—suggesting some expectation of success—and again attracted a clientele from Boston. In his *History of the State of Rhode Island*, Samuel Arnold tells us that in 1762 "Douglass had moved his company from Newport, built a theatre, and commenced playing in Providence, where large numbers of people came from Boston to attend the performances."[37]

The same population who threatened the theater supported it. Boston papers covered the players whenever they were performing in the area, such as in Newport in 1761, and in Providence in 1762. After the amateur production of *The Fair Penitent* was performed, one worried op-ed rebutted:

[The] acting of plays and tragedies in this town is now practiced with impunity [...] P.S. It is apprehended that when the American Company of Comedians, who are now at

New York or Philadelphia, hear there is so great an inclination for such entertainments in this place, they will endeavor to introduce themselves[38]

If the fear was that Boston knew too much of the professional threat from the American Company—which the American Company would soon know of them—then the fear was too late. Boston audiences knew all about the theater, having witnessed it for a generation through academic drama.

By the end of the decade, even soldiers were following the student's lead and producing their own amateur plays under the guise of practicing "rhetoric." The most level-headed critique came from the Worcester physician William Paine, who wrote to Isaac Smith in 1769:

I am entirely of your Opinion with Regard to Theatrical Performances (viz.) That this Country in its present Circumstances cannot Support a Playhouse without manifest Disadvantage to the Community. But yet I think that the Stage affords the most rational Entertainment that I know of, and I look upon a well regulated Theatre to be of real Service, as it tends to promote Virtue and Discourage Vice [...] (But as you observe) I never should have Thought of Soldiers for Actors. Can it be supposed that a Person utterly unacquainted with The beauties of Language, can enter enough into the spirit of a Performance, which abounds with all the Flowers of Rhetoric, as to set up for an Actor? Certainly not. And I think they are a proper Subject for Ridicule for their attempting it.[39]

William Paine had already internalized both the argument and the language of the American Company's David Douglass: "a well-regulated theatre" is "the most rational entertainment." These are phrases that appear on the handbills that Douglass circulated whenever introducing himself to a new town:

A well regulated theater has ever been held, by the wisest and most learned men of the present age, a matter of the highest utility; not only, as the most rational entertainment human nature is capable of enjoying, but, in being highly conducive to enlarge the mind, polish the manners, and while it entertains and improves, is as it were, to use the words of that great judge of nature, Shakespeare, to "shew virtue her own image."[40]

Not only had theater arrived through the academic tradition, but through the same tradition it had already commandeered the rhetoric of objection.

Notes

1   Simon Gratz, "Some Material for a Biography of Mrs. Elizabeth Fergusson," *Pennsylvania Magazine of History and Biography* 39 (1915): 309.

2   Alexander Quesnay refitted the playhouse in late November, and its opening on 2 January is reported in Philadelphia's *Freeman's Journal* on 28 November

1781 and 2 January 1782. It was closed after the one performance.

3 Many of Clinton's letters are published in Benjamin Franklin Stevens, ed., *The Campaign in Virginia, 1781*, 2 vols. (London, 1888).

4 The best example is, or course, the British army's performance of the *Blockade of Boston*, during which the American forces counter-attacked Boston and surprised the British inside the playhouse.

5 See Marius B. Péladeau, ed., *The Prose of Royall Tyler* (Montpelier: Vermont Historical Society, 1972), 149 ff.

6 In the young Aaron Burr's household, for example, his sister recorded for 20 January 1755: "Something happened to make us extreamly merry this eve. You will wonder what it should be, so to put you out of pain I'll tell you—I had orders from Cousin Billy Vance to dress Brother Sammy (this is my Brother you know) in womens cloths, in order to act part of a play, which was done quite privately, and with no other desighn [*sic*] than to lern the young sparks a good delivery"; see *The Journal of Esther Edwards Burr: 1754–1757*, ed. Carol F. Karlsen and Laurie Crumpacker (New Haven: Yale University Press, 1984), 82–3.

7 Stephen Greenblatt, *Will in the World: How Shakespeare Became Shakespeare* (New York: W.W. Norton, 2004), 27.

8 In 1761, Smith composed *An Exercise consisting of a Dialogue and Ode Sacred to the Memory of His late Gracious Majesty, George II* (Philadelphia: by Andrew Steuart and Hugh Saine, 1761), and the following year he wrote and his students performed a similar exercise, marking the ascension of King George III; see Arthur Hobson Quinn, *A History of the American Drama, From the Beginning to the Civil War*, 2d edn. (New York: Appleton-Century-Crofts, 1951), 27.

9 Lawrence Lewis, Jr., "Edward Shippen, Chief Justice of Pennsylvania," *Pennsylvania Magazine of History and Biography* 7 (1883): 16.

10 Paul Goring, *The Rhetoric of Sensibility in Eighteenth Century Culture* (Cambridge: Cambridge University Press, 2005), 112.

11 Goring, *The Rhetoric of Sensibility*, 102.

12 Richard Beale Davis, *Intellectual Life in the Colonial South, 1585–1763*, 3 vols. (Knoxville: University of Tennessee Press, 1978), 3.1284, who claims there were two performances on the occasion, one in English, one in Latin. See also Lyon G. Tyler, *Williamsburg, The Old Colonial Capital* (Richmond: Whittet & Shepperson, 1907), 224–31.

13 "The Statutes of the College of William and Mary, Codified in 1736," reprinted in *William and Mary Quarterly* 22 (1914): 288.

14 Hugh Garland, "School Days of John Randolph," *William and Mary Quarterly* 24.1 (1915): 3; reprinted from Hugh Garland, *Life of John Randolph of Roanoke*, 2 vols. (New York: D. Appleton & Company, 1850).

15 *Virginia Gazette*, 10–17 September 1736.

16 Samuel Arnold concurs, whose *History of the State of Rhode Island and Providence Plantations*, 2 vols. (New York: D. Appleton, 1878), 2.238, tells

us that in 1762 "Douglass had moved his company from Newport [in 1761], built a theatre, and commenced playing in Providence, where large numbers of people came from Boston to attend the performances."

17 The deposition dates from 2 July 1755 that the students had performed a play about seven months earlier, "Records of the Linonian Society, Yale College, 1753–1870," Yale University, MS. 206, series 2, box 2, folder 1. The records are abstracted in Arthur W. Bloom, "A History of the Theatre of New Haven, Connecticut before 1860" (Ph.D. Thesis, Yale University, 1966), 8.

18 Bloom, "A History of the Theatre," 19, 26, from a meeting of 18 June 1756.

19 Bloom, "A History of the Theatre," 31.

20 Bloom, "A History of the Theatre," 44, 53–4, 66–7.

21 Robert Brand Hanson, ed., *The Diary of Dr. Nathaniel Ames of Dedham, Massachusetts, 1758–1822*, 2 vols. (Rockport: Picton Press, 1998), 1.12–14.

22 Cf. *Publications of the Colonial Society of Massachusetts* 48 (1974): 295.

23 Hanson, *Diary*, 1.28–30.

24 *The Boston News Letter*, 27 December 1759.

25 The 27 March 1760 issue of the *Maryland Gazette* reprints a letter from "a late Boston Paper," which offers an account of a company of gentlemen who "amused themselves and their friends by a representation of [...] *Cato*." See also *Boston Post-Boy*, 7 January 1760; and Hanson, *Diary*, 1.44–7.

26 Hanson, *Diary*, 1.44, 1.45, 1.47.

27 How's Tavern, run at the time by Ezekiel How, was later immortalized as the Wayside Inn, where Longfellow recuperated after the death of his wife and composed his famous *Tales*. It is still, the brochures tell us, the oldest operating inn in America.

28 In Hanson, *Diary*, 1.244–5, Ames records his "General Prologue which I wrote for *The Toy Shop*, acted at Battles the 20th April 1772."

29 "College Book," Harvard University, Harvard College Library Archives, vii (16 November 1762), 101.

30 Hanson, *Diary*, 1.244–5.

31 Anne Rowe Cunningham, ed., *Letters and Diary of John Rowe: 1759–1762, 1764–1779* (Boston: W.B. Clarke, 1903), 77.

32 Heather S. Nathans, *Early American Theatre from the Revolution to Thomas Jefferson: Into the Hands of the People* (Cambridge: Cambridge University Press, 2003), 24.

33 *The Boston Evening Post*, 9 March 1767.

34 *Boston Gazette*, 13 April 1767.

35 B.W. Brown, *The Colonial Theatre in New England* (Newport: Newport Historical Society, 1930), 17.

36 Hanson, *Diary*, 1.63, 1.69.

37 Arnold, *History of the State*, 2.238.

38 *The Boston Evening Post*, 6 April 1767.

39 "Letters of William Paine," *Proceedings of the Massachusetts Historical Society*, third series, 59 (1926): 424.

40 From a handbill in New York, 1762; see also the *Pennsylvania Chronicle* 26 January to 2 February 1767; *Maryland Gazette*, 6 September 1770, 4 October 1770; *South Carolina Gazette*, 20 September 1773; and *Cornwall Chronicle* (Montego Bay, Jamaica), 15 February 1777.

Collected Bibliography

Agnew, Jean-Christophe, *Worlds Apart: The Market and the Theater in Anglo-American Thought, 1550–1750* (Cambridge: Cambridge University Press, 1986).

Allen, Nancy Gayle Myers, "A Critical Edition of Two Tudor Interludes: *Nice Wanton* and *The Disobedient Child*" (Ph.D. Thesis, Texas Tech University, 1984).

Altman, Joel, *The Tudor Play of Mind: Rhetorical Inquiry and the Development of Elizabethan Drama* (Berkeley: University of California Press, 1978).

Archer, Jayne Elisabeth, and Sarah Knight, "Elizabetha Triumphans," in *The Progresses, Pageants, and Entertainments of Queen Elizabeth I*, ed. Jayne Elisabeth Archer, Elizabeth Goldring, and Sarah Knight (Oxford: Oxford University Press, 2007), 1–23.

Ardolino, Frank, "'Thus Glories England Over All the West': Setting as National Encomium in Robert Greene's *Friar Bacon and Friar Bungay*," *Journal of Evolutionary Psychology* 9.3–4 (1988): 218–29.

Aristotle, *Posterior Analytics*, in *The Complete Works of Aristotle*, 2 vols., ed. and trans. Jonathan Barnes (Princeton: Princeton University Press, 1984), 1.114–66.

Arnold, Samuel, *History of the State of Rhode Island and Providence Plantations*, 2 vols. (New York: D. Appleton, 1878).

Ascham, Roger, THE SCHOLEMASTER *Or plaine and perfite way of teachyng children [...]* (London: by Iohn Daye, 1570).

_____, *The Scholemaster, 1570*, ed. R.C. Alston (Menston: Scolar Press, 1967).

Aston, Margaret, *The King's Bedpost: Reformation and Iconography in a Tudor Group Portrait* (New York: Cambridge University Press, 1993).

Atkins, J.W.H., *English Literary Criticism: The Renascence* (New York: Barnes and Noble, 1947).

Axton, Marie, *Three Tudor Classical Interludes* (Cambridge: D.S. Brewer, 1982).

Babb, Lawrence, *The Elizabethan Malady: a study of melancholia in English literature from 1580 to 1642* (East Lansing: Michigan State College Press, 1951).

B., W., *The Court of good Counsell* (London: by Raph Blower, 1607).

Bacon, Francis, *The Advancement of Learning*, ed. Michael Kiernan (Oxford: Clarendon, 2000).

_____, *Novum Organum*, ed. and trans. Peter Urbach and John Gibson (Chicago: Open Court, 1994).

_____, *The Works of Francis Bacon*, 14 vols., ed. James Spedding, R.L. Ellis, and D.D. Heath (London: Longman, 1857–74).

The Barbers Playe, in *The Chester Mystery Cycle*, 2 vols., ed. R.M. Lumiansky and David Mills (London: Oxford University Press, 1974), 1.56–79.

Barish, Jonas A., *The Antitheatrical Prejudice* (Berkeley: University of California Press, 1981).

Beaumont, Francis, and John Fletcher, *Comedies and Tragedies* (London: for Humphrey Robinson and Humphrey Moseley, 1647).

Becon, Thomas, *The Catechism of Thomas Becon with Other Pieces Written by him in the Reign of King Edward the Sixth*, ed. John Ayre (Cambridge: Cambridge University Press, 1844).

Best, Thomas W., "Introduction," in Edmund Stubbe, *Fraus Honesta*, prep. Thomas W. Best (Hildesheim: Georg Olms Verlag, 1987), 11–23.

Bevington, David, and Eric Rasmussen, "Introduction," in Christopher Marlowe, *Doctor Faustus, A- and B-Texts*, ed. David Bevington and Eric Rasmussen (Manchester: Manchester University Press, 1993), 1–102.

Bland, Desmond, ed., *Gesta Grayorum* (Liverpool: Liverpool University Press, 1968).

Blencowe, John, *Mercurius Sive Literarum Lucta*, prep. Heinz J. Vienken (Hildesheim: Georg Olms Verlag, 1981).

Bloom, Arthur W., "A History of the Theatre of New Haven, Connecticut before 1860" (Ph.D. Thesis, Yale University, 1966).

Blundell, Mary Whitlock, *Helping Friends and Harming Enemies: A Study in Sophocles and Greek Ethics* (Cambridge: Cambridge University Press, 1989).

Boas, Frederick S., *Shakespeare and the Universities and Other Studies in Elizabethan Drama* (New York: D. Appleton and Company, 1923).

_____, *University Drama in the Tudor Age* (Oxford: Oxford University Press, 1914).

Bourdieu, Pierre, *The Logic of Practice*, trans. Richard Nice (Stanford: Stanford University Press, 1990).

Brenner, Robert, *Merchants and Revolution: Commercial Change, Political Conflict, and London's Overseas Traders, 1550–1653* (Princeton: Princeton University Press, 1993).

Bright, Timothy, *Treatise of Melancholie* (London: by Thomas Vautrollier, 1586).

Brown, B.W., *The Colonial Theatre in New England* (Newport: Newport Historical Society, 1930).

Bryan, Emily D., "In the Company of Boys: the Place of the Boy Actor in Early Modern English Culture" (Ph.D. Thesis, Northwestern University, 2005).

Burr, Esther Edwards, *The Journal of Esther Edwards Burr: 1754–1757*, ed. Carol F. Karlsen and Laurie Crumpacker (New Haven: Yale University Press, 1984).

Burton, Robert, *The Anatomy of Melancholy* (Oxford: by Iohn Lichfield and Iames Short, for Henry Cripps, 1621).

_____, *The Anatomy of Melancholy*, 6 vols., ed. Thomas C. Faulkner, Nicholas K. Kiessling, and Rhonda L. Blair, intro. J.B. Bamborough (Oxford: Clarendon, 1989–2000).

_____, *The Anatomy of Melancholy*, ed. Floyd Dell and Paul Jordan-Smith (New York: Tudor, 1938).

Bushnell, Rebecca, *A Culture of Teaching: Early Modern Humanism in Theory and Practice* (Ithaca: Cornell University Press, 1996).

Capp, Bernard, *English Almanacs 1500–1800: Astrology and the Popular Press* (Ithaca: Cornell University Press, 1979).

Cartwright, Kent, *Theatre and Humanism: English Drama in the Sixteenth Century* (Cambridge: Cambridge University Press, 1999).

Chambers, E.K., *The Elizabethan Stage*, 4 vols. (Oxford: Clarendon, 1923).

Charlton, Kenneth, *Education in Renaissance England* (London: Routledge and Kegan Paul, 1965).

Christopherson, John, *An exhortation to all menne to take hede and beware of rebellion* (London: by John Cawood, 1554).

_____, "Ιεφθάε," St. John's College, Cambridge, MS. 284.H.19.

_____, "Ιεφθάε," Trinity College, Cambridge, MS. 0.1.37.

_____, *Jephthah*, ed. and trans. Francis Howard Fobes (Newark: University of Delaware Press, 1928).

_____, "Tragœdia Iephte," Bodleian Library, MS. Tanner 466.

Church of England, Diocese of Lincoln, Bishop [Thomas Cooper], *Thesaurus linguae Romanae & Britannicae tam accurate congestus, vt nihil penè in eo desyderari possit [...]* (London: by Henry Denham, 1584).

Cicero, *De Oratore*, 3 vols., ed. Augustus S. Wilkins (Oxford: Oxford University Press, 1881).

Clark, Ira, *Comedy, Youth, Manhood in Early Modern England* (Newark: University of Delaware Press, 2003).

Clarke, Samuel, *The Lives of Sundry Eminent Persons in This Later Age in Two Parts. I. Of Divines. II Of Nobility and Gentry of Both Sexes* (London: for Thomas Simmons, 1683).

_____, *The Lives of Two and Twenty Eminent Divines* (London: by A.M. for Thomas Underhill and John Rothwell, 1660).

"College Book," Harvard University, Harvard College Library Archives, vii (16 November 1762).

A Comedy Called Susenbrotus, ed. and trans. Connie McQuillen (Ann Arbor: University of Michigan Press, 1997).

Comensoli, Viviana, *"Household Business": Domestic Plays of Early Modern England* (Toronto: University of Toronto Press, 1996).

"Commonplace Book of Anthony Scattergood," British Library, Additional MS. 44963, Scattergood Collections, vol. XXXII.

The Compleat CLERK, Containing the best FORMS Of all sorts of PRESIDENTS, for CONVEYANCES and ASSURANCES; and other INSTRUMENTS now in use and practice, 4th edn. (London: by G. Sawbridge, T. Roycroft, and W. Rawlins, for H. Twyford, O. Blagrave, J. Place, and R. Harford, 1677).

Cook, Anne Jennalie, *The Privileged Playgoers of Shakespeare's London, 1576–1642* (Princeton: Princeton University Press, 1981).

Costello, William T., *The Scholastic Curriculum at Early Seventeenth-Century Cambridge* (Cambridge: Harvard University Press, 1958).

Cowell, John, *The Interpreter* (Cambridge: by Iohn Legate, 1607).

Crane, Mary Thomas, *Framing Authority: Sayings, Self, and Society in Sixteenth-Century England* (Princeton: Princeton University Press, 1993).

Cressy, David, "Educational Opportunity in Tudor and Stuart England," *History of Education Quarterly* 16 (1976): 301–20.

_____, "The Social Composition of Caius College, Cambridge 1580–1640," *Past and Present* 47 (1970): 113–15.

Curtis, Mark H., *Oxford and Cambridge in Transition, 1558–1642: An Essay on Changing Relations Between the English Universities and English Society* (Oxford: Clarendon, 1959).

Davids, Thomas William, *Annals of Evangelical Nonconformity in the County of Essex* (London: Jackson, Walford, & Hodder, 1863).

Davis, Richard Beale, *Intellectual Life in the Colonial South, 1585–1763*, 3 vols. (Knoxville: University of Tennessee Press, 1978).

Dear, Peter, *Discipline and Experience: The Mathematical Way in the Scientific Revolution* (Chicago: University of Chicago Press, 1995).

_____, "Jesuit Mathematical Science and the Reconstitution of Experience in the Early Seventeenth Century," *Studies in the History and Philosophy of Science* 18 (1987): 133–75.

de Roover, Florence Edler, "Early Examples of Marine Insurance," *Journal of Economic History* 5 (1945): 172–200.

de Roover, Raymond, *Business, Banking, and Economic Thought in Late Medieval and Early Modern Europe*, ed. Julius Kirshner (Chicago: University of Chicago Press, 1974).

Dick, Hugh G., "Introduction," in Thomas Tomkis, *Albumazar: A Comedy*, ed. Hugh G. Dick (Berkeley: University of California Press, 1944), 1–70.

Dillon, Janette, *Language and Stage in Medieval and Renaissance England* (Cambridge: Cambridge University Press, 1998).

Dollimore, Jonathan, *Radical Tragedy: Religion, Ideology, and Power in the Drama of Shakespeare and His Contemporaries*, 2d edn. (Durham: Duke University Press, 1993).

Duffy, Eamon, *The Stripping of the Altars: Traditional Religion in England 1400–1580* (New Haven: Yale University Press, 1992).

Durning, Louise, ed., *Queen Elizabeth's Book of Oxford*, trans. Sarah Knight and Helen Spurling (Oxford: Bodleian Library, 2006).

Earle, John, *The Autograph Manuscript of Microcosmographie* (Leeds: Scolar Press, 1966).

Edgerton, William L., *Nicholas Udall* (New York: Twayne, 1965).

Edwards, Richard, *Damon and Pithias: A Critical Old Spelling Edition*, ed. D. Jerry White (New York: Garland, 1980).

Elliott, John R., Jr., "Plays, Players and Playwrights in Renaissance Oxford," in *From Page to Performance: Essays in Early English Drama*, ed. John A. Alford (East Lansing: Michigan State University Press, 1995), 179–94.

_____, "Queen Elizabeth at Oxford: New Light on the Royal Plays of 1566," *English Literary Renaissance* 18 (1988): 218–29.

_____, and Alan H. Nelson (University), Alexandra F. Johnston and Diana Wyatt (City), eds., *Records of Early English Drama: Oxford*, 2 vols. (Toronto: University of Toronto Press, 2004).

Enterline, Lynn, "Rhetoric, Discipline, and the Theatricality of Everyday Life in Elizabethan Grammar Schools," in *From Performance to Print in Shakespeare's England*, ed. Stephen Orgel and Peter Holland (New York: Palgrave Macmillan, 2006), 173–90.

Erasmus, Desiderius, *Ciceronianus*, trans. Izora Scott, in Izora Scott, *Controversies Over the Imitation of Cicero as a Model for Style and Some Phases of their Influence on the Schools of the Renaissance* (New York: Teacher's College, Columbia University, 1910).

_____, *The Colloquies of Erasmus*, trans. Craig R. Thompson (Chicago: University of Chicago Press, 1965).

_____, *De pueris statim ac liberaliter instituendis declamatio*, trans. Beert C. Verstraete, in *Collected Works of Erasmus: Literary and Educational Writings 4*, 86 vols., ed. J.K. Sowards (Toronto: University of Toronto Press, 1978), 26.295–346.

Euripides, *Bacchae*, ed. E.R. Dodds, 2d edn. (Oxford: Clarendon, 1960).

Feingold, Mordechai, *The mathematicians' apprenticeship: Science, universities and society in England, 1560–1640* (Cambridge: Cambridge University Press, 1984).

Ferrar, John, and Doctor Jebb, *Nicholas Ferrar. Two Lives by his Brother John and Doctor Jebb*, ed. J.E.B. Mayor (Cambridge: Cambridge University Press, 1855).

Finkelpearl, Philip J., *John Marston at the Middle Temple* (Cambridge: Harvard University Press, 1969).

Fischer, Sandra K., "'He means to pay': Value and Metaphor in the Lancastrian Tetralogy," *Shakespeare Quarterly* 40 (1989): 149–64.

Fleay, Frederick Gard, *A Chronicle History of the London Stage, 1559–1642* (New York: Stechert, 1909).

Fletcher, Harris Francis, *The Intellectual Development of John Milton*, 2 vols. (Urbana: University of Illinois Press, 1956–61).

Foucault, Michel, "What Is an Author?," in *Textual Strategies: Perspectives in Post-Structuralist Criticism*, ed. and trans. Josué V. Harari (Ithaca: Cornell University Press, 1979), 141–60.

Fowler, Laurence, and Helen Fowler, eds., *Cambridge Commemorated: An Anthology of University Life* (Cambridge: Cambridge University Press, 1984).

Gager, William, *The Complete Works*, 4 vols., ed. Dana F. Sutton (New York: Garland Press, 1994).

Garland, Hugh, *Life of John Randolph of Roanoke*, 2 vols. (New York: D. Appleton & Company, 1850).

Gascoigne, George, *The Glasse of Governement*, in *The Complete Works of George Gascoigne*, 2 vols., ed. John W. Cunliffe (Cambridge: Cambridge University Press, 1910), 2.1–90.

Gatti, Hilary, *The Renaissance Drama of Knowledge* (New York: Routledge, 1989).

Gentili, Alberico, and John Rainolds, *Latin Correspondence by Alberico Gentili and John Rainolds on Academic Drama*, trans. Leon Markowicz (Salzburg: Institut für Englische Sprache und Literatur Universität Salzburg, 1977).

Gesta Grayorum 1688, ed. W.W. Greg (Oxford: Oxford University Press, 1914).

Goldberg, Jonathan, *Sodometries: Renaissance Texts, Modern Sexualities* (Stanford: Stanford University Press, 1992).

_____, *Writing Matter: From the Hands of the English Renaissance* (Stanford: Stanford University Press, 1990).

Goring, Paul, *The Rhetoric of Sensibility in Eighteenth Century Culture* (Cambridge: Cambridge University Press, 2005).

Grady, Hugh, "Falstaff: Subjectivity between the Carnival and the Aesthetic," *Modern Language Review* 96 (2001): 609–23.

Grafton, Anthony, and Lisa Jardine, *From Humanism to the Humanities: Education and Liberal Arts in Fifteenth- and Sixteenth-Century Europe* (Cambridge: Harvard University Press, 1986).

Granger, J.A., *A Biographical History of England*, 4 vols., 2d edn. (London: 1775).

Grantley, Darryll, *Wit's Pilgrimage: Drama and the Social Impact of Education in Early Modern England* (Aldershot: Ashgate, 2000).

Gratz, Simon, "Some Material for a Biography of Mrs. Elizabeth Fergusson," *Pennsylvania Magazine of History and Biography* 39 (1915): 257–321.

Gray, Arthur, *Jesus College* (London: F.E. Robinson & Co., 1902).

Green, A. Wigfall, *The Inns of Court and Early English Drama* (New Haven: Yale University Press, 1931).

Greenblatt, Stephen, *Renaissance Self-Fashioning: From More to Shakespeare* (Chicago: University of Chicago Press, 1980).

_____, *Will in the World: How Shakespeare Became Shakespeare* (New York: W.W. Norton, 2004).

Greene, Robert, *Friar Bacon and Friar Bungay*, ed. Daniel Seltzer (Lincoln: University of Nebraska Press, 1963).

Gurr, Andrew, *Playgoing in Shakespeare's London*, 2d edn. (Cambridge: Cambridge University Press, 1996).

_____, *The Shakespearian Playing Companies* (Oxford: Oxford University Press, 1995).

Guy, John, *Tudor England* (Oxford: Oxford University Press, 1988).

Halliwell, Stephen, *The Aesthetics of Mimesis: Ancient Texts and Modern Problems* (Princeton: Princeton University Press, 2002).

Halpern, Richard, *The Poetics of Primitive Accumulation: English Renaissance Culture and the Genealogy of Capital* (Ithaca: Cornell University Press, 1991).

Hammond, N.G.L., and H.H. Scullard, eds., *Oxford Classical Dictionary*, 2d edn. (Oxford: Clarendon, 1991).

Hanson, Robert Brand, ed., *The Diary of Dr. Nathaniel Ames of Dedham, Massachusetts, 1758–1822*, 2 vols. (Rockport: Picton Press, 1998).

Happé, Peter, *English Drama before Shakespeare* (London: Longman, 1999).

Harbage, Alfred, ed., *Annals of English Drama 975–1700*, rev. by S. Schoenbaum, 3d edn. rev. by Sylvia Stoler Wagonheim (London: Routledge, 1989).

Harris, Richard, Paul Cattermole, and Peter Mackintosh, *A History of Norwich School* (Norwich: Friends of Norwich School, 1991).

Hausted, Peter, *Senile Odium*, ed. and trans. Laurens J. Mills (Bloomington: Indiana University Press, 1949).

Healy, Thomas, "Doctor Faustus," in *The Cambridge Companion to Christopher Marlowe*, ed. Patrick Cheney (Cambridge: Cambridge University Press, 2004), 174–92.

Helgerson, Richard, *The Elizabethan Prodigals* (Berkeley: University of California Press, 1976).

Heywood, Thomas, *AN APOLOGY for Actors* (London: by Nicholas Okes, 1612).

Hill, Christopher, *Economic Problems of the Church: From Archbishop Whitgift to the Long Parliament* (Oxford: Clarendon, 1956).

Höfele, Andreas, "'So Potent Art': Magic Power in Marlowe, Greene and Shakespeare," in *The Iconography of Power: Ideas and Images of Rulership on the English Renaissance Stage*, ed. György E. Szónyi and Rowland Wymer (Szeged: JATE, 2000), 53–72.

Holinshed, Raphael, *THE Third volume of Chronicles* (London, 1587).

Holyday, Barten, *ΤΕΧΝΟΓΑΜΙΑ: or the Marriages of the Arts* (London: by William Stansby for Iohn Parker, 1618).

_____, *Technogamia: or the Marriages of the Arts*, ed. Sister M. Jean Carmel Cavanaugh (Washington, DC: The Catholic University of America Press, 1942).

Horace, *Ars Poetica*, in *Satires, Epistles and Ars Poetica*, trans. H. Rushton Fairclough (Cambridge: Harvard University Press, 1999), 451–89.

Horne, David H., *The Life and Minor Works of George Peele* (New Haven: Yale University Press, 1952).

Houlbrooke, Ralph A., *The English Family 1450–1700* (London: Longman, 1984).

Ingelend, Thomas, *The Disobedient Child*, in *The Dramatic Writings of Richard Wever and Thomas Ingelend*, ed. John S. Farmer (London: n.p., 1905).

James VI and I, *A Counterblaste to Tobacco* (London: by R.B., 1604).

_____, *Basilicon Doron*, in *King James VI and I: The Political Writings*, ed. Johann P. Sommerville (Cambridge: Cambridge University Press, 1994), 1–61.

Jardine, Lisa, "The Place of Dialectic Teaching in Sixteenth-Century Cambridge," *Studies in the Renaissance* 21 (1974): 31–62.

Jones, Ann Rosalind, and Peter Stallybrass, *Renaissance Clothing and the Materials of Memory* (Cambridge: Cambridge University Press, 2000).

Jonson, Ben, *Timber: Or, Discoveries*, in *Ben Jonson*, 11 vols., ed. C.H. Herford, Percy Simpson, and Evelyn Simpson (Oxford: Clarendon, 1925–52), 8.555–649.

Kahn, Victoria, *Rhetoric, Prudence and Skepticism in the Renaissance* (Ithaca: Cornell University Press, 1985).

Kearney, Hugh, *Scholars and Gentlemen: Universities and Society in Pre-Industrial Britain, 1500–1700* (Ithaca: Cornell University Press, 1970).

Keenan, Siobhan, "Spectator and Spectacle: Royal Entertainments at the Universities in the 1560s," in *The Progresses, Pageants, and Entertainments of Queen Elizabeth I*, ed. Jayne Elisabeth Archer, Elizabeth Goldring, and Sarah Knight (Oxford: Oxford University Press, 2007), 86–103.

Kerr, Heather, "Sir Thomas Elyot, 'Marcus Geminus' and a Comedy for Elizabeth I at Oxford, 1566," *AUMLA: Journal of the Australasian Universities Language and Literature Association* 73 (1990): 141–55.

King, Ros, *The Works of Richard Edwards: Politics, Poetry and Performance in Sixteenth-Century England* (Manchester: Manchester University Press, 2001).

Knapp, Margaret, and Michal Kobialka, "Shakespeare and the Prince of Purpoole: The 1594 Production of *The Comedy of Errors* at Gray's Inn Hall," in *"The Comedy of Errors": Critical Essays*, ed. Robert S. Miola (New York: Routledge, 1997), 431–45.

Knapp, Robert S., "The Academic Drama," in *A Companion to Renaissance Drama*, ed. Arthur F. Kinney (London: Blackwell, 2002), 257–65.

Knight, Sarah, "'He is indeed a kind of Scholler-Mountebank': Academic Liars in Jacobean Satire," in *Shell Games: Studies in Scams, Frauds, and Deceits (1300–1650)*, ed. Mark Crane, Richard Raiswell, and Margaret Reeves (Toronto: Centre for Reformation and Renaissance Studies, 2004), 59–80.

Lanier, Douglas, "'Stigmatical in Making': The Material Character of *The Comedy of Errors*," *English Literary Renaissance* 23 (1993): 81–112.

Laslett, Peter, *The World We Have Lost* (New York: Scribner's, 1965).

Leinwand, Theodore B., *Theatre, Finance, and Society in Early Modern England* (Cambridge: Cambridge University Press, 1999).

Leishman, J.B., ed., *The Three Parnassus Plays (1598–1601)* (London: Ivor Nicholson & Watson Ltd., 1949).

Lemnius, Levinus, *De Habitu et Constitutione Corporis* (Antwerp: apud Guilielmum Simonem, 1561).

Levine, Nina, "Extending Credit in the *Henry IV* Plays," *Shakespeare Quarterly* 51 (2000): 403–31.

Lewis, Gillian, "The Faculty of Medicine," in *The Collegiate University*, ed. James McConica (Oxford: Clarendon, 1986), 213–56, vol. 3 of *The History of the University of Oxford*, 8 vols., 1984–97.

Lewis, Lawrence, Jr., "Edward Shippen, Chief Justice of Pennsylvania," *Pennsylvania Magazine of History and Biography* 7 (1883): 11–34.

Linton, Anna, "Sacrificed or Spared? The Fate of Jephthah's Daughter in Early Modern Theological and Literary Texts," *German Life and Letters* 57 (2004): 237–55.

Lloyd, Michael, *The Agon in Euripides* (Oxford: Clarendon, 1992).

Lorenz, Hendrik, *The Brute Within: Appetitive Desire in Plato and Aristotle* (Oxford: Clarendon, 2006).

Lyly, John, *Campaspe*, in *The Complete Works of John Lyly*, 3 vols., ed. R. Warwick Bond (Oxford: Clarendon, 1902), 2.302–60.

MacCaffrey, Wallace, *Elizabeth I* (London: Edward Arnold, 1993).

Manning, Thomas John, "The Staging of Plays at Christ Church, Oxford, 1582–1592" (Ph.D. Thesis, University of Michigan, 1972).

Marlowe, Christopher, *Doctor Faustus, A- and B-Texts*, ed. David Bevington and Eric Rasmussen (Manchester: Manchester University Press, 1993).

Martin, Frederick, *The History of Lloyd's and of Marine Insurance in Great Britain* (London: Macmillan and Co., 1876).

Martin, Julian, *Francis Bacon, the State, and the Reform of Natural Philosophy* (Cambridge: Cambridge University Press, 1992).

Matthews, Victor H., *Judges & Ruth* (Cambridge: Cambridge University Press, 2004).

Mayor, J.E.B., *Early Statutes of the College of St. John the Evangelist in the University of Cambridge* (Cambridge: Cambridge University Press, 1859).

Mazzio, Carla, "Sins of the Tongue," in *The Body in Parts: Fantasies of Corporeality in Early Modern Europe*, ed. David Hillman and Carla Mazzio (New York: Routledge, 1997), 53–80.

_____, "The Three Dimensional Self: Geometry, Melancholy, Drama," in *The Arts of Calculation: Quantifying Thought in Early Modern Europe*, ed. David Glimp and Michelle R. Warren (New York: Palgrave Macmillan, 2004), 39–65.

McCarthy, Kathleen, *Slaves, Masters, and the Art of Authority in Plautine Comedy* (Princeton: Princeton University Press, 2000).

McCoy, Richard C., "Lord of Liberty: Francis Davison and the Cult of Elizabeth," in *The Reign of Elizabeth I: Court and Culture in the Last Decade*, ed. John Guy (Cambridge: Cambridge University Press, 1995), 212–28.

McNulty, Robert, "Bruno at Oxford," *Renaissance News* 13 (1960): 300–305.

Mercurius Rusticans: A Critical Edition, ed. Ann J. Cotton (New York: Garland Publishing, 1988).

Middleton, Thomas, *The Second Maiden's Tragedy*, ed. Anne Lancashire (Manchester: Manchester University Press, 1978).

Milton, John, "An Attack on the Scholastic Philosophy," in *Complete Prose Works*, 8 vols., ed. Don M. Wolfe, et al. (New Haven: Yale University Press, 1953–82), 1.240–48.

_____, *Apology for Smectymnuus*, in *Areopagitica and Other Prose Works*, ed. C.E. Vaughan (London: J.M. Dent, 1927), 105–61.

Misogonus, in *Six Anonymous Plays*, second series, ed. John S. Farmer (London: Early English Drama Society, 1906), 133–243.

Montrose, Louis Adrian, *The Purpose of Playing: Shakespeare and the Cultural Politics of the Elizabethan Theatre* (Chicago: University of Chicago Press, 1996).

Morgan, Victor, "Cambridge University and 'The Country' 1560–1640," in *The University in Society*, 2 vols., ed. Lawrence Stone (Princeton: Princeton University Press, 1974), 1.183–245.

Mortenson, Peter, "*Friar Bacon and Friar Bungay*: Festive Comedy and 'Three-Form'd Luna,'" *English Literary Renaissance* 2 (1972): 194–207.

Motter, T.H. Vail, *The School Drama in England* (London: Longmans, Green and Co., 1929).

Mulcaster, Richard, *Positions Concerning the Training Up of Children*, ed. William Barker (Toronto: University of Toronto Press, 1994).

Muldrew, Craig, *Economy of Obligation: The Culture of Credit and Social Relations in Early Modern England* (New York: St. Martin's Press, 1998).

Mullinger, J. Bass, *The University of Cambridge* (Cambridge: Cambridge University Press, 1873).

Nagy, Gregory, *The Best of the Achaeans: Concepts of the Hero in Archaic Greek Poetry*, rev. edn. (Baltimore: Johns Hopkins University Press, 1999).

Nashe, Thomas, *The Vnfortvnate Traveller*, in *The Works of Thomas Nashe*, 5 vols., ed. Ronald B. McKerrow (New York: Barnes & Noble, 1966), 2.187–328.

Nathans, Heather S., *Early American Theatre from the Revolution to Thomas Jefferson: Into the Hands of the People* (Cambridge: Cambridge University Press, 2003).

Nelson, Alan H., "Cambridge University Drama in the 1580s," in *The Elizabethan Theatre 11*, ed. A.L. Magnusson and C.E. McGee (Port Credit: P.D. Meany, 1990), 19–31.

_____, "Contexts for Early English Drama: The Universities," in *Contexts for Early English Drama*, ed. Marianne G. Briscoe and John C. Coldewey (Bloomington: Indiana University Press, 1989), 137–49.

_____, "Drama in the 1520s: Cambridge University," *Research Opportunities in Renaissance Drama* 31 (1992): 67–8.

_____, *Early Cambridge Theatres: University, College, and Town Stages, 1464–1720* (Cambridge: Cambridge University Press, 1994).

_____, ed., *Records of Early English Drama: Cambridge*, 2 vols. (Toronto: University of Toronto Press, 1989).

Newton, Thomas, *The Touchstone of Complexions* (London: by Thomas Marsh, 1576).

Nichols, John, *The Progresses and Public Processions of Queen Elizabeth*, 3 vols. (London: Printed by and for J. Nichols and son, 1823).

Noonan, John T., Jr., *The Scholastic Analysis of Usury* (Cambridge: Harvard University Press, 1957).

O'Gorman, Ned, "Aristotle's Phantasia in the *Rhetoric*: Lexis, Appearance, and the Epideictic Function of Discourse," *Philosophy and Rhetoric* 38 (2005): 16–40.

Ong, Walter J., *Rhetoric, Romance and Technology: Studies in the Interaction of Expression and Culture* (Ithaca: Cornell University Press, 1971).

Orgel, Stephen, *The Illusion of Power: Political Theater in the English Renaissance* (Berkeley: University of California Press, 1975).

_____, *The Jonsonian Masque* (Cambridge: Harvard University Press, 1965).

_____, "The Poetics of Spectacle," *New Literary History* 2 (1971): 367–89.

Orlin, Lena Cowen, ed., *Material London, ca. 1600* (Philadelphia: University of Pennsylvania Press, 2000).

Orrell, John, *The Human Stage: English Theatre Design, 1567–1640* (Cambridge: Cambridge University Press, 1988).

_____, "The Theatre at Christ Church, Oxford, in 1605," *Shakespeare Survey* 35 (1982): 129–40.

_____, *The Theatres of Inigo Jones and John Webb* (Cambridge: Cambridge University Press, 1985).

Paine, William, "Letters of William Paine," *Proceedings of the Massachusetts Historical Society*, third series, 59 (1926): 422–424.

Palingenius, Marcellus, *The Zodiake of Life*, trans. Barnabe Googe, intro. Rosamund Tuve (New York: Scholars' Facsimiles, 1947).

Palliser, D.M., *The Age of Elizabeth: England Under the Later Tudors, 1547–1603* (London: Longman, 1983).

Péladeau, Marius B., ed., *The Prose of Royall Tyler* (Montpelier: Vermont Historical Society, 1972).

Philip, Ian, *The Bodleian Library in the Seventeenth and Eighteenth Centuries* (Oxford: Clarendon, 1983).

Plato, *Crito*, in *Four Texts on Socrates*, trans. Thomas G. West and Grace Starry West, rev. edn. (Ithaca: Cornell University Press, 1998).

Plautus, *Amphitryon*, in *Three Plays by Plautus: Miles Gloriosus, Amphitryon, and The Prisoners*, ed. and trans. Paul Roche (New York: Mentor Books, 1968), 17–106.

Plummer, Charles, ed., *Elizabethan Oxford: Reprints of Rare Tracts* (Oxford: Clarendon, 1887).

Porter, H.C., *Reformation and Reaction in Tudor Cambridge* (Hamden: Archon, 1958).

Porter, Joseph A., *Shakespeare's Mercutio: His History and Drama* (Chapel Hill: University of North Carolina Press, 1988).

Postlewait, Thomas, "Theatricality and Antitheatricality in Renaissance London," in *Theatricality*, ed. Tracy C. Davis and Thomas Postlewait (Cambridge: Cambridge University Press, 2003), 90–126.

_____, and Tracy C. Davis, "Theatricality: An Introduction," in *Theatricality*, ed. Tracy C. Davis and Thomas Postlewait (Cambridge: Cambridge University Press, 2003), 1–39.

Potter, Ursula, "Cockering Mothers and Humanist Pedagogy in Two Tudor School Plays," in *Domestic Arrangements in Early Modern England*, ed. Kari Boyd McBride (Pittsburgh: Duquesne University Press, 2002), 244–78.

_____, "The Naming of Holofernes in *Love's Labour's Lost*," *English Language Notes* 37 (2000): 13–26.

_____, "Performing Arts in the Tudor Classroom," in *Tudor Drama Before Shakespeare, 1485–1590: New Directions for Research, Criticism, and Pedagogy*, ed. Lloyd Kermode, Jason Scott-Warren, and Martine Van Elk (New York: Palgrave Macmillan, 2004), 143–65.

Prest, Wilfrid R., *The Inns of Court under Elizabeth I and the Early Stuarts, 1590–1640* (Totowa: Rowman and Littlefield, 1972).

Puttenham, George, *The Arte of English Poesie. Contriued into three Bookes: The first of Poets and Poesie, the second of Proportion, the third of Ornament* (London: by Richard Field, 1589).

Queen Elizabeth I, "Queen Elizabeth's first reply to the Parliamentary petitions urging the execution of Mary, Queen of Scots, November 12, 1586" (version 2), in *Elizabeth I: Collected Works*, ed. Leah S. Marcus, Janel Mueller, and Mary Beth Rose (Chicago: University of Chicago Press, 2000), 190–96.

Quinn, Arthur Hobson, *A History of the American Drama, From the Beginning to the Civil War*, 2d edn. (New York: Appleton-Century-Crofts, 1951).

Rackin, Phyllis, "Androgyny, Mimesis, and the Marriage of the Boy Heroine on the English Renaissance Stage," *PMLA* 102 (1987): 29–41.

Raffield, Paul, *Images and Cultures of Law in Early Modern England: Justice and Political Power, 1558–1660* (Cambridge: Cambridge University Press, 2004).

"Records of the Linonian Society, Yale College, 1753–1870," Yale University, MS. 206.

Richards, Jennifer, *Rhetoric and Courtliness in Early Modern England* (Cambridge: Cambridge University Press, 2003).

Ricketts, John, *Byrsa Basilica, Seu Regale Excambium: A Latin Academic Comedy of the Early Seventeenth Century, by J. Rickets*, ed. and trans. R.H. Bowers (Louvain: C. Uystpruyst, 1939).

Rivlin, Elizabeth, "Theatrical Literacy in *The Comedy of Errors* and the *Gesta Grayorum*," *Critical Survey* 14 (2002): 64–78.

Robertson, Roderick, "Oxford Theatre in Tudor Times," *Educational Theatre Journal* 21 (1969): 41–50.

Rossi, Paolo, *Francis Bacon: From Magic to Science*, trans. Sacha Rabinovitch (London: Routledge & Kegan Paul, 1968).

Rowe, John, *Letters and Diary of John Rowe: 1759–1762, 1764–1779*, ed. Anne Rowe Cunningham (Boston: W.B. Clarke, 1903).

Ruggle, George, "Ignoramus," Bodleian Library, MS. Douce 43.

_____, "Ignoramus," Bodleian Library, Rawlinson MS. D1361.

_____, *Ignoramus [...] Translated into English by R.C.* (London, 1662).

_____, *Ignoramus*, ed. John Sidney Hawkins (London, 1787).

_____, *Ignoramus: Or, the English Lawyer: A Comedy*, trans. Edward Ravenscroft (London: W. Feales, 1736).

_____, *Ignoramus (1615)*, ed. and trans. Dana F. Sutton, *The Philological Museum*, 5 September 2000, University of Birmingham, 8 November 2007 <http://www.philological.bham.ac.uk/ruggle/>

_____, *Ignoramus*, ed. E.F.J. Tucker (Hildesheim: Georg Olms Verlag, 1987).

Ruggles, Henry Stoddard, "The Lineage of George Ruggle, a Member of the Virginia Company," *William and Mary College Quarterly Historical Magazine* 5 (1896–97): 203–4.

Sacks, David Harris, "London's Dominion: The Metropolis, the Market Economy, and the State," in *Material London, ca. 1600*, ed. Lena Cowen Orlin (Philadelphia: University of Pennsylvania Press, 2000), 20–54.

Schmitt, Charles B., "Experience and Experiment: A Comparison of Zabarella's View with Galileo's in *De Motu*," *Studies in the Renaissance* 16 (1969): 86–92.

_____, *John Case and Aristotelianism in Renaissance England* (Kingston: McGill-Queen's University Press, 1983).

Segal, Erich, *Roman Laughter: The Comedy of Plautus* (Cambridge: Harvard University Press, 1968).

Shakespeare, William, *The First Part of King Henry the Fourth*, ed. Barbara Hodgdon (Boston: Bedford Books, 1997).

_____, *Hamlet*, ed. Harold Jenkins (London: Routledge, 1993).

_____, *Hamlet*, ed. Ann Thompson and Neil Taylor (London: Arden Shakespeare, 2006).

_____ [*sic*], *The London Prodigal* (London: by T.C. for Nathaniel Butter, 1605).

_____, *Love's Labor's Lost*, ed. H.R. Woudhuysen (Walton-on-Thames: Thomas Nelson and Sons, 1998).

_____, *The Merchant of Venice*, in *The Riverside Shakespeare*, ed. G. Blakemore Evans, et al. (Boston: Houghton Mifflin Company, 1974), 250–85.

Shapiro, Michael, *Children of the Revels: The Boy Companies of Shakespeare's Time and Their Plays* (New York: Columbia University Press, 1977).

Shell, Marc, *The Economy of Literature* (Baltimore: Johns Hopkins University Press, 1978).

Shenk, Linda, "Queen Solomon: An International Elizabeth in 1569," in *Queens and Power in Medieval and Early Modern England*, ed. Robert Bucholz and Carole Levin (Lincoln: University of Nebraska Press, forthcoming).

_____, "'To Love and Be Wise': The Earl of Essex, Humanist Court Culture, and England's Learned Queen," *Early Modern Literary Studies* 13.2, Special Issue 16 (2007): 3.1–27.

_____, "Transforming Learned Authority into Royal Supremacy: Elizabeth I's Learned Persona in Her University Orations," in *Elizabeth I: Always Her Own Free Woman*, ed. Carole Levin, Jo Eldridge Carney, and Debra Barrett-Graves (Burlington: Ashgate, 2003), 78–96.

Shepard, Alan, *Marlowe's Soldiers: Rhetorics of Masculinity in the Age of the Armada* (Burlington: Ashgate, 2002).

Sidney, Sir Philip, *A Defence of Poetry*, ed. J.A. Van Dorsten (New York: Oxford University Press, 1966).

Simon, Joan, *Education and Society in Tudor England* (Cambridge: Cambridge University Press, 1966).

_____, "The Reformation and English Education," *Past and Present* 11 (1957): 48–65.

_____, "The Social Origins of Cambridge Students, 1603–1640," *Past and Present* 26 (1963): 58–67.

Smith, Bruce R., *Ancient Scripts and Modern Experience on the English Stage 1500–1700* (Princeton: Princeton University Press, 1988).

Smith, G.C. Moore, *College Plays Performed in the University of Cambridge* (Cambridge: Cambridge University Press, 1923).

Smith, William, *An Exercise consisting of a Dialogue and Ode Sacred to the Memory of His late Gracious Majesty, George II* (Philadelphia: by Andrew Steuart and Hugh Saine, 1761).

Sophocles, *Oedipus Rex*, ed. R.D. Dawe (Cambridge: Cambridge University Press, 1982).

Sowernam, Esther, *Esther hath hang'd Haman [...]*, in *Half Humankind: Contexts and Texts of the Controversy about Women in England 1540–1640*, ed. Katherine Usher Henderson and Barbara F. McManus (Urbana: University of Illinois Press, 1985), 217–43.

Spenser, Edmund, *The Faerie Queene*, ed. Thomas P. Roche, Jr. (Harmondsworth: Penguin, 1987).

"Statutes of the College of William and Mary, Codified in 1736," *William and Mary Quarterly* 22 (1914): 288.

Steggle, Matthew, "Varieties of fantasy in 'What You Will,'" in *The Drama of John Marston: Critical Re-Visions*, ed. T.F. Wharton (Cambridge: Cambridge University Press, 2000), 45–59.

Stevens, Benjamin Franklin, ed., *The Campaign in Virginia, 1781*, 2 vols. (London, 1888).

Stewart, Alan, *Close Readers: Humanism and Sodomy in Early Modern England* (Princeton: Princeton University Press, 1997).

Stone, Lawrence, "The Educational Revolution in England, 1560–1640," *Past and Present* 28 (1964): 41–80.

_____, "Social Mobility in England 1500–1700," *Past and Present* 33 (1966): 16–55.

Stubbe, Edmund, *Fraus Honesta*, prep. Thomas W. Best (Hildesheim: Georg Olms Verlag, 1987).

Stubbes, Phillip, *The Anatomie of Abuses* (London: by Richard Iones, 1583).

Sturley, D.M., *The Royal Grammar School, Guildford* (Guildford: n.p., 1980).

Swinburne, Henry, *A Treatise of Spousals, or Matrimonial Contracts* (New York: Garland, 1985).

Tanner, J.R., *The Historical Register of the University of Cambridge* (Cambridge: Cambridge University Press, 1917).

Tennenhouse, Leonard, *Power on Display: The Politics of Shakespeare's Genres* (New York: Methuen, 1986).

"Theater at Christ Church, Oxford, August 1605," British Library, Additional MS. 15505, fol. 21a.

Thomas, Keith, *Religion and the Decline of Magic: Studies in Popular Beliefs in Sixteenth and Seventeenth Century England* (London: Weidenfeld & Nicolson, 1971).

Thompson, Craig R., *Schools in Tudor England* (Washington, DC: Folger Shakespeare Library, 1958).

Tilley, Arthur, "Greek Studies in England in the Early Sixteenth Century," *The English Historical Review* 53 (1938): 221–39.

Tomkis, Thomas, *Albumazar: A Comedy by Thomas Tomkis*, ed. Hugh G. Dick (Berkeley: University of California Press, 1944).

_____, LINGVA: *Or The Combat of the Tongue, And the fiue Senses For Superiority* (London: by G. Eld, for Simon Waterson, 1607).

Tremlett, T.D., ed., *Calendar of the Manuscripts belonging to the King's School, Bruton, 1297–1826* (Dorchester: Friary, 1939).

Tucker, E.F.J., "Ruggle's *Ignoramus* and Humanistic Criticism of the Language of the Common Law," *Renaissance Quarterly* 30 (1977): 341–50.

Tyler, Lyon G., *Williamsburg, The Old Colonial Capital* (Richmond: Whittet & Shepperson, 1907).

Upton, Christopher, prep., *John Christopherson IEPHTE, William Goldingham HERODES* (Hildesheim: Georg Olms Verlag, 1988).

Vickers, Brian, *Francis Bacon and Renaissance Prose* (Cambridge: Cambridge University Press, 1968).

Vives, Juan Luis, *The Education of a Christian Woman: a sixteenth-century manual*, ed. and trans. Charles Fantazzi (Chicago: University of Chicago Press, 2000).

_____, *Tudor School-boy Life: The Dialogues of Juan Luis Vives*, ed. and trans. Foster Watson (London: Frank Cass, 1970).

Walker, John, *The Sufferings of the Clergy During the Great Rebellion, Part II* (Oxford: John Henry and James Parker, 1862).

Walkington, Thomas, *The Optick Glasse of Humours* (London: by Iohn Windet for Martin Clerke, 1607).

Wall, Wendy, "'Household Stuff': The Sexual Politics of Domesticity and the Advent of English Comedy," *English Literary History* 65 (1998): 1–45.

Watson, Foster, *The Beginnings of the Teaching of Modern Subjects in England* (London: Pitman, 1909).

Weaver, F.W., "Bruton School," *Somerset & Dorset Notes & Queries* 3 (1893): 241–8.

Webster, John, *Academiarum Examen, or the Examination of Academies*, in *Science and Education in the Seventeenth Century: The Webster-Ward Debate*, ed. Allen G. Debus (London: Macdonald & Co., 1970), 67–192.

Wertheim, Albert, "The Presentation of Sin in 'Friar Bacon and Friar Bungay,'" *Criticism: A Quarterly for Literature and the Arts* 16 (1974): 273–86.

West, William N., *Theatres and Encyclopedias in Early Modern Europe* (Cambridge: Cambridge University Press, 2002).

Whigham, Frank, *Ambition and Privilege: The Social Tropes of Elizabethan Courtesy Theory* (Berkeley: University of California Press, 1984).

White, Beatrice, ed., *The Vulgaria of John Stanbridge and the Vulgaria of Robert Whittinton* (London: Kegan Paul, Trench, Trubner & Co., Ltd., 1932).

White, Martin, *Renaissance Drama in Action: An Introduction to Aspects of Theatre Practice and Performance* (London: Routledge, 1998).

White, Paul Whitfield, *Theater and Reformation: Protestantism, Patronage and Playing in Tudor England* (Cambridge: Cambridge University Press, 1993).

Wiesel, Elie, *Sages and Dreamers: Biblical, Talmudic, and Hasidic Portraits and Legends* (New York: Summit, 1991).

Williams, Penry, "Elizabethan Oxford: State, Church and University," in *The Collegiate University*, ed. James McConica (Oxford: Clarendon, 1986), 397–440, vol. 3 of *The History of the University of Oxford*, 8 vols., 1984–97.

Williams, Raymond, *Marxism and Literature* (Oxford: Oxford University Press, 1977).

Wilson, Thomas, *A Discourse Upon Usury*, ed. R.H. Tawney (New York: A.M. Kelley, 1963).

Winter, William D., *A Short Sketch of the History and Principles of Marine Insurance*, 2d edn. (New York: Insurance Society of New York, 1935).

Wittkower, Rudolf, and Margot Wittkower, *Born Under Saturn: The Character and Conduct of Artists* (New York: Norton, 1969).

Wood, Anthony à, *Athenæ Oxonienses*, 4 vols., ed. Philip Bliss (London: for F.C. and J. Rivington, 1813–20).

Woudhuysen, H.R., *Sir Philip Sidney and the Circulation of Manuscripts, 1558–1640* (Oxford: Clarendon, 1996).

Wright, Andrew, *Court-Hand Restored: or, the Student's Assistant in Reading Old Deeds, Charters, Records, etc.* (London: H.G. Bohn, 1846).

Yates, Frances A., *Giordano Bruno and the Hermetic Tradition* (Chicago: University of Chicago Press, 1964).

Young, Alan R., *The English Prodigal Son Plays: A Theatrical Fashion of the Sixteenth and Seventeenth Centuries*, ed. James Hogg (Salzburg: Universität Salzburg, 1979).

Index